OVERDRIVE

OVERDRIVE

Managing in Crisis-Filled Times

MICHAEL SILVA

TERRY McGANN

JOHN WILEY & SONS, INC.

New York • Chichester • Brisbane • Toronto • Singapore

Library of Congress Cataloging-in-Publication Data:
Silva, Michael A., 1951–
    The leader in crisis : managing in crisis-filled times / Michael
Silva, Terry McGann.
        p.   cm.
    Includes index.
    ISBN 0-471-51549-3
    1. Crisis management.   I. McGann, Terry.   II. Title.
HD49.S57   1995   94-38593
658.4—dc20   CIP

Printed in the United States of America
10 9 8 7 6 5 4 3 2

To our families,
  who provide purpose,
  support,
  and a fair amount of crisis.

ACKNOWLEDGMENTS

A number of people have contributed their time and talent to *Overdrive*. Once again, we deeply appreciate the efforts of Michael Snell and John Mahaney. We have worked together for so long on so many projects, that it is hard to imagine a book without the professional guidance of Michael and John.

Special thanks to Mary Kowalczyk for her patience with endless revisions and to Danalyn Adams for keeping the project on schedule. Neither individual can be praised enough.

Craig Hickman, as always, deserves appreciation for his continued vision of writing as a worthwhile endeavor. In addition, we are grateful to Jim Cooley for not being politically correct, for not being too smooth, and for not favoring image over substance.

Finally, we would like to acknowledge fellow crisis consultants Bruce Christensen, Peter Bennett, Pete Schutz, Marlon Berrett, Rob Higginson, Doug Jeffe, John Beck, David Swope, Gary Neese, Herb Nobriga, Barry Brokaw, and Chris Beck for their contribution under contrary conditions.

CONTENTS

Contents

PREFACE

Some crises strike with warning and with predictable timing. Others strike suddenly and unexpectedly. Either way, crisis turns an ordinary day at the office into an annoying day at best, but at its worst, crisis is a corporate nightmare.

On just such an ordinary day, Lucja Szymczakowska happily set up for business outside the Skydome in Toronto. For three years she had supported herself, her sister, and three children by selling hot dogs from her own vending cart. Then, suddenly and without notice, five new hot dog carts showed up to compete in the already overcrowded market. Lucja's nightmare had just begun, however, for the new carts were owned and operated by McDonald's, *the* McDonald's.

That same day, Edward Schmidt, president and chief executive officer of Alpha Solarco Inc., blithely arrived at his office only to hear a political announcement that threatened the very existence of his Cincinnati-based company. In light of China's sales of missiles and other technology to Pakistan, the United States slapped trade sanctions on China, which banned the transfer of certain technologies with potential military applications. Since Alpha Solarco had been deriving 75 percent of its total sales from exports to China, the government's ban posed real problems.

Much like Szymczakowska and Schmidt, executives of the nation's various cellular telephone companies strolled into their offices one day only to learn that ATT and McCaw Cellular Communications had merged in pursuit of the lucrative wireless communication market. Like the five new McDonald's carts, the merger poses more than a minor challenge to future profits for the cellular phone companies because behemoth ATT plans to sink over $20 billion into acquisitions in a quest to dominate the cellular market. As a result, some cellular companies will have gone out of business before this book goes to press.

These three examples of crises (and at least 18 others) recently appeared in a *single* edition of *The Wall Street Journal.* Friday, August 27th, was a day like any other day, just an ordinary business day in America, filled with crisis. In fact, crises have become so pervasive that a survey of executives conducted by the American Management Association indicates that they spend well over 70 percent of their time each day "putting out fires."

But the sheer volume of crisis alone doesn't justify another book on corporate problem solving. What fascinates us is the relationship between crisis, which is so prevalent in modern organizations, and vision, which is so important to organizational success.

It is a relationship of seeming opposites. Vision, on one hand, is a creative, inventive, and insightful process, while crisis, on the other hand, is chaotic and uncontrolled, at best merely disruptive, but often extremely destructive to organizations and careers. So how can the two possible coexist? The answer lies in a stark and simple, yet extremely revealing, piece of common sense: *Every crisis is a violation of vision.*

Just as the concept of *light* helps us define and comprehend the meaning of *darkness, fast* contrasts with *slow, long-term* thinking puts *short-term* thinking in perspective, so also does the mental picture of things going *right* illuminate all that is going *wrong.* In other words, only by constantly contrasting how things *should be* with how things really *are* does an organization feel flush with success or confronted with crisis.

If we consider vision and subsequent strategy as a collection and schedule of organization *should be*s, then any falling short of the mark is a crisis of some degree. We should be number two in our market; a crisis is being number four. We should be first in the stores with new products; a crisis is getting beaten to the shelves by the competition. We should be 65 percent of plan by August 10th; a crisis is when net profit is under plan by 17 percent. We should be operating with 10,000 fewer employees; a crisis is the inability to downsize effectively. We should be shipping 100 cases by the end of the shift; a crisis is when the line stalls, forcing a delay. We should be submitting our proposal by next Friday; a crisis occurs when the study promised by the New York office by 5 P.M. Thursday is not faxed as promised. In countless day-to-day examples such as these, common sense suggests that crisis is when life does not live up to plan.

The intertwined relationship between vision and crisis begs an important question. How can an organization or executive hope to develop an effective and functional vision without being equally effective at the management of crisis? If, as we believe, every crisis is a violation of vision, then *every crisis solution demands, to some extent, a modification of vision.*

Think of vision as if it were a masterpiece being painted in the middle of a construction site. The circumstance dictates that the artist must not only conceive and create the delicate blend of form and color, but, simultaneously, must also paint over the accumulation of smudges, splatters, and spills that assault the masterpiece from the surrounding activity. It is even conceivable that the artist might have to start from scratch if the damage is too severe. Using this analogy, it might be argued that some Fortune 500 companies are in need of a new canvas, not merely a touch-up here and there.

The simultaneous need to create and then modify vision suggests a demand for executives that are visionary but also hard-nosed practical crisis managers. In reality, an organization's vision is assaulted by crisis from the moment of inception, whether the crisis is as common as the need to re-engineer or as unthinkable as the next environmentally lethal oil spill. Consequently, we are alarmed that while so much is ventured about vision, so little is committed to understanding the dynamics of crisis. Unfortunately for companies like Exxon, whose vision dominates its industry, its seeming lack of effective crisis management skill during the spill of the *Exxon Valdez* cost its shareholders added billions.

To further appreciate why developing a more effective crisis management capacity is vital to a leader's success, consider briefly four crisis concepts.

First, the more ambitious a vision, the more frequent the crisis. Even the most basic organization pursues a vision, but not all visions are basic. As visions grow more complex, the potential for crisis also escalates. Think of the beverage stand at the local elementary school carnival. The simple structure of the vision, to sell drinks for a quarter, leaves little room for things to go wrong. You can run out of drinks, cups, ice, and maybe change, but that's it. Coca-Cola, on the other hand, also shares a vision of selling beverages. But the complexity of Coke's vision invites potential problems not found at the school carnival, such as varying national health codes, environmental regulation, patent infringement, and even small wars.

The linkage between the complexity of a vision and the frequency of crisis suggests that an organization with a visionary leader, but one that cannot effectively manage a multitude of crises, is in deep trouble. The very skill of the leader in crafting a complex vision simultaneously ensures the constant flow of crisis that can potentially bring the vision down, *unless* the leader is equally skilled in crisis management.

Second, how you go about solving a crisis has become even more important than any specific solution, no matter how effective it may be. In a very real way, current methods of crisis management leave a legacy that surrounds every organization, for better and for worse, long after the actual crisis has passed. This reality drives our attempt to probe more deeply into the anatomy of crisis and to propose a radically new methodology that will prepare leaders to counter the inevitable crises, large and small, that affect organizations every day. Consider one deceptively simple, yet revealing, example.

Lake Powell was created by damming up the Colorado River near the Utah-Arizona border. The resulting coastline stretches from the Wahweep Marina in Arizona to the Bullfrog Marina in Utah, a distance of 182 miles, making Lake Powell more of an inland ocean than a land-locked reservoir. Given its size, severe storms can whip up winds exceeding 50 knots and waves cresting over 10 feet. One such storm tore loose two of the four anchors securing our 74-foot boat to the beach. During the crisis, 16 passengers, including 6 children, watched as we struggled to secure the two broken anchor lines. What they saw was not merely the mechanical efforts of splicing line and resetting anchors; rather, they observed the whole dynamics of the process, not out of detached curiosity, but for some sign that safety would be regained. Should they remain calm, or should they panic? Were the efforts to solve the problem deliberate or random? Did we focus all our effort on solutions, or were we wasting time placing blame on those who set the anchors? The answers to these sorts of questions would linger, for better or for worse, long after the actual crisis had passed.

If you extend this example to the corporate world, you can better appreciate our point. While an organization wrestles with crisis, its shareholders, directors, and employees watch, and, more important, remember. Their impressions determine if a particular leader and management team is one that they really want at the helm when the next storm blows.

Third, the best and the brightest are paid to manage crisis. During a time when stockholders berate seemingly obscene executive salaries, the competent crisis manager is a bargain. Whether the crisis is a major league players' strike or a major chemical spill, the impact of incompetence, or even mediocrity, begs for strong strategy and a skilled touch when the heat is on. So it is no surprise that the daily routine of corporate leadership is hardly routine. Rather, the best are paid in anticipation of the next organizational flare-up or meltdown. Ironically, this suggests that a promising career headed for the top is simultaneously headed for crisis-filled times.

Fourth, no one appreciates your crisis more than your competition. Let's face it. When IBM fell from grace, you could hear the cheers from the smallest Silicon Valley techno-think tank to the Tokyo boardroom of Toshiba. Every micro and macro crisis that Big Blue weathers is a potential weak link in their market domination of the computer industry where business is war and no prisoners are taken, no matter how grand their corporate legacy.

During crisis, particularly a major crisis, an organization has no friends, only varying degrees of enemies. From the moment the *Exxon Valdez* spilled its first drop of oil to the legal confrontations five years later, Exxon has stood alone. Its only supposed friends are the legion of lawyers and specialists whose short-term loyalty has been bought by millions of dollars in fees. And always lurking is the competition, whose best interests are served by your worst crisis nightmare. Circumstances such as these demand that crisis bring out the best in leadership and management, not the worst.

The relationship between crisis and vision, and the impact that crisis has on the success of an organization, prompts a career wake-up call for all leaders and those that aspire to leadership. This is because crisis has become a permanent player in the game of management for all companies, not just for the elite of the Fortune 500, but for the corner hot dog stand as well. On an ordinary day, in union shops, assembly lines, distribution centers, and plush boardrooms across the country, executives must match wits to defend their vision against challenges of all types and all sizes. If they manage poorly, they jeopardize their company's very existence. If they manage well, they can conquer even the most serious crisis.

In the battle between McDonald's and Lucja Szymczakowska, Szym-czakowska did not have the benefit of a Harvard M.B.A. or years of formal career training. But her crisis management was so common-sense street-smart, her resolve so fierce, that George Cohon, chairman of McDonald's Canadian unit, respectfully and graciously conceded, "We've got five hot dog carts we'd like to sell."

OVERDRIVE

Crisis Myths and Crisis Realities

Five widely accepted myths of crisis management, based on partial or distorted truths, influence how today's executives approach crisis. In order to fully understand the dangers associated with these five myths, you must think about these factors: first, the kernel of truth each myth contains; second, the way the myth distorts reality; and third, the truth that dispels the myth.

Myth Number One: Crisis Results from Someone's Mistake

Certainly, human error causes or contributes to many crises, but other factors, such as mutual disasters, changing technology, shifting consumer trends, and organizational aging play ever greater roles. This myth propels executives to seek scapegoats or conduct witch hunts to identify a target that can receive full blame for the crisis. Of course, you may slaughter your scapegoat or burn your witch at the stake and still find yourself up to your neck in crisis.

1

Myth Number Two: A Lot of Crisis in an Organization Indicates an Inability to Manage Crisis Effectively

Obviously, a new crisis will camp out on the doorstep of an organization that handles an old crisis poorly, because one unresolved crisis almost automatically leads to the next. However, our own observations lead us to conclude that the volume of crisis stems more from management's vision than from its inability. Ironically, if management sets low objectives, then less can go wrong. Therefore, the best organizations, those with the most aggressive visions, tend to encounter the most crisis.

When you embrace a loftier vision, three dynamics come into play: your vision becomes more dependent on the cooperation of others, competition increases as you go up against the best and the brightest, and timing becomes more crucial. Therefore, this myth stimulates executives to set their sights low, and keeps their organizations off the cutting edge in fear that the increased crisis will cost too much.

Myth Number Three: Crisis Always Destroys

While every crisis does disrupt an organization, not every crisis destroys it. In fact, more often than not, crisis can regenerate an organization as it invigorates management to *focus* on what really counts, to *innovate* solutions to problems and to *reevaluate* everything the culture believes and does. In reality, this myth itself inflicts the real destruction because it impels management to avoid crisis as a means of preserving policies and procedures that may have long since ceased to be productive.

Myth Number Four: Contingency Plans Equal Crisis Management

While every organization must anticipate and prepare itself for crisis, most contingency plans amount to little more than wishful thinking because most such plans assume that when crisis strikes, it will follow predictable paths. If a crisis is truly predictable, it isn't a crisis at all. Genuine crisis management allows you to deal with crisis *wherever* and *however* it surprises you. This math keeps management in an imaginary comfort zone where it can be blindsided and destroyed by even the smallest unthinkable crisis.

Myth Number Five: Lone Wolves Resolve Crises Best

The best crisis management involves team play. It works best when a motivated group addresses a challenge with focus, unity, and cooperation, and nothing damages *organizational* crisis management more than the lone wolf, the solo player who struts into the situation as if taking center stage in a one-player show. Yet, this sort of act almost always mesmerizes the business press whose reviews make good stories, even when the performance fails. The press, as much as anything, fosters the myth that lone wolves, not teams, solve crisis best.

Accepting this myth ignores the backstage workers and the supporting cast of actors and actresses that actually do the dirty work of confronting crisis. Admittedly, there are individuals that perform exceptionally well under crisis conditions. In fact, some exploits are legendary. But for most organizations whose CEO is a leader, not a legend, the myth is deadly and needs debunking.

CHAPTER 1

The Four Horsemen of Crisis: Technology, Shifting Trends, Corporate Aging, and Global Capitalism

"It's All Part of the Game"

In July 1993, San Francisco Forty-Niners' quarterback Steve Young became the highest-paid player in the National Football League, earning $5 million per year. But before the season began, the franchise player broke his thumb, forcing him to miss preseason games. Fortunately for the Forty-Niners, they boasted one of the league's best backup quarterbacks in the form of Steve Bono. During his first game replacing the injured Young, Bono lived up to his billing until a crushing tackle broke his collarbone, effectively ending the season for the talented replacement. With the third-string QB already injured, the team turned to their fourth-string rookie, who, on his first start, guided the football team to its only loss of the preseason. Head Coach George Seifert put the crisis in perspective when he sighed, "It's all part of the game."

No matter what kind of an organization you run, and no matter how well you run it, you can expect crisis to be part of your game. And since corporations, nonprofit institutions, and government agencies alike tend to attract trouble like lightning rods, executives have developed a whole vocabulary to describe the phenomenon: They try to extricate their organizations from "between a rock and a hard place"; they move to higher ground when

5

they find themselves "knee deep in alligators"; they duck when "it hits the fan"; and they struggle for the winning play on "fourth and long." Whatever metaphor they use, they know that trouble lurks around every corner.

As the cherished Canadian summer waned in 1993, school kids trudged back to class clutching millions of dollars worth of their favorite candies. However, two parents, alarmed over the candy's odd taste and the slight mouth irritation it caused, alerted the government about a potential problem with Smarties, one of the most popular candies in Canada. The candy's manufacturer, Nestle, acted quickly, pulling all of its products from the shelf, even though only two minor cases had been reported. The company set up two toll-free hot lines and ran national ads in Canadian papers that advised consumers to turn in their Smarties for a full refund.

After extensive investigation and testing, and in consultation with the Health Protection Branch of Health Canada (a government agency), it turned out that the two kids who complained about the candy suffered from slight allergies to the particular type of ink used to print the "Cool Dude" purple packaging Nestle had designed as part of a back-to-school promotion. The company simply replaced that ink and immediately restocked supermarket shelves with the popular Smarties.

Like the Forty-Niners' quarterback crisis, Nestle faced a challenge caused, not by some specific human error, but by a routine happenstance that arose from merely "playing the game." In football, no matter how careful, well trained, and well prepared the player, the threat of injury always exists, and, in business, no matter how cautious, astute, and decisive the executive, the threat of crisis attends every decision.

In today's complex world of hypercompetition, multiple markets, and instantaneous media scrutiny, scores of circumstances and conditions might lead to crisis every day, and human error causes few of them. Nevertheless, the myth persists that, somehow, crisis flows from someone's mistake. That's understandable, of course, because a handful of dramatic crises have indeed resulted from sheer management negligence.

The Truth Behind the Myth

On March 24, 1989, the feedwater pumps supplying water to the steam generators went down at the Three Mile Island nuclear power plant. While the crisis clearly fell within the limits of established contingency plans, technicians, in the course of fixing the feedwater pumps, did not notice that the valve controlling the water used to cool the reactors had stuck in the open position. That human oversight proved costly.

For 2 hours and 22 minutes, vitally needed coolant drained from the system until Three Mile Island flirted with a meltdown that could have radiated a fourth of Pennsylvania. Though technicians narrowly averted a meltdown, dangerous levels of radiation had leaked into the atmosphere.

The General Public Utilities Corporation, which owned and operated the nuclear facility, took six years to settle the 300 claims filed against it. One settlement paid out $1.9 million for a child born with Down's Syndrome within a year of the radiation; another awarded $855,000 to the parents of an infant born with cerebral palsy. Evidence linked both conditions to fetal radiation exposure, but the root cause of these defects, according to the Kemeny Commission, was "management error."

Similarly, on a muggy September evening in 1991, two AT&T technicians overlooked a power transfer that shut down telephone lines up and down the East Coast. The resultant lack of long-distance telephone service isolated individual airports that depended on AT&T to carry communications as air traffic controllers handed off jumbo jets from one airport's airspace to another's. The breakdown left planes crowding the East Coast flight corridor with virtually no guidance. Luckily, the incident did not provoke an accident—but the potential for catastrophe was dangerously real.

People remember these two particular incidents, Three Mile Island and the AT&T breakdown, because they made national headlines. Every day in communities across the United States, human error creates some sort of crisis, which feeds the myth that most crises result from human failures. Admittedly, a statistical analysis might point out that error does account for a high percentage of crises, particularly common crises that stalk managers on a daily basis. However, the most serious crises, especially the unthinkable kind, often flow from sources beyond human control. Thus, if you focus on rooting out the human error in every crisis, you might very well miss the real sources of the calamity.

Four Horsemen of Apocalypse

Ancient mythology imagined four horsemen who rode the wind, sowing death and destruction across the world that would ultimately end all existence on the planet. Since no one could actually see these mythical horsemen, one could only judge their presence by the symptoms of their activities, often in disease, poverty, war, and death. The myth held particular power in the Dark Ages when fleas spread Black Death through rat-infested towns.

Modern organizations face their own version of the four horsemen. Far from mere figments of the imagination, however, these horsemen are deadly killers, born of the massive changes sweeping organizational environments everywhere, and they create crises far more devastating than any attributed to human error. The modern-day four horsemen are technology, shifting trends, organizational aging, and global capitalism.

Technology

This horseman wields two deadly weapons. First, technology can transform one small miscalculation into major misfortune for masses of people. Three Mile Island and the AT&T breakdown demonstrate how the mathematics of a technological mistake can take on geometric proportions, with one oversight ultimately endangering thousands. The potential for this kind of disaster escalates daily, but so does danger from situations involving no human oversight at all.

In Utah, a small tribe of Native Americans, whose numbers had dwindled from twenty thousand to mere hundreds, struck it rich on land the state of Utah originally thought was worthless. With complete autonomy over the barren tract of sand, salt, and waterless earth, the tribe foresaw profit where others saw only a dump for hazardous waste. With enthusiastic support from the federal government, millions of dollars have been spent on research and proposals to build a toxic waste disposal facility on the land that would become the dumping ground for the Western states. Of course, the state of Utah panicked at the prospect of a potential disaster that could wipe out Salt Lake City, the state's largest city, a mere 50 miles away. However, the Native American tribe holds the deed to the land and, like other Native American groups, completely controls the use of its property beyond the restrictions of state and federal laws. If the facility comes on line, the tribe will indeed strike paydirt, while the state of Utah will find itself sitting on a technological time bomb just waiting to explode.

In another example, the post–Cold War tendency toward full disclosure of risks to the public has turned old technology into new technological dangers. The Pentagon reported that, somewhere in the swamps of South

Carolina, it lost a thermonuclear warhead, the result of a crash of an Air Force bomber in the late 1950s. Although the bomb cannot possibly detonate, another danger does exist: that the device will become a delayed (and long-term) source of nuclear pollution threatening both wildlife and people who have built homes as the swamp gave way to suburbia. Unfortunately, since no one knows the precise location of the bomb, animals and people will likely suffer disease and death long before someone finally digs it up.

This horseman's second weapon, the fact that the rate of technological change claims as its victims the very organizations that profit from technology, can visit equally dire consequences on the unsuspecting.

Richard Wurman, author of the book *Information Anxiety*, observes that the amount of information available to the world doubles every four years. This phenomenon results in technology for which Karlheinz Kaske, CEO of Siemans AG, suggests an average life span of 48 months, from inventor's table to consumer's shelves to the trash heap.

The implications of a 48-month life span for new technology pose a dire threat to organizations whose lifeblood depends on technology, and that threat certainly does not come about as a result of human error. The rapid rate of change can result in serious crisis for some very big names in global competition. For instance, in the 1970s, competitors in the computer business earned the nicknames "Snow White and the Seven Dwarves." IBM, of course, played Snow White, while Sperry Rand, Control Data, Honeywell, Burroughs, General Electric, RCA, and NCR played the dwarves. Without exception, the dwarves and even Snow White herself fell victim to the very technology that had propelled their growth. Now, these former giants languish in the shadows of much younger players with names unheard of in 1970: Apple, Microsoft, and Compaq.

While you might cite a thousand contributing factors in the story of the decline of Snow White and her entourage, you must admit one common denominator in each: that technology outraced their ability to harness it for profit. They were, as Shakespeare put it, "Hoisting by their own petard."

Virtually every organization on earth comes under the rule of this same dynamic. Not even the most mundane product or service remains immune. Rockport reduces the weight of its dress shoes, making them almost 75 percent lighter than Florsheim's. Interplak revolutionizes the toothbrush, producing a high-tech version with swiftly counter-rotating brushes that duplicate two hours of brushing in two minutes. Sharper Image sells a television that projects an image on specially made eyeglasses. Timex introduces a watch that lights up like a lamp. Coors pioneers a beer can that can talk to consumers. The exhilarating and deadly list goes on, spelling doom and destruction for any organization that clings to its traditional technology. Every little breeze of technological change visits a hurricane of crisis on some company that responds just a split second too late. Executives at Baldwin Piano & Organ Company are learning this lesson the hard way.

How could the venerable piano get caught with its keys down in a techno-war? Hasn't the basic concept behind the piano remained unchanged for centuries, making it the epitome of a product with a "mature market"? Sure, until the Japanese came along, combining baby grands and extension cords in a product Baldwin assumed consumers would never accept. Baldwin, however, misjudged the appeal of the technology, and electronic pianos quickly became the rage in families with young children, the biggest market segment buying pianos. Older generations tended to hold on to their old Baldwins, which, to its credit, the company had made virtually indestructible. As a result, Baldwin, a name synonymous with the piano industry, now holds only a 3 percent share of the electric keyboard market. Baldwin chairman, George Castrucci, sees the need to commit his company to new technology, so Baldwin may once again be making sweet music, but only after a bruising clash with one of the modern-day horsemen.

Shifting Trends

In 1990, when traces of benzene were detected in bottles of Perrier spring water, the concerned company pulled all the bottles off the shelves and improved the filtration process to prevent another occurrence of contamination. Perrier's swift response earned it high marks for crisis management, but the company soon faced another crisis far more deadly than mere benzene contamination.

When the nation turned the corner into the '90s, Perrier did not make the curve. Sticking with its '80s image of aging yuppies toasting yet another leveraged buyout, Perrier watched its sales evaporate by 50 percent in five short years.

Perrier only remains popular with the over-45 crowd, the survivors of the go-go '80s. In younger circles, with ever-increasing disposable incomes, the once premier brand has been replaced by Snapple, diet soda, bottled iced tea, and Clearly Canadian. If the younger crowd thirsts for spring water, it orders a Pellegrino. The resulting market share crisis forced Perrier into the arms of Nestle, which began pushing the company into the lucrative soft drink market where a mere two percentage points represents nearly $1 billion in sales.

Getting caught with your guard down by the horseman of shifting trends spells certain crisis. If your existing product or service declines in value because consumers have fallen for a new fad, you cannot profitably follow that fad yourself, nor can you easily create a new one overnight. Rather, you find yourself languishing in the worst kind of limbo, stuck between your customer's cold shoulder and a hot trend. Human error? Not really.

Heinz's feisty chief executive officer Anthony O'Reilly identifies the same type of shifting trend in the processed (canned and bottled) food business: "We perceived two years ago that there was a big change among consumers who were shell-shocked by the recession." He was talking about a new acceptance among consumers of private label products and a reluctance on their part to pay more money simply for a product with a big name. Signals of this crisis came to O'Reilly's attention in the form of three years of flat stock prices after its blockbuster performance between 1980 and 1990.

Philip Morris received similar signals in 1993, then shocked the industry by dropping the price of a pack of Marlboros by 40 cents in an attempt to compete with less expensive private label cigarettes.

Unlike the horseman of technological change, which strikes rather suddenly, the horseman of shifting trends tends to turn down the screws so slowly as to make the threat almost imperceptible.

In 1960, the heyday of unionism, the United Auto Workers (UAW) claimed an astounding 31.4 percent of the adult American workforce as members. By 1970, the number had dropped to 27.3 percent, in 1980, to only 21.9 percent. Finally, in 1991, the number fell to a mere 16.1 percent. At no time during the 20-year decline did the union suffer a single debilitating crisis. Rather, three or four evolving attitudes undermined the value of what the union provided to its members. First, management's increased sensitivity toward workers downgraded the UAW's role as protector. Second, the union's success in driving wages and benefits up alienated the general public. The fact that in 1992 the union was striking at Caterpillar for a compensation package that exceeded the then–current level of $34 per hour evoked no sympathy from a recession-plagued nation. Third, global competition and the availability of cheaper labor offshore made union demands anticompetitive. Fourth, the UAW was increasingly losing showdowns with management. The Caterpillar strike, which some observers saw as the UAW's last stand, ended with the union agreeing to concessions after the company began to hire new workers. Finally, the UAW had grown so powerful and unwieldy that it became just another bureaucratic entity to the very members it was originally formed to serve. The resulting drop in membership sent unmistakable signals that shifting trends, while they had not run over and crushed the union, were slowly but surely bypassing it.

Organizational Aging. Everything alive eventually ages and dies. No individual or organization can escape such passages, but in the case of a company, the process can result in rebirth rather than certain death.

When touring a devastated Japan in 1947, James Michener interviewed the plant manager of one of the few surviving steel operations. The manager worried, "We're in desperate trouble here. All our competitors had their plants destroyed by your bombs. Now they'll rebuild using the latest heavy machinery from Sweden and Canada. If we let them get a head start on everything new, we may never catch up. It is often more sensible to scrap old ways, even at great expense, so that you can start fresh with new procedures; if you cling tenaciously to the old, you will become as outmoded as this decrepit plant." The wisdom of the Japanese manager applies not only to hard assets such as machinery and equipment, but to softer assets, such as management skills.

Companies, like people, respond to aging differently. Some grow old gracefully, recognizing that they no longer possess the physical and mental quickness to compete in a world of upstart youngsters full of vim and vigor. Such companies remain clearheaded enough to realize that they must either regenerate or die. Some, however, handle the passage less gracefully, clinging to a view of the world as it was, becoming defenders of the status quo, and burning up scarce energy swatting at those who threaten their strategic myopia.

In a tense conversation between Bill Gates, the chairman of Microsoft Corp., and Jim Cannavino, head of IBM's personal-computer business, Cannavino threatened, "I wouldn't want to be in your shoes. I wouldn't want to have to compete with the IBM company." At the time Cannavino uttered that statement, he had no idea just how old and rickety IBM had become. Further, Cannavino did not know just how hard it would be to compete against the fresh legs (and ideas) of Bill Gates' Microsoft. Cannavino and IBM would not age gracefully.

12

Aging looks even uglier when a once sleek and vibrant competitor does not recognize its sagging gut, impaired eyesight, and hardening arteries. As so often happens to a former heavyweight champion taking to the ring after retirement, the early and easy fights produce little more than bangs and bruises, but eventually the aging fighter faces a tough young bully and never sees the knockout punch coming. This kind of punch blindsided America's bankers.

Faced with a changing world, the bankers just could not relinquish their view of the financial world as it once was. Decades of waiting for borrowers to beg for loans had eliminated any need for marketing skills, skills in desperate demand when good borrowers become as rare as good bankers.

The industry's total reliance on asset-based lending produced generations of managers unable and unwilling to analyze anything that wasn't bolted to the floor or constructed of brick and mortar. Thus, the new service and high-technology industries—where cash flow, not buildings and inventory, creates success or failure—so mystified conventional lenders that the more creative and aggressive money managers scooped up the good loans, leaving only bad loans for the old fogies.

Unable to cope with this change, many banks headed to South America where lenders still operated the old way, only this time they sat behind their desks listening to entire governments beg for money at even the most outrageous interest rates. What should have been a relatively common crisis of changing market conditions and financial attitudes escalated into the unthinkable: billions of bad loans written off and egg on the face of U.S. banking. In a scant 20 years, the entire banking industry went from the peak to the gutter, only a step behind the savings and loan industry. Now U.S. banks, which once dominated the world, count only one among the top ten.

Graceful passages require more than new procedures and policies, they demand brand-new thinking to back them up. General Motors almost countered the trend with a top-to-bottom imaginatively designed, state-of-the-art Saturn facility. Everything in the plant was brand spanking new, except the attitudes of General Motors itself. Eventually, Saturn, like its parent, would begin recalling its products to correct defects.

Executives often fail to see the crisis dynamics of organizational aging because their eyes have grown so clouded with the cataracts of control. The old guard bravely marches into the new world all but blind to the need for the innovative, the nontraditional and the unique. To this group, the future must look like the past against the new crop of hungry, disrespectful, focused, and

13

flexible competitors. That future will become the past even before tomorrow arrives.

Global Capitalism. Competition, by no means a new organizational phenomenon, shapes the heart and soul of capitalism. And competition breeds surprises. James Fallow, editor of *The Atlantic,* explains that our economic system, by definition, courts the unexpected crisis. In order to achieve more vibrant economic activity, some things in the system must inevitably be "chewed up and destroyed." Such chewing up and destroying is what Joseph Schumpeter affectionately calls "creative destruction—the heart of capitalism." But if the teeth have sunk into your own ankles, you'd most likely call the situation a crisis.

The logic is straightforward. For every company that thrives, 10 stumble into the graveyard. During a nine-month period in the early 1990s, roughly 49,000 U.S. companies failed. Particularly hard hit was the East Coast, where Massachusetts suffered a 261 percent increase in failures, followed by Rhode Island with a 163 percent increase, New Hampshire with 162 percent, and Maryland with 160 percent. Creative destruction, indeed. New York posted the best performance in terms of preventing business failure by scoring a relatively mild 70 percent increase in failure.

When you hear these numbers, you probably think first of small businesses, and you're right—80 percent of startups fail their first year. But the airlines industry reminds us that size provides no safe haven from predators in the corporate food chain. Pan American, Eastern, and Midway lead the list of nutrients that fed the growth of Delta, United, and American Airlines. For the unemployed worker and dismissed executive, corporate death has become far more painful than any abstract government statistic.

In the coming years, the already voracious competitive feeding frenzy will take an unimaginable global turn for the worse, and the two most influential contributing factors flow from the demise of the Soviet empire.

First, the transition to capitalism of former communist economic systems adds to the sheer volume of capitalist competition. The volume increase occurs in several ways. Initially, there comes an increased demand for goods and services from markets formerly closed to capitalists. Consider this revealing calculation: if the combined population of the former Eastern Bloc and the Soviet Union owned as many telephones per person as do the citizens of Great Britain, that demand would require an additional 200 million telephones. This type of market explosion will certainly expand the size

14

of current competitors as well as attract a host of newcomers, both of which stimulate greater competition. But that is only the beginning.

Eventually, perhaps measured in decades, when the population of Cuba will own as many cars, telephones, and VCRs as do Americans, then Cuban manufacturers will be competing with U.S. and Korean companies for shares of that, as well as the Canadian market—instantly, more competitors. In time, the increased volume will be chewed up by capitalistic competitors in a violent round of creative destruction and crisis. This time, the winners will not always be Japanese, U.S., and West German companies, but just as easily companies or conglomerates headquartered in Poland, Hungary, or North Korea. Whatever mosaic the victors form, it all adds up to more competition.

However, the second source of increased competition is even more intriguing, albeit less obvious. For years, American economists have ventured that a good portion of Japan's competitive advantage stems from the fact that the Japanese spend relatively little yen on armaments. All the effort, energy, and resources that have gone into nuclear weapons in the United States and the Soviet Union go, in Japan, to the making of cars, computers, and home electronics. So what happens when the U.S. (and former Soviet) defense industries turn their attention to products such as air conditioners, copiers, and golf clubs? The transition will result in a radical increase in competition. Already a manufacturer of sonar for nuclear submarines has targeted bass fishermen as likely customers, offering them a state-of-the-art fish finder once reserved for the *Nautilus*. Transitions such as these will result in a radical increase in competition in all industries as dollars (and rubles), previously dedicated to defense, will seek and destroy more consumer-oriented targets.

The Cold War may have come to a crashing halt, but a new and different kind of war has just commenced: the war for consumers worldwide. In that war, companies will face formerly unthinkable crises every day in a "bet your company, fight for your life" struggle for corporate dominance.

Each of the four horsemen creates its own unique havoc in organizations, but real hell breaks loose when all four strike simultaneously and without remorse.

Getting Trounced

In its heyday, Wang Laboratories, makers of Wang computers, once boasted $3 billion in annual sales and over 31,000 employees. Wang was one of the

15

first companies to market electronic-imaging products that scan paperwork and store it electronically. But then it completely missed the personal computer revolution and the movement towards networked systems. As a result, Wang dove under the protection shield of Chapter 11.

Wang provides the sad example of a good company getting trounced by all four horsemen at the same time. More important, Wang's woes demonstrate how each horseman incites the others, escalating a bad dream into a horrible nightmare.

It started with technology. Founder An Wang had engineered excellent hardware and software that could efficiently compete in the market against the likes of IBM and Digital Computers (DEC). But the technology was evolving like wildfire, moving relentlessly toward smaller, quicker, and more flexible machines. Although the company tried to keep up, its very success had brought increased size and bureaucracy, both of which hampered it responsiveness.

The changing technology put computer power in the hands of individual users, and the personal computer exploded into U.S. offices and living rooms. While Wang struggled to keep on the forward edge of technology, consumer preferences were demanding smaller, lighter, and more mobile machines. To make matters worse, the rate of technological change and shifting trends joined forces to attack an aging organization.

Chronologically, Wang was a relatively young company, but managerially it operated like a rest home. The founder, slow to change and not sufficiently responsive enough to signals from the market, ruled the company with an iron fist. He seemed to operate as if his original innovative approach to computing would be the last innovation of the industry, an assumption proven wrong by upstarts such as Apple, Grid, and Compaq.

Each round of new challenges increased the tension between the founder and the investment community, until finally he agreed to step down. However, he appointed his son, a proverbial chip off the old block, as his successor. Consequently, the company never escaped the clutches of its own geriatric culture, and its rebirth into a more flexible and responsive organization would take two long years of incubation in the bankruptcy court.

The final horseman administered the coup de grace. Holding its own against the onslaught of IBM and Digital Computers while attempting to whisk away pesky Apple and Compaq had already proven more than Wang could handle. The added pressure applied by offshore newcomers NEC,

16

Toshiba, and Canon knocked the company off the playing field and into Chapter 11.

Yes, Wang eventually emerged from Chapter 11, but as merely a shell of its former self, with fewer than 6,000 employees, anticipated annual revenues of less than $1 billion, and an emphasis on software and service rather than hardware.

The myth of linking all crisis to human error reduces sensitivity to the presence of the four horsemen. Since the challenges brought on by technology, trends, passages, and global capitalism tend to accrue gradually, you must monitor them closely and constantly. Otherwise, they'll gallop over you, wielding weapons no amount of effort and wisdom can stand against.

CHAPTER 2

Not Just Another Day at the Office: Why Being on the Cutting Edge Generates Crisis

Laid-back Lorin

A quick glance at Lorin Pugh's daytimer would suggest the epitome of managerial incompetence. At 9:30 A.M., there's the meeting with the Environmental Protection Agency. Pugh's company, Cummins Intermountain, a distributor for truck and mining engines, is being investigated for the improper dumping of hazardous waste. At 11:30 A.M., Pugh meets with his lawyers to discuss a sexual harassment suit being filed against the company from one of his branch operations in Nevada. At 3:00 P.M., there's the meeting with company president, Bain McMillan, to review the computer foul-up that delayed the posting of last month's financial reports by nine days. Finally, the day ends in a tense negotiation with a disgruntled customer who wants three new mining engines, at $130,000 a piece, claiming improper servicing on the part of Pugh's company.

Incompetent? Hardly. Pugh is one of the most competent and respected distributors for Cummins Diesel, the world's premier manufacturer of diesel engines. In operation for over 50 years, the company is productive, prosperous, and innovative. So why the seeming cavalcade of crisis?

More a malicious judgment than a mere myth, assuming that the volume of crisis somehow suggests a management flaw is pure fallacy. Look more closely at Lorin Pugh's world.

The hazardous waste that concerns the EPA is ordinary motor oil, drained during common oil changes. For years, Cummins Intermountain used a company that was officially approved by the EPA to legally handle oil disposal. It turns out that the disposal company did not follow all the rules, unbeknownst to Cummins Intermountain and the 25 other companies that paid for their services. So in a bizarre application of the environmental Superfund law, the government lawyers are putting the touch on all the former clients of the disposal company to foot the bill for its improper disposal techniques. The sexual harassment suit involved a female employee whose employment was terminated on suspicion of embezzlement. The word suspicion is not to be taken lightly. Pugh, like other street-smart CEOs knew that it was easier and far less costly to simply terminate the employee than drag her to court, although the funds embezzled would never be recovered. The employee retaliated with charges of sexual harassment. Her charges were dropped when she was confronted with the company's evidence of embezzlement.

The data processing snafu was not the result of improper management, but rather originated with the quest to raise the level of customer service by improving the inventory control system. To accomplish Pugh's vision, a new computer system was brought in, complete with the standard set of "bugs" that disrupted the financial reporting subroutine during implementation. The last meeting of the day was with a valued customer who, for the last 15 years, made the same type of "you've got to fix it" demands on the company, regardless of who had responsibility for the problem. The customer, a tough-talking miner, despite the ritual negotiation over major repairs, always brings his business to Cummins Intermountain.

Silver-haired, laid-back, old-fashion-valued, and toothpick-chomping, Pugh is one of thousands of small-business CEOs (a business is officially designated "small" by the Department of Commerce if it has less than 500 employees) that literally navigate a minefield of challenges to produce a profit in the '90s, and it's not easy. The government surrounds Cummins Intermountain with the IRS, the EPA, the EEOC, OSHA, Social Security, and health-care requirements that make keeping up with Washington a full-time job, in addition to delivering quality products and services. Then there is the competition itself, hitting from two directions. Above are the national players like Detroit Diesel and Caterpillar and below are the mom-and-pop shops, all appealing to fickle customers. Then there are issues over which Pugh has little control. A soft economy motivates a national company to stretch out payables, intentionally causing a check destined for Cummins to "float" through the system for 90 days, and increased fuel taxes have truckers moaning about poor mileage and blaming it all on the engine. For Lorin Pugh, crisis is merely ordinary work on an ordinary day.

The Truth Behind the Myth

Let's face it, not all CEOs and management teams are competent, so a fair volume of crisis can be expected due to lousy management. Often, incompetence and crisis are linked together in high-profile business failures that create the impression that *all* companies in crisis are hurting for qualified management. This is particularly true when a large established company is on the path toward mediocrity or death.

Sometime during the first two decades of the twentieth century, 15 well-known companies came into existence. For the sake of this example, we selected companies fairly well known to the public: General Electric, American Express, Johnson & Johnson, Procter & Gamble, Dow Jones, International Harvester, USX, New York Central, R.C.A., Montgomery Ward, JCPenney, Bank of America, Western Union, and Borden. All 15, at one time or another, seemed destined for greatness. But as we approach the next century, only 5 seem to be capable of pushing on to new levels of performance, while the remaining 10 stalemate or cease to exist altogether. Since each of the 10 marginal companies captured a lion's share of media exposure over the years, the decline in management competence was pretty well documented, leaving a legacy that a company in decline was a crisis cauldron boiling up one destructive challenge after another. With this type of perception, it is pretty easy to understand why an ordinary day in Lorin Pugh's life looks strikingly similar to a day in the life of an executive managing a sinking ship. But looks are deceiving.

The crisis faced by Cummins Intermountain does not flow from mediocrity, shallow strategy, or incompetence. Rather, much of Lorin Pugh's crisis flows directly from the ambitious vision that drives his organization.

The relationship between vision and crisis creates an interesting dilemma. If you set relatively low, easily achieved objectives, you will encounter fewer and less severe crises. But if you aim for ambitious and harder to reach destinations, you will experience more frequent and more severe crises.

The dilemma stems from the bit of country philosophy expressed in the Chinese proverb, "If you do not know where you are going, then you will not worry about not getting there." The message? Few roadblocks get in the way of low expectations, but when you dream big dreams, you invariably find a lot of big hurdles in your path. Contrary to this fact, organizations, and the men and women who manage them, *routinely* set their sights on very aggressive and intense objectives, *routinely* inviting more occurrences of crises.

People tend to view the relationship between vision and crisis as mere "pop" psychology, especially when they think in terms of proverbs and cliches. But a little common sense can clarify this thinking. Consider this book, for example.

If we intentionally set an easily achieved vision, we might decide to write this book and have 100 copies privately printed, with the aim of giving copies to each member of our immediate family, our closest friends, and one or two key people who can positively influence our career. With this limited vision, it is easy to list circumstances that might pose a crisis:

Mental or physical disability

Lack of concrete ideas to fill a book

Not enough money to have 100 books privately printed

With such a low set of objectives, few things can really block our vision. In order to be successful, all we have to do is translate some thinking into 200 pages of writing, then find a print shop that will typeset, print, and bind our book for a fee. Not much can go wrong with such a modest approach.

However, suppose we radically raise our vision, choosing instead to write a major contribution to the understanding of crisis that will attract the interest of an internationally recognized New York publishing house, as well as the attention of the national media propelling the book onto *The New York Times* best-sellers list and into 20 foreign languages. The increased objectives automatically increase the number of things that can go wrong:

Lack of original thinking or strong writing

Inability to secure a publishing contract

No interest from the Book-of-the-Month Club

Publication of a direct competitor by a name-brand author

No print reviews

No interviews on talk shows

Low orders from bookstores

Books not given good "visibility" on shelves

High returns of unsold books and no reorders

Not enough copies sold to warrant a paperback edition

No interest from foreign publishers

Clearly, the number of potential crises has grown proportionally to our increase in expectations. This happens for three very good reasons: dependency, timing, and competition.

Why Good Companies Have More Crisis

Contrary to the vague fuzziness of the pop psychology logic that tries to explain why "bad things happen to good people," the concepts of dependency, timing, and competition provide very concrete explanations of why good companies experience so much crisis. Further, each concept can be used in a form of crisis audit to actually determine the most vulnerable areas where a crisis will have more of a tendency to strike, though this should in no way be considered a tool of predictability.

Dependency

The grander the vision, the more a company must depend on the cooperation of others. Funeral homes have long maintained a small-town aura even in the biggest cities. The typical funeral parlor is a small business, usually family owned. The funeral director and his family often live in the facility, keeping the whole business of death a low-overhead affair.

In business terms, you can count on a certain number of "customers" to break even. But here comes Service Corporation International with much larger aspirations. The nation's biggest funeral services company operates 660 funeral homes and 160 cemeteries in the United States and Canada. Because of its size, attracting new consumers to its 22 new funeral homes in construction or on the drawing board is a big challenge. Such high expectations have forced SCI's CEO Bill Heiligbrodt to consider expanding overseas, primarily in Europe and Asia. As it does so, SCI becomes more dependent and, subsequently, vulnerable to a whole range of factors that would never affect an old-fashioned, family-run parlor.

For starters, the company must enlist the aid of international law firms and CPAs to juggle licenses, income, and taxes. Over 160 cemeteries put the growing company into the high-density real estate business, creating a property management challenge that would tax the management skills of the world's best golf courses. Finally, here comes the Environmental Protection Agency which worries about what people burn and bury in the environment. Each additional requirement brought on by SCI's ambition brings with it an added dependency on some lawyer, consultant, government agency, or Wall Street banker. (J. P. Morgan owns 10 percent of the company's stock.)

Few organizations can boast of their dependency on so many factors as does the Hawaii State Office of Tourism. Run by Mufti Hannemman, the Office of Tourism is responsible for spending state money and coordinating island-wide efforts toward keeping a steady stream of tourists headed for the idyllic beaches of Waikiki. Since tourism is Hawaii's largest source of income, Hannemman's charge is no small task. But success is wrapped up in a myriad of factors, some controlled by the state, some influenced by the state, and some totally out of anyone's control.

For example, keeping Hawaii a clean and pleasant place to visit, sort of like a big Disneyland, is a task directly controllable by Hannemman's office. Details such as street sweeping, keeping transients out of hotel lobbies, and ensuring adequate parking at popular scenic viewpoints are tracted by Hannemman's staff. They even ran a media campaign to teach residents to be more courteous to visitors. But some factors can only be influenced by the state of Hawaii. When United Airlines and Delta Airlines kept summer airfares high in 1993, Hannemman could only plead for lower fares to attract more visitors. As a strike of the island's hotel workers seemed almost certain, the state could only strongly suggest a mediated settlement. And, when the car rental companies pondered reducing their fleets, creating higher demand for cars but also longer lines and frustrated travelers, Hannemman could only look on in frustration.

Perhaps most frustrating are those factors totally out of the control of the Office of Tourism. When the Japanese economy went into a tailspin in 1992, visitor traffic from Tokyo declined dramatically. This was made worse by the fact that Japanese tourists tend to outspend other visitors, so a decline in their number was particularly painful.

Finally, when the eye of Hurricane Iniki passed dead center over the island of Kauai, all of the island's major hotels were closed for almost a full year for repairs. As a result of the damage, which amounts to billions of dollars, tourism was down 50 percent on Kauai, even after the hotels reopened a year later.

The dependency relationship brought on by complex and ambitious vision is unavoidable. In its simplest terms, billions of dollars of gross sales require at least hundreds of thousands of paying customers. Continued sales require a dependency on each customer, sometimes putting a company in stick positions as did the "Save the Whales" movement.

Sometime in the late 1980s, environmental activists incited public sympathy toward dolphins (and other animals) that were endangered by the net-fishing methods of catching tuna. The environmental groups demanded that methods safer to dolphins be developed or the public would boycott tuna sales. The crisis caught Starkist between two conflicting set of dependencies. On one side were consumers demanding dolphin-safe tuna. On the other side were those who made their living from fishing, an independent breed of small businesspeople who didn't take well to the environmental movement. Not meeting consumer demands would result in declining sales, but not buying tuna caught by methods unsafe for dolphins would simply push independent fishing operations to sell their tuna overseas where many consumers were not as sensitive to the plight of dolphins and, in fact, considered dolphins and other whales part of the food chain. Both dependencies threatened the success of Starkist's corporate vision.

Timing

Cooking up that great backyard hamburger takes a lot of skill. First, the coals that haven't reached the right state can produce burger bonfires. Second, you have to toast the buns carefully or you'll end up with black ones rather than toasty brown ones. Finally, you have to expertly tend the cooking patties in order to ensure that Uncle Sol gets a rare one and Grandma Jones gets one that's well-done. Timing is everything. And the timing challenge escalates in the kitchen of an exclusive French restaurant. Everything must come together on schedule or the lamb chop dries, the bernaise sauce settles and thickens, the broccoli becomes soggy, and the soufflé falls. In French cooking, the more ambitious the meal, the trickier the timing.

24

Borland International, Inc., invested heavily to develop software for high-end computers operating in the Microsoft Windows market. They did everything right but the timing and they showed up late for the software parade. As a result, the company earnings sank.

America West Airlines, Inc., faced a similar timing problem, but with much higher stakes. With 104 airplanes and 12,000 employees, the airline went into bankruptcy in order to reorganize and emerge a more efficient operation. Unfortunately, after a year of Chapter 11 protection, just as the new airline was ready to emerge, the industry savaged itself with fare wars that wounded even such giants as American, United, and Delta. For America West, the timing could not have been worse and its survival hinged not only on its reorganization efforts, but on a battle in the skies that they could do nothing about.

The summer of 1993 posed a particularly sticky timing problem for producers and directors that make a living in Hollywood. That summer saw the release of over 50 new movies, a summer release record. Given the box-office traffic jam, when to release a movie became almost as important as the movie itself. The anticipation and advertising budgets of movies such as *Jurassic Park, The Fugitive,* and *The Firm* could spell death for a lesser-known movie making its debut on the same weekend. After risking millions of dollars on single movie, producers confronted the difficult issue of what night, what week, and what cities.

Perhaps nowhere is timing more crucial than in the health-care market. Each new device and drug must meet with government approval which means running the logjam at the Food and Drug Administration. Take, for example, a 510(k) device. In order to qualify for 510(k) approval, you must demonstrate that the device is "substantially equivalent" to what is already on the market. Applications for 510(k) approval more than doubled in 1993 to 3,950 as compared to 1,900 the previous year. The increase in applications has stretched the average approval period from 98 days to 170 days. This poses a serious crisis to those organizations that have sunk significant sums into product development and then must twiddle their thumbs waiting for approval. Dynatronics Laser Corp. of Salt Lake City waited 13 months before getting the go-ahead to market its therapeutic ultrasound machine. The company estimates it lost $1 million in sales—a crisis in a company with annual revenues of $7 million. But it is not only the little companies that suffer. Hewlett-Packard waited for almost two years for approval to sell separately two fetal monitors that were already approved and marketed as a single unit.

25

For some, the FDA timing fiasco can turn unthinkable. Grant Wright, president of Inventive Products, Inc., sought authorization eight years ago for a breast examination device that was approved in three weeks in Canada. The fight for approval has cost his company $2.5 million and forced Wright to lay off most of his workers.

The more complex and grand a vision, the more vulnerable it becomes to a timing miscue. Coordinating human, financial, and industrial resources presents its own set of challenges. However, lurking always on the horizon are timing issues, such as the economy, world events, and the weather, that defy the control of leaders and managers.

Competition

Running for president of the local PTA, while itself a task, pales by comparison with running for president of the United States. Not only do the stakes become huge, so does the competition.

Increasing competition forces the computer industry into its own version of genocide, as the battle for the personal computer market wounds even the most powerful manufacturers, while completely destroying the weaker players. When the war began in the fall of 1991, pc prices spiralled down 40 percent in a six-month period.

Crisis stalks every organization, regardless of size, but when you run with the fiercely competitive crowd, the probability of crisis soars. Coke would "like to sing in perfect harmony" at the funeral of Pepsi and, when Coke sales decline, Pepsi "likes it like that." The jingles are cute, but the intensity behind the scramble for soft-drink consumers is anything but pleasant. Carbonated soft drinks are a $48-billion-a-year business that attracts the best and the brightest of competition. While we become mesmerized by the Pepsi vs. Coke battles, we tend to forget that giants the likes of Seagrams, Nestle, and Cadbury Schweppes are also slugging it out. The newest battleground seems to be "designer drinks." After years of cola wars, consumers seem drawn to clear carbonated drinks with a fruity base. Clearly Canadian Beverage Corp. dominated the early market with a range of clear sodas, boasting about one third less calories than the colas, although not a diet drink. But motivated by Clearly Canadian's success, the giants moved in. In a single year, sales of Clearly Canadian plummeted a shocking 25 percent. Stock prices followed sales, and shares dropped from a peak of $25.80 a share in 1992 to a dismal $5.50 a year later. Of course, the more attractive the numbers, the more talented the competition. Sales of pre-washed, prepared, and packaged produce, such as ready-to-eat salads, sky-rocketed 76 percent in a single 13-week period across America in 1993. Setting the pace was Dole Food Co., whose prepared salad sales increased 64 percent in a single year. Dole's major competition is Fresh International, another California-based company. But the two won't dominate the market for long. Sensing the opportunity, London giant, Grand Metropolitan, is seriously considering entering the market using its Green Giant label. Can Kraft Foods be far behind?

The escalation of competition is not only an issue of volume, but of violence. Five or six companies going after the same market results in a certain level of competition, but a handful of companies the likes of Sony, GTE, or Merck produce a quantum leap in competition. In other words, the quality of the players, not the quantity of the players, can really turn up the heat.

The multinational market for voice and data transmission services totals $10 billion a year and is growing at a 15 percent annual clip. The sheer size of the market and the rate of growth are motivating big telecommunications companies to forge global alliances in an effort to hone a razor's edge in international competition. In 1993, MCI announced a $5 billion plan to join forces with British Communications. Under this pact, British Telecommunications will pay cash for a 20 percent stake in MCI, which is the second-largest long-distance carrier in the United States. AT&T recently concluded negotiations with numerous foreign partners to strengthen its network from Singapore to Spain. This level of cutthroat competition pushes Spring closer to crisis, as it now stands as a single company in a den of very powerful alliances. In global telecommunications, it's not just how many competitors there are that is alarming, but who they are is particularly unnerving, leaving little room for error.

While it is easy to talk about, cutting-edge competition jolts even the very best. Honda Motor Co. skyrocketed to success in the 1980s, guided by a unique culture called the "Honda Way." Middle managers hammered out decisions in bull sessions called *waigaya,* which loosely translated means "noisy-loud" and engineers were given almost free rein to design the cars. But as American car makers became more competitive and global auto manufacturers concentrated on building "world cars," the Honda Way was no longer good enough to maintain Honda's competitive edge. So while sales remained high, profits crimped, forcing a debt rating review by Standard & Poor's. So the car maker revamped its traditional management approach, no small feat for a Japanese company. The old leadership was thrown out and Nobuhiko Kawamoto, the newly installed president, instituted the "Kawamoto Way" or top-down management. This radical departure from traditional Japanese management is less a change in strategy than it is an attempt to build a more effective corporate culture to turn up the heat in global car competition.

In the same industry, but 10,000 miles apart, two other motor companies were being squeezed by the escalation in competition. Both France's Renault and Sweden's Volvo experienced record earnings as the '80s gave way to a new decade, but neither had a minivan nor the resources to start development from scratch. Following Lee Iacocca's revolutionary combination of a sedan and a station wagon into a minivan, car makers jumped on the bandwagon and pushed out model after model of the popular suburban transport. Renault and Volvo, on the other hand, continued to make and sell "breadboxes on wheels." Still without a minivan as 1993 drew to a close and facing a global depression in auto sales, the companies announced plans to pursue a full-fledged merger, turning Renault and Volvo into a single company.

A good organization's vulnerability to the nuances of dependency, timing, and competition put productive managers into a bad light, making them appear less talented than they are because they face so many crises. Further, the often short-term outlook of lenders and investors turns the vulnerability into a seed bed of misperception.

False Judgment and the Business within a Business

Lawrence Bossidy, chairman of Allied Signal, Inc., runs two related but uniquely separate businesses. The first is Allied Signal, the company, and the second is Allied Signal, the stock. Both businesses sell products, create jobs, and demand expert managerial guidance, but that is where the similarities end.

Allied Signal, the company, employs 88,000 workers in fields as diverse as chemicals and aerospace. In 1992, the company did just over $12 billion in sales with a net income of $535 million. The major portion of Bossidy's time is spent keeping the company profitable. To that end, he has trimmed the workforce, implemented an acquisition strategy, and restructured the factory floor to increase productivity. Bossidy's competition reads like a mini who's who: United Technologies, General Electric, Rockwell, ITT, DuPont, Monsanto, ICI, Bosch, and Westinghouse.

Allied Signal, the stock, is also a booming business that demands attention. With over 140 million shares selling at $72.25 per share (September 1993), this operation churns through over $10 billion dollars in stock value. While none of the employees of Allied Signal actually report to Bossidy, they do owe their very existence to his management abilities. These are the tens of thousands of stock brokers, analysts, economists, traders, and secretaries that make a living selling Allied Signal stock to private and institutional investors. In a quirky way, Allied Signal, the stock, makes a profit and shows a loss. When a single share is sold for more than it was bought, that is a profit. A share unloaded for less than was originally paid is a loss. The swings of profit and loss are not insignificant. On the day before Bossidy took over as CEO on July 1, 1991, Allied Signal's shares traded at $33.25— less than half of the highest price paid per share in 1993. If bought at $33 and sold at $73, some investor would be a very happy camper.

We are obviously playing a game in defining the trading of Allied Signal stock as a separate business, independent of the Allied Signal's operation that manufacturers chemicals, jet engines, and automobile parts. However, it's not a game to Bossidy. In fact, he must perform in both businesses. A string of years when Allied Signal's stock stays at depressed levels will cost Bossidy his job as sure as three years of consecutive losses on the bottom line. To make matters worse, some employees of Allied Signal, the stock, conduct a management evaluation of Bossidy every three months in the form of the quarterly report analysis and pass judgment on his activities with three simple words: buy, sell, and hold.

Wall Street's quarterly analysis ritual plays a key role in how crisis is perceived. If an analyst buys into the myth that the volume of crisis somehow indicates a management shortcoming, then the result might be a false judgment that sends stock prices tumbling and management scrambling. That is why it is important that analysts be able to differentiate crisis as it flows from ineptitude and that which flows from a competitive vision that is subject to the stresses of dependency, timing, and competition.

Buying into the myth forces managers to lower long-term vision in the attempt to lower the incidence of crisis. By reducing the stresses of dependency, timing, and competition, they simultaneously reduce the potential for future growth and profitability. In short, the very activities that protect a stock's short-term value may be undermining its long-term potential. A partial protection against this type of myopia would be for Wall Street to can the myth, avoid the false judgment, and learn to differentiate that crisis which indicates a powerful vision and that which indicates visionless management.

CHAPTER 3

A Fine Line:
Crisis That Destroys and
Crisis That Creates

Déja Vù

Bankruptcy doesn't necessarily kill a company. More often than not, it inflicts slow torture, degrading and draining the organization as creditors flay its skin one strip at a time. Even the toughest executives pale at the thought of Chapter 11. So why then did Continental Airlines do it twice in a seven-year period?

On September 23, 1983, the unions threatened Continental Airlines, then the nation's eighth-largest carrier, with a total work stoppage. The next day, the airline ceased operations and filed for bankruptcy, citing "excessive labor costs" among its reasons. With losses of $219 million for the preceding 18 months, Continental argued that it could not continue with labor costs that exceeded one-third of its total operating expenses, a fact that had turned the airline industry, as a whole, into a money-losing proposition ever since 1979.

By September 28, however, Continental was flying again, with its seats filled to over 60 percent capacity. To staff its operations, Continental rehired 4,200 of its 12,000 workers but at compensation levels roughly half of what they were the week before. The unions cried foul, with Donnie Cox, a spokesperson for the flight attendant's union, calling Continental Chairman Frank Lorenzo a "gangster" for using Chapter 11 to bust the unions.

31

In 1990, it was déja vù. Continental again filed for Chapter 11 bankruptcy protection from creditors. Again it asked for, and got, wage concessions from its workers, although it did not lay any workers off as it did in 1983. And again, the airline emerged from bankruptcy to compete once more.

More than any other myth, the assumption that crisis always destroys comes closest to the truth. In fact, as we have examined this myth, we have sometimes found it hard to detect the distortion that makes this a myth at all. However, the somewhat dated example of Continental sheds light on the distortion.

Continental's crisis, which still exists, has been a running gun battle between the company and previously powerful and then deposed unions, escalating jet fuel costs and cutthroat competition. Led by a high-profile senior executive that *Fortune* magazine once labeled one of the 10 toughest bosses in America, Continental has, over seven long years and two bankruptcies, taken its share of buckshot, each time losing some feathers. But the story takes a remarkable turn in 1993.

Buffeted by consumer concerns over the economy, air travel stagnated during the summer of '93, prompting a fare war in the fall. The major airlines, already reeling from high costs and depressed earnings, and observing two competitors, Southwest and Morris (both regional midgets in the world of mega-flyers) racking up profits with no-frills "peanut" fares, tried to follow suit. Colleen Barrett, Southwest's executive vice president for customers, believed that a new airline could more easily duplicate the Southwest system than an established giant such as United or American, but, according to *The Wall Street Journal,* the "best candidate among the major airlines" to pull off the low-cost, low-frills approach was, in fact, Continental. Following the two bankruptcies, Continental emerged with the third-lowest labor rate in the industry, behind Southwest and America West. Also due to its bankruptcy, the airline did not have to support expensive but unprofitable routes, most of which it sold off to raise cash. These maneuvers left Continental in a perfect position to create the only kind of airline operation that can actually make money in the '90s.

Crisis doesn't necessarily destroy. Consider the difference between a star athlete losing a leg, or that same athlete undergoing surgery to repair cartilage damage to a knee joint. In the former case, the event destroys a career, ending the vision and dreams of the unfortunate victim. But in the latter case, the event only disrupts a career, allowing the athlete, after recovering, to perform once again, and perhaps even more successfully. In hindsight, the union affiliation of Continental's workers was an icon from a prehistoric era of management-labor relations. Union power and pride created an entrenched system that drained vital energy from the sagging airline and prevented the changes it needed to make in order to survive. Continental underwent what amounted to reconstructive surgery, ridding itself of what had become an unproductive relationship.

A word of caution. We do not offer the Continental example to sell the benefits of filing bankruptcy or busting unions. Instead, we cite it to emphasize our view that crisis need not destroy an organization. In many cases, an organization can commit the initial destruction visited by crisis into a downright beneficial situation.

A Fine Line

A fine line exists between crisis that destroys and crisis that provides a new lease on life. Some degree of destruction attends every crisis. A late shipment of parts, delayed for a day by a winter storm, destroys planned production quotas. An airline flight, delayed by mechanical failure, destroys a portion of a frequent flyer's goodwill, so carefully purchased with advertising and promotional dollars. A truck recalled due to a faulty fuel system destroys the potential for a repeat customer. Such examples occur with such regularity that the myth, "crisis destroys," can be very hard to dispel. And, of course, some crises deal fatal blows. If you look again, look to the airline industry. Pan American and Eastern found no silver lining in the dark cloud but were, instead, killed by the lightning bolt.

To understand the problems caused by this myth, you must test the assumptions underlying the definition of destruction. Farming provides an excellent case in point.

In seasonal climates, fruit farmers prune their trees in the spring in preparation for a bountiful fall harvest. The actual pruning is a clear act of destruction, as the farmer lops off entire branches until the trees look barren and near death. But when the fruit arrives, the tree transforms into a production machine, channeling nutrients to fewer branches bearing much bigger and more profitable fruit. If you don't prune your trees, they will yield a larger crop, but the smaller, less appealing fruit will not command top dollar. The analogy applies to organizations. Organizations, like trees, can

grow to the extent where they channel valuable resources in many directions at once. During times of prosperity, such expenditures cause no harm,
but during a corporate crisis, when resources grow scarce, their willy-nilly
distribution can lead to stilted, mediocre performance.

Many managers do not grasp the value of pruning. Almost instinctively,
they work to protect all parts of an organization as if each were equally
important. Thus, in the normal course of events, corporate pruning does not
occur. When crisis strikes, it takes over the job of the pruner, forcing managers to cut off a piece here and a piece there, as they struggle for the organization's survival. Such forced pruning can be an extremely painful process,
but it can free vital energy for those areas of the organization that should
receive the utmost attention.

In high profile downsizing, such as has taken place at General Motors
and IBM, thousands of workers felt the cut of the pruning saw, most of
them permanently. It may sound callous to compare the disruption and
uncertainty faced by thousands of families to the pruning of fruit trees, but
don't give in to the temptation to shoot the messenger. Place the blame
where it really lies, with the managers who allowed their organizations to
expand beyond their productive capacities and waited for a crisis to force a
pruning. Too many employees, like too many inches around the midriff of a
middle-aged athlete, do not appear overnight. They accumulate a little here,
a little there, until the organization looks in the mirror and confronts its
own obesity. In the case of IBM, the 40 percent of the workforce it cut back
did not become unnecessary in an instant. They had been sapping corporate
energy for years before Big Blue's financial crisis forced some quick and
dirty pruning.

When viewed with a long-term perspective, immediate destruction
may provide a new lease on life. Crisis forces the harsh task of determining
the unproductive branches of the organization. The task may inflict short-
term pains, but if you do it right, you can create a leaner and more competitive organization.

The myth that all crisis destroys propels management into a defensive
mode as they try to save every part of the organization from the pruning
sheers. It produces a mind-set that assigns equal weight to every product,
policy, procedure, asset, and operating plan, but when, during crisis, you try
to protect them all, you greatly reduce the chances of long-term success.
During crisis, you must prune, but you must do so with a skilled and sys-
tematic hand.

Downsizing: The Right Way

While crisis forces pruning, there is a big difference between wise trimming and blind hacking. One requires wisdom and skill, the other only muscle. Jim Saras knows the difference.

Saras runs TriValley, a unique agricultural cooperative, as its chairman and CEO. Founded over 60 years ago, TriValley ranks in the Fortune 500, boasts a first or second national market position for most of its canned fruit products, and competes effectively against the likes of Del Monte. Owned by farmers and run by a farmer (Saras is a Stanford-educated peach grower), TriValley has gained remarkable insight into the art of pruning.

Because canned fruit is a commodity, the fortunes of TriValley ride up and down on cycles of supply, demand, competition, weather patterns, environmentally safe pesticides, and consumer preferences. With each rise and fall of the company's performance, Saras must make sure the organization does not grow too fat during times of plenty, nor too lean during times of famine. The task gets even more complex when you consider that TriValley operates some of the largest canning facilities in the world, staffed by thousands of full-time and seasonal workers. In this type of organization, you cannot turn momentum on and off like a garden hose. Take peaches, for example.

When the demand for peaches decreases, Saras cannot simply decrease the production of peaches. Peach farming does not measure productivity in 120-day cycles (the average growth period of a tomato crop) but rather in cycles of seven to eight years, the time it takes to establish a productive peach tree. Cutting the volume of peaches processed, while solving a short-term decline in demand, creates a consequence almost a decade into the future, if, as a result of discussed processing capacity, growers pull trees out of the ground to keep production down. You can't effectively manage such a delicate situation with a slash-and-burn mentality. Unfortunately, too many managers mistake slash and burn for legitimate downsizing. Proper pruning should incorporate three factors: focus, innovation, and reevaluation.

Focus

Crisis creates abundant problems for an organization, but it seldom affords managers the time, energy, and resources needed to solve every problem.

Crisis conditions force management to identify essential needs and concentrate solely on those areas, selling or abandoning everything else.

In 1986, AmeriCare, a Sacramento-based health maintenance organization (HMO), was acquired through a leveraged buyout by a miniconsortium of investors. The debt piled on the company as a result of the acquisition forced the organization into a financial crisis, motivating management to search out the most important operating units and to redline the rest for termination. The search uncovered two businesses with little relevant relationship to health care: a manufacturing operation making plastic plants and a furniture business. In addition, health-care operations outside of the state of California did not perform nearly as well as those geographically located near the Sacramento headquarters. As a result, AmeriCare dumped the plastic plant and furniture businesses and trimmed back non-California operations. The company's new CEO, Dan Cowley, then focused on increasing business in the western United States. In the end, Foundation Health Corporation (the new name for AmeriCare) bid for and won the Department of Defense CHAMPUS contract to provide health care for military dependents in California and Hawaii. The contract exceeded $5 billion over a four-year period and increased stockholder value from the purchase price of $13 per share to over $40 per share in 1993. The crisis brought on by the stifling debt load resulted in a companywide focus on a single profitable area. This same type of focus has benefited Nashville, the spiritual center of country music.

Not long ago only "yokels in the boondocks" listened to country music, but now even the most sophisticated denizens of Manhattan tap their toes to the sound of Garth Brooks and Wynonna Judd. Indeed, the twang of Garth Brooks' guitar now reverberates in Paris bistros. At the center of this boom in country music's popularity sits Gaylord Entertainment. Gaylord relies on a simple strategy: Concentrate on the country franchise. But the company learned this lesson the hard way.

Following the purchase of the Grand Ole Opry and two country cable networks, Gaylord's stock has risen at a 72 percent annual rate. Its hotel, the Opryland, boasts an occupancy rate of almost 90 percent, 20 points higher than the national average. And operating income at TNN, the premier country cable channel, has been growing 20 percent annually. However, basking in success, the company also purchased four TV stations unrelated to the country music movement. Locked in a mature industry, the stations performed dismally compared to Gaylord's country music affiliated businesses, prompting CEO W. "Bud" Wendell to refocus and "make sure Gaylord stays country to the core."

During crisis, focus should channel corporate energy in the form of time, money, meetings, vision, operating objectives, and all the other variables that affect success to a narrow segment of the organization. This mimics the human body's reaction to crisis when it reduces blood flow to the hands and feet in order to divert needed oxygen to the brain and internal organs. Cutting off circulation to the limbs can cause painful side effects, but the body executes it instinctively and quickly in order to protect its vital elements. Crisis managers must learn to do the same because delay can cause more damage than the crisis itself.

RJR Nabisco Holdings gained the scorn of Wall Street analysts for moving too slowly. Ironically, the criticism came on the same day that the company announced plans to cut 10 percent of its workforce. S. Leigh Ferst, a tobacco analyst at Prudential Securities, observed that RJR wasn't moving quickly enough and that "they have a lot of fat they need to cut." Notice the irony. The company reluctantly announces layoffs, feeling good about taking the tough approach, while the outside community complains that the company still carries too much fat. Delay during a crisis signals an attitude of protectionism, and eventual action does little to stem the tide of criticism. Even elite organizations can make this mistake.

When Volkswagen announced that its subsidiary in Spain would require a $1 billion infusion to stay alive, the announcement placed newly appointed chairman Ferdinand Piech in a bad light, having previously said that the Spanish operation would break even by year-end 1993. Volkswagen's delayed response to the problem caused the real damage. John Lawson, research director at DRI/McGraw Hill in London, citing previous problems at VW's Brazilian and U.S. plants, observed that "it seems to be another case of VW finding out rather late about the problems at overseas subsidiaries." Deserved or not, Volkswagen has attracted a reputation for always moving a step too late in its effort to focus on a crisis.

Beware of confusing this emphasis on focus during a crisis with the '80s concept of "sticking to the knitting." Tom Peter's axiom that companies should concentrate on what they do best applies to skills, and it makes eminent sense where talent does, in fact, exist. In contrast, our concept of focus applies to how companies spend their energy. In no way do we suggest that a company in crisis should streamline its product line or service and concentrate on a single activity. General Electric maintains an extremely clear focus, yet it competes in a variety of markets. Rather, we are suggesting a company should direct energy, a scarce commodity during crisis, to the most important and productive areas of the company. The application of energy need not necessarily relate to the strategic decision of determining what business(es) the company should emphasize. Bear in mind the most important issue here: Crisis usually prevents continued concentration on *all* organizational activities, so you must choose your emphasis wisely.

Innovation

During crisis you must determine whether a particular product, service, department, or policy should undergo the pruning shears or whether the crisis really cries out for innovation. When Johnson & Johnson faced the horror that someone was lacing Tylenol with cyanide, the company did not abandon its product. Instead, it revolutionized the industry with safety-sealed containers and caplets, forcing the competition to follow suit. The destruction of a specific product, packaging, distribution, or marketing method can turn into a positive opportunity if it leads to the creation of a far more effective alternative. To its credit, Greenpeace, an activist environmental group, has proved its organization has innovation as its driving force.

Founded in Vancouver, Canada, in 1971, by former anti-Vietnam protesters turned environmental activists, Greenpeace evokes images of yellow speedboats harassing whaling ships and Patagonia-clad volunteers spray-painting white seal pups to make their fur unusable to hunters. In its activist heyday, Greenpeace made such a nuisance of itself that the French government authorized intelligence agents to sink a Greenpeace ship anchored in a New Zealand harbor, which had been monitoring France's nuclear research in the Pacific. Now the environmental group faces a crisis far more dangerous than French commandoes: apathy.

After 20 years, Greenpeace's confrontational tactics no longer shock the public into awareness, but seem like a throwback to the '60s. The organization's original financial supporters have turned fifty-something and are scrapping it out as lawyers, investment bankers, and company presidents—hardly a group that wants the public to associate their contributions with fanatics ramming Japanese drift-net boats. Further, Greenpeace's absolute and predictable political stands no longer influence Capitol Hill, which all but ignores the group's strong-arm tactics. After all, Vice President Al Gore has emerged as the model environmental activist: informed, balanced, visionary, and acceptable to mainstream America. As a result of all this, contributions to Greenpeace have sunk faster than the ship the French agents scuttled, and the loss of revenue has forced a 15 percent cutback in staff, the closing of offices, limitations on field work, and an overall 25 percent shrinkage of U.S. operations. Paul Watson, a founding member, suggested that donations floundered because Greenpeace was "flogging the original myth to death."

In response to the decline of public support, the organization has reconsidered its confrontational tactics and has begun taking the radical approach (for an activist organization) that efforts to prevent environmental abuse should be driven by solid scientific research. The new lower-profile philosophy has already convinced the European Community (EC) to phase out the dumping of industrial pollutants into the North Sea, Mediterranean, and North Atlantic by 1995, and it has successfully dissuaded major countries from mining and developing Antarctica. More importantly, the trend toward softer lobbying, research, and instructional media make Greenpeace, once again, acceptable to contributors driven away by the confrontational tactics that worked well in the organization's early days but which fell out of step with the softer values of the "fifty-somethings."

Unlike slash and burn, innovation provides the additional value of creating a significant competitive advantage. This holds particularly true when a crisis strikes a company that does not lead its market. Look again at Johnson & Johnson. The conversion to tamper-resistant packaging and caplets has become an industrywide standard, not limited merely to Tylenol products. J & J's innovation forced every competitor to spend the capital required to make the changes that Johnson & Johnson initiated. A similar approach could help a company like Exxon.

The *Exxon Valdez* oil spill left a foul coating on the company's image. Even after spending billions of dollars on cleanup costs and additional billions on legal settlements, Exxon still looks to many people like an archenemy of the environment. The company could reverse that image with a bit of innovation.

A few years before the wreck of the *Valdez*, Exxon had researched the feasibility of converting its fleet to double-hull vessels. Two hulls would require that an accident must rupture both layers before oil could escape into the environment. While the concept seemed perfectly sound, the investment required to make the conversion soured management on the idea. Now, *what if*, in the wake of the *Valdez* incident, Exxon announced that it would take the initiative, paying the price to convert its entire fleet to double-hulls? *What if* the company broadcast the message that the more risk of another environmental disaster outweighed the costs of conversion? *What if* Exxon assumed that the U.S. government would make the same conversion mandatory for all other oil companies shipping in American waters? Conversion would cost a pretty penny, but the sheer size of the company would ensure that the project hardly dented earnings. On the other hand, smaller competitors would find it extremely difficult to meet the new standards. In the end, Exxon might enjoy a new Exxon image as a friend of the environment, while at the same time wreaking havoc on the competition.

Innovation places the concept of pruning in a new light because cutting back with an innovative objective eliminates just enough deadwood to pave the way for splicing a healthy new branch onto the company in the form of updated technology, new policies, or a different marketing plan. The new potential created by innovation can thereby more than offset the destruction caused by the original crisis.

Reevaluation

The likelihood that a crisis may strike any given organization at any given moment opens up the possibility of using crisis as a motivation for reevaluating everything an organization does, especially its approach to those problems that seem to occur over and over again. Smart reevaluation uncovers weak and unproductive branches, hard to identify during periods of relative calm and stability, that the organization ought to prune.

During the Reagan administration, U.S. troops invaded the tiny island of Grenada in a supposed effort to protect American citizens and assets. The postinvasion analysis uncovered glaring problems with the technology that the Navy, Army, and Air Force used to communicate with each other. You would think, then, that the Grenada experience would have led someone to correct these problems, but, in fact, while someone did somewhat lessen them, the same difficulties cropped up during U.S. participation in the Gulf War. Only this time, the inability of the different service branches to communicate with each other resulted in American lives lost to "friendly fire."

Reevaluation of the Grenada and Gulf War crises can now reveal an ugly side of the American military. During times of peace, the different branches of service do all that they can to remain separate and distinct from one another. The military bases this strategy not on effective management principles, but rather on age-old battles for turf. The traditional military mentality perceives that any combining of service branches would open the door to eventual shared authority and shared funds, both feared by the military bureaucracy. Such a problem doesn't cause trouble until a crisis erupts and claims lives that otherwise might have been spared.

American automobile manufacturers face the same circumstance of recurring problems that only come to light when a crisis illuminates them. In 1979, the year Lee Iacocca began his high-profile tenure at Chrysler, Detroit recalled the following cars: 15,000 Mustangs and Capris for defective power steering; 3,400 Mustangs for unsafe engine fans; 77,700 Ford vans for defective brake hoses; 400,000 Capris for seat backs that could collapse; 70,000 Ford light trucks for wheel assembly defects; 390,000 full-sized Mercurys and Continentals for steering defects; 172,000 Monzas, Sunbirds, and Starfires, also for steering problems; 430,000 Pontiacs for defective pollution-control devices; 372,000 Cadillacs for defective accelerator pedals; 1,800,000 of GM intermediate-sized cars and pickup trucks for defective bearing assemblies; 41,500 Cadillac Sevilles for fuel injection systems that could catch fire; and 1,300,000 full-sized GM cars for front seat belts that can come loose under stress. In 1993, 14 years later, Iacocca officially ended his affiliation with Chrysler, legitimately claiming he had successfully turned the ailing automaker into a winner. However, that same year, the combined automotive geniuses of America recalled, repaired, or compensated owners for almost the same number of defects listed for 1979. In fact, every year between 1979 and 1993 American automobiles recalled millions of cars to repair relatively small engineering and production defects they could have prevented on the assembly line, saving Detroit billions of dollars. The recall process has become such an accepted phenomenon that it hardly makes the news any more. Indeed, the practice has become so commonplace that a prominent television network resorted to artificially jury-rigging a flaming GM truck wreck to attract public attention and ratings.

The lack of quality control on the American automotive assembly lines represents a low-grade crisis condition that has remained unchanged for the last 20 years. As profits ebb and flow, the companies lay off workers, close facilities, reduce shifts, cut and slow down assembly lines, but no company has bit the bullet and addressed a problem that diverts billions of dollars from the bottom line. Management apparently accepts recalls as an absolute of nature, much like gravity. While recalls strike all auto manufacturers in all countries, they do not strike with the regularity that affects Detroit.

Detroit's crisis condition screams for reevaluation and pruning. If management continues to ignore this problem, preferring to concentrate on other crises they can more easily address, the problem will never go away. They will settle for appearance of effective activity, while, in a sense, they are simply wallowing in "the thick of thin things."

In order to make pruning effective, management must reevaluate its organization regarding those problems that seem to crop up time and time again. Such problems are truly destructive and hard to solve, which explains why management allows them to constantly recur. On the other hand, when an organization commits itself to rooting out entrenched problems, it can limit the destruction caused not only by that problem, but by any future crisis that comes along.

One Twinkie Too Many

While the power lunch may now require low-cal California nouvelle cuisine, the working lunch still subsists on a Diet Pepsi, Doritos, and a Twinkie. While not particularly damaging as a single meal, a 30-year diet of working lunches will eventually take its toll, sometimes pushing an individual over the edge and into the hospital, the victim of one Twinkie too many.

A cardiac arrest or a stroke provides sufficient motivation for the victim to take a hard look at priorities and make some crucial lifestyle changes. Lying in your hospital bed, you can clearly see the cycle of schedule, calories, lack of exercise, jetlag, and long days with short sleepless nights that have put you there. You must, you conclude, make some changes and prune out some of your old lifestyle choices.

Organizations, like people, often find themselves one Twinkie over the line. Years of routine activity have accumulated, until the organization becomes a corporate couch potato, spending vast amounts of energy simply keeping itself alive, but hardly vibrant. When crisis arrives, it stuns the organization like a stroke, motivating management to rethink its organizational lifestyle and get rid of what has made it sick. The process can be a painful one, and the recovery can be excruciating, but the right changes can result in a longer life, adding a spring to the corporate step that may have been missing for years.

CHAPTER 4

When the Wings Fall Off: Why Contingency Plans Don't Work

When the Wings Fall Off

At 2:44 P.M., Aloha Flight 777 had flown to the midpoint of a routine 20-minute jump from Honolulu International Airport to Kahalui, Maui. The entire trip, one of 16 flights between Honolulu and Maui that Aloha Airlines would fly that day, would normally last only 22 minutes. At 2:45 P.M., the flight crew felt the Boeing 727 shudder slightly, and then "all hell broke loose." A 32-foot chunk of the aircraft's cabin had disappeared, leaving a gaping view of the sky. With the plane careening at 500 miles per hour, the suction pulled a flight attendant through the hole to her death and forced passengers to cling to mangled seats and each other to avoid a similar fate. The wind sheer exploding through the cabin fused a metal plate to the face of one passenger, sitting just aft of the damage. Frantically, the captain and copilot ransacked the emergency procedure manual for guidelines to correct the situation, but the search proved fruitless. Engineers of Boeing, the manufacturer of the 727, never imagined that more than a third of the passenger cabin could rip away and the plane remain airborne.

The lack of a contingency plan left the crew of Aloha Flight 777 to its own devices, struggling against the laws of aerodynamics that should have sent the aircraft plummeting to earth. Amazingly, they improvised a procedure that brought the aircraft to a safe landing, saving the lives of 136 passengers.

We do not replay the crisis of Flight 777 to fault Boeing for the lack of a contingency plan dealing with an entire section of cabin ripping off an airplane. If Boeing had developed an option for such an unlikely occurrence, it would also have had to write similar detailed instructions for every conceivable, yet improbable, circumstance that could befall a 727, such as the pilots passing out from food poisoning or a missile striking a plane during a landing at Phoenix. Such a contingency plan would look like the *Encyclopedia Britannica.* In other words, developing contingencies for every possible outcome, no matter how improbable, creates a condition of preparation paralysis. Consequently, organizations construct contingency plans based on the statistical chances that a particular type of manageable crisis might occur. For example, aircraft manufacturers publish very detailed contingency plans to deal with the possibility that an aircraft cabin will depressurize, leaving the passengers without oxygen. The manual teaches aircraft crews exactly how to handle this particular contingency, and the crews brief passengers on the use of oxygen masks before the plane takes off. But they do not tell passengers what to do if the wings fall off the aircraft in midair, because that will not likely happen, and even if it should happen, it defies any attempt at management. When the wings fall off at 30,000 feet, you might as well settle back and enjoy the last and most thrilling ride of your life.

Contingency plans play a crucial role in management's capacity to deal with circumstances that have gone awry. For example, in the United States, every hospital that provides surgical services or intensive care maintains a standby electrical generator that automatically fires up the instant the facility loses normal electrical power. Without this type of contingency protection, a delicate coronary bypass procedure could turn to disaster when life support equipment stops functioning, and a premature baby could lose its life when its artificially controlled environment ceases to exist for even 30 seconds.

However, contingency planning, while important, can actually become a liability when management mistakenly relies on it in all circumstances. Contingency plans do not equal crisis management. Like the standby generator in a hospital, an organization's contingency plans may automatically fire up, even when the crisis falls outside the scope of the plans. When this occurs, an organization places itself in double jeopardy. Not only does it face the dangers and destruction of the crisis itself, but it also finds that its contingency plans hamper efforts to resolve the crisis effectively.

Where Contingency Plans Fail

In order to explode this myth that contingency plans equal crisis management, you must consider the initial truth from which it springs. Every organization will encounter certain inevitable and, thus, highly predictable crises. For example, the sheer volume of automobiles registered in California allows the California Highway Patrol (CHP) to anticipate those factors that might snarl rush-hour traffic on a certain stretch of freeway. In anticipation, the CHP has created contingency plans to deal with accidents that might force traffic to a grinding halt. This type of crisis response abounds in most organizations. Exxon has designed a plan to deal with oil spills, Delta Airlines has developed strict procedures to deal with a plane crash, and Federal Express has proposed extensive options to deal with the prospect of foul weather. The Secret Service, the Federal Bureau of Investigation, and the Pentagon maintain hundreds of contingency plans to deal with all the likely crises that might affect their respective areas of responsibility. In this sense, you might argue that a contingency plan, once implemented, becomes crisis management.

But the truth behind the myth gets distorted when the crisis exceeds the capacity of the contingency plan to provide an effective solution. When the unthinkable crisis occurs, the effectiveness of the contingency plan drops dramatically in an inverse ratio to the effort put into the plan itself. In other words, the more effort you invest in implementing a predesigned contingency plan during an unthinkable catastrophe, the less effective the plan becomes. In order to understand why this occurs, you must look at two factors that most often create the sort of crisis that exceeds the capacity of established contingency plans: catastrophic events and rapid revolutionary change.

Catastrophic Events

In the summer of 1993, intense rainfall caused the Mississippi River to overflow its banks. The resulting flood lasted for six weeks and caused an estimated $20 billion in damage. Of that amount, the U.S. government kicked in over $10 billion in relief, loans, and tax breaks for the devastated area.

Since the lay of the land, as the Mississippi winds its way through the Midwest, lends itself to seasonal flooding, every city and town along its banks has created some type of contingency plan it can activate when the

45

water pushes up against the levees that line the banks for hundreds of miles. But the flood of '93 exceeded even the most wild-eyed worst-case scenario. As a result, the preexisting contingency plans proved virtually worthless. They were not ill-conceived, they simply did not deal with the real crisis, which cascaded far beyond an issue of water—that being the need to reconstruct an entire section of the country from scratch: homes, businesses, farms, roads, bridges, and schools. This same type of catastrophe does not restrict itself to natural occurrences, as the National Aeronautics and Space Administration sadly learned.

The inherent dangers of space travel motivated NASA to keep on hand contingency plans for dealing with a mission turned sour, but NASA never expected that a catastrophe would play itself out on prime-time television. The fiery destruction of the *Discovery* shuttle on global television not only immediately suspended NASA's space flight agenda, it went far beyond the logistics of the launch. In a flash of light, the agency found itself in a fight for financial survival as Congress used the crisis as a springboard to review NASA's performance, procedures, budget, and mission. This particular turn of events caught NASA with its contingency plans around its ankles, fighting for its very existence.

Whether you fear a natural or man-made catastrophe, you must weigh three factors that set it apart from an ordinary crisis and render all normal contingency plans obsolete.

First, consider magnitude. A catastrophe obliterates everyday life, subordinating all normal activities to its immediate effects. When the city of Los Angeles erupted in riots in the aftermath of a racially charged trial of police officers accused of using unlawful restraint, the turmoil caught police by surprise. Although trained in riot tactics, they were caught off guard by the number of people who took to the streets. Faced with the immense size of the uprising, they found their usual tactics rendered so useless that most officers spent the initial stages of the riots sitting in their cars, at a safe distance from the conflagration.

Second, consider a catastrophe's scope. Hurricane Andrew not only directly inflicted damage on Miami with its high winds and destructive waves, it also sent the construction industry into turmoil as it struggled to meet the demand for basic building materials such as plywood, the price of which increased over 40 percent immediately after the hurricane struck Florida. The effects of a catastrophe spread like the ripples on a pond after you toss a rock into it. Hurricane Andrew and the 1993 Mississippi flood will affect housing and food and transportation costs for years after the winds and waters have receded.

Finally, consider a catastrophe's longevity. Catastrophes disrupt normal lifestyles for a longer period of time than do normal crises. The Chernobyl nuclear reactor failure in the former Soviet Union did more than spill radiation into the countryside. Entire towns and tracts of farmland for hundreds of miles around the now defunct nuclear power station became uninhabitable for at least the next 50 years.

Revolutionary Change

In 1989, ecstatic East Germans celebrated the raising of the Iron Curtain and the fall of the Berlin Wall. In 1990, just as the world adjusted to a free East Germany, the Soviet Empire suddenly disbanded, sending shock waves throughout the international community. This beginning of a new world order may have spelled the end of a host of old conflicts, but it also visited catastrophe on the entire defense industry. None of the major players in the defense industry, such as Northrop, Raytheon, and Rockwell International had considered the possibility that the Cold War would end so abruptly and with so little warning. Thus, they developed no contingency plans to address the possibility that the public would scream for a peace dividend at the expense of their future stock dividends. The resultant "Great Defense Shakeout" cost hundreds of thousands of workers their jobs and pushed the states of California and Connecticut deeper into recession.

Just as a catastrophe differs from a mere disaster, so does revolutionary change differ from normal change. Two major differences render contingency plans designed for normal change ineffective during revolutionary change.

First, revolutionary change strikes like lightning. Most Westerners take for granted Japan's status as a world economic power, and they also equate Japanese-produced goods and services with quality. However, few can identify exactly when Japan transformed "made in Japan" from a derisive term to one synonymous with incomparable quality. Japan's transformation took place so suddenly, Westerners went to bed with an image of that country as a low quality producer and woke up with a pretense of the new Japan as a zero-defects manufacturing society. To the manufacturers of U.S. television

47

sets, Japan's change came so quickly that it cost RCA and Magnavox their industry dominance. The same story unfolded in computer chips, stereos, banking, and automobiles.

The quickness of revolutionary change outraces even the best contingency plans, if any existed at all. In 1973, the gaze of U.S. automobile manufacturers remained fixated on oil. Unable to wage a serious military war against Israel, Arab nations turned to waging economic warfare on the world, with oil as the principal weapon. While Detroit prepared elaborate plans for every conceivable variation in the flow and price of oil from the Middle East, they completely ignored any threat that might originate from Japan. After all, who would really want to buy a stupid Japanese car? However, by 1980, a mere seven years later, Toyotas, Nissans (Datsuns), and Hondas had replaced countless Fords, Chryslers, and Chevys in American carports.

Second, revolutionary change brings surprise. At the end of 1992, pharmaceutical companies were enjoying their best-ever decade in the history of U.S. healthcare. In 1993, just eight months later, newly elected President Bill Clinton presented a plan to nationalize American health care, setting drug company profits as his number one target. Surprise!

Often the surprise hides in plain sight, as demonstrated by Generation X. In the 1980s, the "forty-somethings," or baby boomers, ruled, but that group has lost its luster as the "twenty-somethings," or Generation X, have taken over the '90s. Boomer bosses, so accustomed to propelling the leading edge of change, now find themselves accused by their Generation X subordinates of behaving like "knotheads" and "control freaks." Worse still, and perhaps the ultimate irony, the Xers see the boomers as techno-illiterate, light years behind the computer and communications revolution. Most cuttingly, Generation X complains that the boomers refuse to "walk the talk." For all of the forty-something talk of empowerment and participatory management, the Xers see the boomers as hierarchical, rigid, and status-quo-seeking dinosaurs. What a slap on the face to the generation that look over the Berkeley campus, ended the Vietnam War, challenged IBM with a garage-built computer called Apple, and otherwise saw themselves as the antithesis of the status quo! And what a surprise to the soothsayers who saw the baby boomers, with their icon Bill Clinton, as the vanguard of change, that younger upstarts, raised on Nintendo and feeling hampered by the boomers who block their way to a neater, cleaner techno-world, have moved to center stage.

Understanding the Details of Disaster

When you study a list of the unique characteristics of catastrophe and revolutionary change, you quickly get a clear picture of why contingency plans do not equal effective crisis management. The elements of magnitude, scope, longevity, quickness, and surprise erect barriers to developing practical options that will work in every crisis situation. Each element presents its own unique challenge to traditional contingency thinking.

Magnitude

The magnitude of a crisis figures greatly in the insurance industry, which provides perhaps the best example of how magnitude can render contingency plans useless. Lloyds of London insures worldwide ocean shipping more than any other carrier. As a routine part of the company's business plan, executives have assumed that a certain percentage of the ships that they insure will sink or suffer another form of major damage. Lloyds' actuaries make fairly specific predictions about the relationship between potential damages that might occur and the amount of money to charge as a premium. However, the actuaries did not imagine the prospect that over 30 percent of the ships that it insures would sink in the same year.

No contingency plan can address a crisis of this magnitude. Oh, you could develop one, but preparing for a 30 percent loss would ruin the company. Since shippers would not pay the outrageous premiums, developing a contingency for such gargantuan losses would be futile. While doing so might intrigue an accountant, planning an organization's tragic demise does not represent a wise use of management time.

Scope

The breadth of President Clinton's health-care reform left the entire industry breathless. Not in their wildest imaginations did the insurance companies, hospitals, HMOs, the American Medical Association, and the drug companies ever conceive that they would find themselves forced to practice a form of socialized medicine. The very scope of the reform rendered all contingency plans ineffective because it involved so many organizations and factors that lay beyond the control of a single company's attempt to implement the reform package. The U.S. health-care system integrates a multi-

49

tude of different parts. While a single hospital, or even the entire insurance industry, could have implemented a contingency plan to deal with Clinton's reforms, any plan would necessarily have to take into account every other player in the health-care field. The scope of such a contingency plan would defeat any industry player on a practical level. In essence, a contingency plan designed to deal with the crisis caused by the reform package would fill the same *Encyclopedia Britannica* the aircraft industry would need to address every unthinkable crisis that could involve an airplane.

The element of scope simply overwhelms existing contingency plans with more factors than an organization can reasonably track. For example, for years America's industrial complex has confronted the onslaught of Japan's productivity. Then, just as American management teams became more proficient in competing with Japan, the unification of Europe posed a brand-new set of competitive dynamics they needed to consider. In late 1993, shortly after the official European unification, Mexico emerged as a legitimate competitive threat with the approval of the North American Free Trade Agreement. Mexico's stock market, the *Bolsa de Valores,* has become the fastest-growing exchange in the world, with capitalization in excess of $140 billion. The cement industry in the United States has already lost dominance to Cementos Mexicanos SA, which has turned its sights on Europe with a $2 billion expansion plan. And Del Monte, which dominates the American market for fresh fruits and canned fruits and vegetables has fallen into Mexican hands. By the end of 1993, more Mexican companies (using ADRs) were traded on the New York and American Stock Exchanges than either German or French companies.

Mexico's emergence as a competitive player expands the scope of global competition beyond the anticipated challenges of Japan and Germany, making all original contingency plans dealing with global expansion wholly inadequate.

Longevity

In reality, no organization can actually plan for consequences 20 to 30 years down the line. For industrialized nations that tend to view corporate life in 3- to 5-year spans (about the longest conceivable to an MBA), the potential impact of a crisis spanning a quarter of a century boggles the mind. Yet, longevity plays a very real role in any organization's survival.

At the height of the Cold War, the U.S. government conducted scores of nuclear tests that fed unanticipated levels of radioactive contamination into the atmosphere. Populations downwind of the test sites might have suffered enough contamination to result in severe medical disorders. Now, some 30 years after the tests, the government faces a barrage of legal accusations from those who hold the military to be financially responsible for acts committed a whole generation earlier. The legal wrangling could push way past the turn of the century. Such lingering consequences affect more than the military.

In the private sector, hazardous waste disposal—from old paint to spent nuclear fuel—has grown into a big business. While the precautions against a disaster seem adequate and certainly high-tech, the industry has done little to grapple with long-term issues. For example, abandoned salt mines have become a prime storage site for nuclear waste hundreds of feet below the earth's surface. The cool, dry, and isolated mines seem ideal, but what if weather conditions radically change 20 years from now and the mines become saturated with groundwater? Such a long-term outcome lies so far beyond the short-term plans of any single organization, public or private, that no one would take such a contingency plan seriously.

Quickness

As an organization, the NCAA stands squarely on the side of gender equality in sports. With no equivocation, the organization staunchly defends the need to make amateur sports gender blind. Yet, the NCAA could not have prepared itself for just how fast it would find itself defending its stated values with action, and more importantly, money. Title IX blindsided the NCAA.

Title IX, a policy enforced by the Office of Civil Rights, basically requires that colleges place equal emphasis on men and women athletes. Although the issue contains great complexities, it boils down to a simple requirement: that colleges spend the same amount of money on female sports as they do on male sports. When you consider that only two sports really matter when you view college athletics in terms of money—football and basketball—equal budgets for male and female athletes will take time, time the NCAA does not enjoy. You can measure equal spending, unlike equal opportunity, and the government wants the measurements performed immediately, if colleges and universities want to retain federal grant and research funds. As a result, either football and basketball programs must cut back on spending, or women's sports will become the best-funded activities on campus.

The mandated rate of change has created much more than a mere administrative annoyance. The women's softball team of Colorado State University took the school to court to demand immediate compliance with Title IX. The quickness demanded by the courts and the government will radically alter the role amateur sports plays on college campuses. If the required funding changes occur, football and basketball will cease to be a prime-time entertainment industry which happens to be associated with education simply because the stadiums sit on college campuses. Instead, they will revert to being *college* sports, of all things.

Every medical exam includes a check of your reflexes. With a gentle tap to the knee, wrist, or elbow, the physician can measure the time it takes for the body to respond to a stimulus. Organizations, like people, respond to stimuli, but the taps do not occur so quickly, a fact that makes the rate of change a particularly sticky issue.

Drawing up a contingency plan that forces an elephant to run a four-minute mile doesn't make sense. In the same way, when conditions demand that an organization immediately achieve an unrealistic pace, planning goes out the window. The rush of competition brought on by the North American Free Trade Agreement (NAFTA) typifies the crisis that forces organizations into a pace that seems impossible. Labor unions, in particular, worry about not being able to keep up with the flood of manufacturers heading south of the border in search of lower costs. Yet, in all candor, no union admits to having developed a contingency plan that deals with the establishment of a free trade zone running from the tip of Alaska down to Tierra Del Fuego, encompassing all in between. Worse still, the unions never dreamed it would happen over a brief five-year span.

Surprise

During the Persian Gulf War the most current, complete, and provocative news coverage did not come from Dan Rather, Tom Brokaw, or Peter Jennings and the venerable networks that they represent. Instead, even George Bush and Saddam Hussein stayed glued to Cable News Network (CNN) for the next breaking story.

CNN's emergence as a global news force beautifully exemplifies how you should measure surprise, not in units of time, but, rather, in terms of realization. Established in May of 1979 by Ted Turner, CNN operated for slightly more than 10 years before the Gulf War illuminated its newly established clout in global news. For 10 years, the networks—ABC, NBC, and CBS—enjoyed ample time to draw up contingency plans that could deal with an upstart competitor that lacked the high-priced faces the nation watched every dinner hour, but when CNN scooped the news world by reporting from *inside* Iraq, that move caught the networks by surprise. In fact, they had done so little to prepare for the challenge to their superiority, that one network attempted to smuggle a news team into Iraq, the capture of which, by Iraq's forces, provided an opportunity for yet another CNN report.

Surprise involves recognition more than chronology. When a mental light bulb flares, it reveals that something different has happened, that the element of surprise has struck. Surprise does not render contingency plans useless. Instead, surprise prevents the development of contingency plans in the first place. How can an organization develop a plan to deal with an event or issue it cannot envision? If it could envision the event, then the event would not surprise it.

Ten years ago, the usual big names dominated the entertainment industry, carving up virtually all movie and television revenues. The likes of Columbia, Paramount, and Time-Warner (owner of HBO) eyed each other with competitive disdain, but no one paid much attention to Disney. After Walt Disney's death, his company's competitors assumed that the company would continue to emphasize children's films and theme parks. They were right, and wrong. Disney, under CEO Michael Eisner, did continue the core business of catering to children, but they also used the core business to break into adult entertainment. In 1994, Disney released a whopping 40 new feature movies, compared to the annual average of 15 to 20 films per major studio.

In television, Disney has become the second-biggest supplier of shows to the networks, including "Home Improvement," the biggest TV hit since "Roseanne." And the video release of *Aladdin* broke records as the single best-selling video of all time.

Now, Disney has been doing business for a number of years, but its sudden dominance took the industry by surprise, causing an industry crisis as a new type of entertainment giant spans markets from retail outlets in fashionable malls to professional hockey. This turn of competitive events never dawned on the likes of 20th Century Fox, leaving it and the rest of the industry without a contingency plan to survive the Disney dance to dominance.

Flying by the Seat of Your Pants

In the pioneer days of aviation, before the cockpit became a cross between Sega Genesis and *Star Wars,* pilots learned to fly "by the seat of their pants." This made sense in an era of flying that placed more emphasis on the pilot than it did on the aircraft, and, during a crisis, a pilot was expected to "wing it." As we mentioned at the beginning of the chapter, a statistically probable, somewhat predictable, and basically manageable crisis lends itself well to pre-conceived contingency plans. This makes contingency planning a valuable management tool. However, management must also learn to put into motion a crisis management approach that deals specifically with a crisis that crashes beyond the barriers of contingency. You manage this type of crisis less with planning than with flying by the seat of your pants. When catastrophe strikes, you must replace the rote implementation of predetermined activities with a more freewheeling approach that races beyond the rules, the training, and experiences of normal flying. In order to survive, a pilot must put it all together in a flash, adopting a flexible approach, pushing the aircraft to the very edge of its capacity. Management must do the same.

The myth that contingency plans equal crisis management (in every situation) becomes destructive when management does not recognize where contingency plans should leave off and seat-of-your-pants flying should take over. Under trying circumstances, most must muster great effort and dedication to weather the storm, but the approach must match the situation.

The hotel industry in America did not show a single profitable year between 1980 and 1993. You cannot blame this poor performance over a 13-year period on mere oversupply or economic trends. Nor can you abate the crisis with traditional contingency methods. Knowing this, Darryl Hartley-Leonard, president of Hyatt Hotels, opted to start flying by the seat of his pants. First, he acknowledged the need for his company to go beyond the conventional stock approach, saying, "Our goal is to redefine what a first-class operation is." Then he began to expand the very definition of a hotel, setting up an experimental hotel in Schaumburg, Illinois, where the company cross-trained employees to accomplish multiple tasks. Hartley-Leonard calls the process *silo busting,* which he modeled after the airline approach in which employees of smaller, more competitive airlines perform multiple tasks to provide better service and save money. In the future, Hyatt employees might all be wearing futuristic watch computers that allow them to check guests in and out from any location in the hotel. Finally, Hyatt may attract guests with virtual-reality marketing, sending prospective customers special glasses with a built-in screen on which they can actually view hotels and resorts.

The Hyatt example illustrates an important line where contingency plans should cease and a more creative, less rigid, more exploratory process should emerge. The shift requires two skills. First, you must know how to identify when a crisis does not lend itself to contingency solutions, and, more importantly, you must develop a new mind-set to "fly by the seat of your pants" when managing such a crisis. This leads to the fifth and final myth of crisis management.

CHAPTER 5

The Myths of the Lone Wolf: Teamwork and Crisis Management

No segment of the health care industry has been growing faster than emergency room medicine. Those who work in the ER must think quick, act fast, and race from one crisis to another without skipping a beat. To gain certification, every new physician must spend a certain amount of time in what ER physician Gary Lambert affectionately calls "hell punctuated by terror." During that time, an observer assesses the fledgling doctor's ability to transfer into specific action all that he or she has learned in medical school. More than anything else, however, the assessors want to see how the aspiring doc runs the ER team.

The best crisis management, like the best ER medicine, involves team play. It works best when a motivated group addresses a challenge with focus, unity, and cooperation, and nothing damages *organizational* crisis management more than the lone wolf, the solo player who struts into the situation as if taking center stage in a one-player show. Yet, this sort of act almost always mesmerizes the business press whose reviews make good stories, even when the performance fails. This, as much as anything, fosters the idea that lone wolves, not teams, solve crises best.

When the media focuses on the star of the performance, it ignores the 20 backstage workers and all the supporting actresses and actors who did all the actual work. Yet, even the audience feels charmed by the star as she or he bows curtain call after curtain call. Admittedly, individuals with great skills perform exceptionally well during crisis conditions. Their exploits give rise to the myth, and they also make debunking an entertainment in itself.

Crisis Styles of the Rich and Famous

Let's face it. The Siskel and Ebert reviews do suggest that a handful of managers possess the golden touch when it comes to managing a crisis. They draw your interest the same way Shaquille O'Neal draws the fascination of basketball fans: they're bigger than life. But that's exactly the point. They fascinate people not because people identify with them but because they are so different. Had "The Shaq" not entered the National Basketball Association, indeed, if teams could only put players under 6 feet tall on the court, would the NBA still play basketball? The show might not be as entertaining without the larger-than-life superstars, but the teams would play the game down and dirty, stressing the basics and functioning like a team. They would get the job done. Crisis forces this same requirement on a company. When the going gets tough and you lack a larger-than-life crisis management star, team work offers the only alternative. Still, the stars can be so entertaining, especially the Number Cruncher, the Spin Master, and the White Knight.

The Number Cruncher

Of all the crisis management stars, you most easily recognize the one who engineers a financial turnaround. When the crisis comes in the form of sagging sales, declining profits, and ebbing investor confidence rather than a gashed oil tanker or a tampered-with painkiller, you can define the solution in terms of the numbers. This type of situation thrusts the number cruncher who excels at ruthlessness and turning corners onto the center of the stage.

Ruthlessness.   The number cruncher cannot afford to project an image of weakness. After crunching the numbers to drive the organization around the corner, real change must occur or the organization will lose all its forward momentum. This basically means that you must ruthlessly examine every asset, then sell, eliminate, or ignore any that does not contribute toward the company's progress. This doesn't take an emotional toll when you're discarding a piece of machinery or a production plant, but when you're dealing with middle managers and their people, it can knock you senseless if you listen to your heart rather than your head. Not surprisingly then, the stars of financial crisis management don't seem to have a heart. Oh, they may care a great deal about people on a personal level, but they conduct business calculatingly, viewing people as just another asset that either helps or hurts the bottom line.

Airline executive Frank Lorenzo typifies the ruthless number cruncher. Smart, tough, and enamored of risk, Lorenzo made enemies on his trek through Texas International, Continental, and Eastern Airlines. His reputation for ruthlessness grew so pervasive that columnist William F. Buckley, Jr., asserted that capitalism and the free-market system, alas, are not perfect and that Frank Lorenzo exemplifies their imperfections. In all fairness, however, take a look at the other side of the coin. Although Eastern Airlines ultimately went belly up and Continental collapsed into Chapter 11 under the weight of its debt, Lorenzo did walk away with some $30 million in his pocket.

Turning Corners.   You know when you've solved a financial crisis, when you've turned the corner, when key negative numbers go positive. Until then, no one knows whether the organization will survive or not. The jury, consisting of bankers, creditors, suppliers, competitors, and customers, waits to see if the company negotiates the corner before passing judgment. The number cruncher hits the books, playing with the figures—adjusting inventories, deferring capital expenses, reallocating general and administrative costs—much like a chef trying to keep a soufflé from falling during an elephant stampede. For a brief moment the soufflé may actually look like it will stay up, with luck, long enough to convince skeptics that the company has successfully turned the corner and can now barrel along on a straight course toward recovery. The pressure for this telltale signal that everything will turn out all right forces a frenetic round of activity during the initial stages of a financial crisis, but the elephants usually end up stealing the show.

The Spin Doctor

These crisis stars inspire business books and magazine articles all over the world. Given the visibility of their efforts, their skill at manipulating public opinion, no wonder they achieve the status of heroes—saviors with a mysterious bag of tricks, who can turn the dullest drama into a Pulitzer Prize–winning play. The so-called spin doctors practice crisis management by manipulating perception. If a crisis begins when the public recognizes its existence, then it ends when the public thinks it has. To be effective, this crisis management approach strives to control three factors: persona, media attention, and short attention spans.

Persona.   More than any other crisis star, the spin doctor exudes personal charisma. Relatively few people can name the current CEO of General Motors, but everyone knows that Lee Iaccoca once ran Chrysler. Typical of this type of crisis manager, Iaccoca and his spin machine created an image that loomed larger than the company's crisis itself, mesmerizing or, to be blunt, distracting the public's attention from the real situation. In the political arena, years after the Nixon administration, some voters might not recall all the details of the Watergate crisis, but few have forgotten Henry Kissinger, a master at presenting a powerful public persona.

The spin doctors surround each crisis with their individual charisma, both positive and negative, until the crisis itself plays second fiddle to their personal performances under the lights. Personality, not plot, makes the play.

Media Attention.   You can't perform without an audience, and the media attracts a most eager audience for the performances of spin doctors during all sorts of crises. Whereas more conventional crisis practitioners try to suppress crisis from public scrutiny, the spin doctor explodes it into the public conscious through books, television, and personal appearances. The crisis becomes a stage set, offering public entertainment night after night on the "CBS Evening News," converting crisis from a collection of one organization's problems into a media event. The spin doctor exploits the excitement of the event to shroud the actual details of the crisis and its management from objective public scrutiny and judgment. The public knew that Chrysler teetered on the brink of bankruptcy, but even though taxpayers willingly shelled out tax dollars to solve the problem, how many voters remember the real nature of Chrysler's predicament? Swept up in the bailout as an event, with Japan pointed as the arch-villain, most people overlooked the most important crisis question: Did America really need three traditional, whining, overmanaged, underproductive car manufacturers?

Short Attention Spans. From the public relations point of view, a crisis ends when public attention ends. PR-oriented crisis managers take advantage of the public's and the media's notoriously short attention spans. Endure the initial heat, and, eventually, the whole episode will naturally melt away. If an organization survives the initial fire, then it has resolved the crisis in the eyes of the public, regardless of the company's true condition at the time of the sordid details of the crisis solution. This phenomenon motivates the spin doctor to put everything into play during the early and most tense moments of the crisis. If the public sees a surge of activity, then it tends to assume the same surge (and same course) will continue throughout the remainder of the crisis. When the Chrysler crisis ceased to satisfy the public's appetite for news, few noticed that the rejuvenated car company immediately invested in Korean and Japanese automobile manufacturing and shifted a significant portion of its own production to Mexico. Iacocca did all this, citing unfair foreign competition as the crisis culprit and arguing that a financial bailout would preserve *U.S.* jobs.

The White Knight

The white knight rides down from the hills with his hired gun drawn to rescue the threatened organization from the big, bad villain. For the most part, white knights shy away from extreme solutions, preferring to do what they logically think should be done, and can be done, but somehow hasn't been done. Michael Eisner, CEO of Disney, rode down from the hills with guns blazing. Not particularly charismatic, and not a ruthless slasher, Mr. Eisner wisely chose to get his organization doing what it should and can do.

Nearly two decades after the death of Walt Disney, Disney Productions found itself mired in a crisis that threatened its very survival. The company's profits had been sliding for three years, shrinking from a high of $135 million in 1980 to just $93 million in 1983. Attendance at the company's theme parks in Anaheim, California, and Orlando, Florida, had fallen for three of the last four years. At Disneyland, its flagship park in Anaheim, attendance in 1983 sank to its lowest point since 1974. Corporate debt had soared dramatically, while sales of Mickey Mouse dolls had shrunk. Saul Steinberg, Irwin Jacobs, and a host of lesser-known takeover raiders had circled the company for months, like cartoon vultures, waiting to pounce on the once vibrant organization. That's when Michael Eisner saddled his horse.

On Saturday, September 22, 1984, at 11:20 A.M., Walt Disney Productions turned over the reins to Eisner. Setting about the task of getting the company to do what it should have been doing all along, Eisner did not merely resolve the crisis, he initiated the beginning of another Disney era that would leave competitors gasping in awe, much as country fair promoters did when they realized on July 7, 1955, that the newly opened Disneyland had ushered in a new era of family entertainment. Eisner's success at Disney illustrates how white knights capitalize on two intertwined factors: mediocrity and magic moments.

Mediocrity.   For the white knight to succeed, conditions must be troublesome but not disastrous. If the situation has gotten totally out of control, then no one, not all the king's horses or all the king's men, can rescue the situation. By the same token, if the situation has not gotten dire enough, then white knights cannot perform their magic. Admittedly, things looked pretty dim for Disney in 1984. Roy Disney, nephew of founder Walt Disney, saw the value of his 1.1 million shares of Walt Disney Productions decline from $85 to $55 million over a 12-month period. In addition, while Hollywood was turning out mega-blockbusters such as *Star Wars* and *Raiders of the Lost Ark,* Disney produced disasters like *Tron* and *Something Wicked This Way Comes.* But the situation wasn't totally bleak. The company had already invested over $80 million in the Disney Channel, to which 1.4 million people had subscribed. In addition, the company had begun developing a fraction of the 28,000 acres it controlled in central Florida, and it had embarked on a five-year plan to transfer the famed Disney movie library onto videocassettes. This hidden upside lay buried deep within the bowels of the organization, largely ignored by the largely unimaginative management that ruled the organization between Walt Disney's death and the arrival of Michael Eisner.

Under Eisner's vision, what others had largely ignored became the raw material for a corporate miracle. With a bit more attention and some "new blood," each underemphasized Disney project exploded to astonishing levels of success. Disney boosted Disney Channel subscribers fivefold, opened thousands of acres surrounding the Disney park in Orlando for codevelopment, and brought to market the film library, which became a golden source of revenue. Eisner himself invented none of these successes. Rather, he took advantage of the latent potential largely overlooked by the mediocre management team he succeeded.

Magic Moments. If location means everything in real estate transactions, then timing means everything to the white knight's success. Time your arrival too early, and people can't comprehend your stratagems. Time it too late, and people may feel that you've come along too late to save the day. The magic of the moment boils down to motivation.

White knights rarely bring to bear radically new strategies or decisions. Rather, like Eisner, they motivate and fine-tune. Like the ghosts in Dicken's *A Christmas Carol,* when white knights appear at the right moment, their mere presence motivates people to buckle down and change things around.

If you could classify any of the crisis management styles as peculiarly American, you might choose this one. It runs like a steady theme through Disney's own movies, with Aladdin and the genie saving Princess Jasmine from marriage to the villainous Jafar, and the heroine Belle saving the Beast from a cursed existence as a malformed mutant. The magic moment unfolds like the Saturday matinee that entertained so many theatergoers over the years. Sooner or later, regardless of how dangerous the situation has become, the mere presence of the hero indicates an eventual happy ending.

Disney thrives because Eisner's management, while not particularly spellbinding in itself, awakened a once creative and radically cutting-edge organization that had temporarily lost its drive and was languishing in early retirement. Like other white knights, Eisner brought out the best in a strong organization that needed only to regain hold of its own destiny.

What's Wrong with this Picture?

Two deficiencies lurk behind this myth and the three styles of crisis management it spawns. First, each style, in its own unique way, can damage the organization more than the crisis itself. Too often, the number cruncher ignores the core values of the organization, while the spin doctor makes perception more important than reality, and the white knight recycles old problems and solutions. Second, none of the three approaches prepares the organization to handle the next crisis more capably. Let's examine these deficiencies more closely:

Soul Slashing

The ruthless slashing tactics of the number cruncher carry with them the risk of cutting not just the fat but the heart and soul out of the organization. Practitioners of this style care little about the organization, only the cold numbers that fleetingly describe it. In the long run, they don't actually solve a crisis, they frequently obliterate it, along with the organization. Following their logic, why not detonate a nuclear device in order to rid Iowa of corn blight? Of course, that will eradicate the blight, but it will also obliterate the corn. With that approach, Carl Icahn kept TWA flying though crisis after crisis, but in the long run, TWA nearly stopped flying all together, and the organization ended up with hardly a feather of its once robust organization.

Raped by the Ratings

The spin doctor judges crisis solutions in terms of the Nielson ratings. As on the late-night talk show war between Jay Leno and David Letterman in 1993, where a joke is a joke only if people laugh at it, a crisis is only a crisis if people notice it. If the public comes to believe that the crisis has passed, then it has passed. Never mind the facts, ma'am.

All too often, a crisis flares up in the media, scorches the surrounding landscape, and then dissipates from inattention. How many times has the media, spurred on by politicians seeking votes, reminded the American people that the country's health-care and education systems have gone to hell in a handbasket, then, once the election draws to a close, let the issues drop?

Frankly, the general public seems to care little about real crisis and real solutions. They just grab their remote controls, pop a bowl of corn, and settle down for a dose of prime-time entertainment. When the crisis drops from the screen, out of sight and mind, however, it continues to smolder until it reaches the flash point again, after exploding into a full-scale disaster. The massive problems that attend health care and education do not ebb and flow with the tide of media attention, but, rather, they will slowly and inexorably surge forward until they form tidal waves of destruction.

The Merry-Go-Round

With a few notable exceptions, white knights seldom solve problems permanently, but merely catch the same problems as they circle round and round. Peter Ueberroth has won fame as the Guy Lombardo of crisis. When you saw Lombardo's band tuning up for "Auld Lang Syne," you didn't need to consult a calendar to know that midnight on December 31st had arrived;

and when you see Peter Ueberroth tuning his management banjo, you know trouble must be lurking just around the corner. First, he took on professional baseball, then the Olympics, then Hawaiian Airlines and riot-torn Los Angeles. His gun's always for hire because the same sort of crises keep coming around. Oh, sure, people work harder and smarter and put out the brushfires, but when the smoke clears, the white knight has ridden over the hill to the next conflagration, often taking the best parts of the management team along for the ride.

While each of the three styles do work to some degree, none of them takes the entire organization to a new level of effectiveness in fighting crisis because taking an organization to a higher plane of crisis awareness has always, and will always, demand a team approach.

Team Managing Crisis

An effective team-based crisis management methodology accomplishes these goals. First, it focuses on extending what the organization does best. Second, it involves all levels of the organization. Finally, it involves management deeply in the process, not merely involving those at the top in number crunching, manipulating perception, or playing the white knight. Each of these goals merits a closer look.

Go with Your Gift

You can easily spot talent, especially when it clearly outshines the competition. During the 1992 Summer Olympics, the United States fielded a basketball team made up of the best professional basketball players in the world. The so-called Dream Team didn't merely beat their opponents, they demolished them in an athletic display that even the losers admired. Even reviewers who knew nothing about the sport followed the Dream Team's exploits in Barcelona. However, when two opponents possess the same skills, you can't spot the real talent so easily. Yet, identifying an organization's unique or dominant talent lies at the heart of effective crisis management.

While some organizations look good or even invincible in certain areas, close scrutiny can usually uncover a unique or dominant gift. To appreciate this point, consider one of our clients, the Napa Valley Wine Association. The Association promotes the interests of its members, a group of prestigious vineyards scattered across the picturesque wine country of Northern California. During our engagement with them, it surprised us to learn that the Ernest and Julio Gallo Winery, Inc., operates very few vineyards and, in fact, buys over 95 percent of its grapes from independent farmers. Maintaining the company's independence from the uncertainty and weather-related risks that naturally attend the raising of grapes, Gallo focuses on its unique advantage, its gift, which involves producing mass quantities of low-cost, medium-quality wine. While Gallo wines win few top awards, they account for roughly 25 percent of all U.S. wine sales. When you strip away the layers of romantic and culinary imagery that so often accompany the purchase of a bottle of wine, Gallo's gift for production becomes obvious.

Like Gallo, each organization possesses its own unique gift, something, among the scores of activities that consume an organization's energy, that the company does best of all. During a crisis, this gift should form the foundation on which the company builds its team solutions.

For example, in 1990, Apple Computer's once sterling performance began to tarnish. After outperforming IBM and DEC in sales growth, the creative company began to stagnate because it began thinking of itself more and more as computer manufacturer, a radical change from its true gift, the enhancement of computer value. The Apple II, which originally propelled the fledgling company to stardom, incorporated components mostly manufactured by other companies. This strategy allowed the company to focus on user-friendliness and ergonomics. But as the company matured, it used more and more internally manufactured components and overly concentrated on the hardware rather than the value-added user-friendliness that made it so successful in the first place. Consequently, Microsoft seized the preeminent role as the user-friendly software provider. Fortunately, Apple possessed enough crisis savvy to refocus on its true gift, forming strategic alliances with Sony, Motorola, and even IBM to produce the hardware components of their products so they could get back to what Apple does best, making the machine user-friendly.

Going with the gift makes sense because the team already knows how to apply that gift in the marketplace. The gift naturally unites the organization in a common cause. Trying to solve a crisis without building on a foundation of strength amounts to trying to drive a car with one foot on the brake and the other on the gas. The management of such an organization, like the driver of the car, senses the brake's resistance and instinctively tries to overcome the stall by applying more gas in the form of effort and energy. Wiser management, however, removes the emphasis from activities that limit the natural strengths of the organization. They take their foot off the brake, freeing the organization from any restraints that might interfere with applying its gift to the crisis solution.

All in the Family

Nothing weakens an organization's crisis response more than the rise of an elite cult of crisis managers, a select group of crisis priests who conduct their ceremonies as a closeted mystery into which only a favored few may be initiated. Like the runaway strategic planning groups of the '70s, cult crisis managers can splinter the organization's culture, dealing out decisions that no one understands, aiming at objectives no one comprehends, and taking steps no one willingly follows.

Cult crisis managers, like the corporate raiders of the '80s, maintain their power by virtue of the mystery of their craft, intentionally making their methods more and more complex and baffling to the uninitiated. A handful of LBO wizards dominated the investment banking environment for so long because they hornswoggled bankers and investors into believing only the wizards could successfully perform the magic of the leveraged buyout.

Allowed to continue in power, cult crisis management results in imbalanced organizational compensation, particularly in private-sector corporations. As crises, both common and unthinkable, become more prevalent, a favored few corner the market on executive pay, floating from one crisis to the next and demanding ever more astronomical fees for practicing their obscure craft.

All effective crisis management programs must include not only the priest but the choir and congregation as well. After all, crisis does not respect degrees and pedigrees but attacks every member of the organization with the same ferocity. When a serious crisis strikes, it attacks everybody's job. Crisis management, therefore, must be as democratic as crisis itself.

To be effective, a crisis solution must involve all the family. An organization under siege cannot afford fence sitters, observers, and skeptics because corporate salvation almost always requires a united effort, much like the one that Celestial Seasonings, the tea company, used.

When Colorado passed legislation, perceived by some as gay-bashing, high-profile Celestial Seasonings became an informal boycott target of gay groups across the nation. Ironically, the corporate culture at Celestial Seasonings is more flexible, tolerant, and diverse than most, making the company an odd target for national hate. But that same culture was also extremely unified, with every employee highly motivated to help hammer out a solution to this particular crisis. In fact, most employees took the potential boycott personally, as if they, not the company, had been attacked. With this kind of internal support, management of Celestial Seasonings took the boycott in stride, with little effect on corporate performance.

Resonance

Still, you must do more than go with your gift and keep crisis all in the family. You must also package your crisis management program in a way that enables it to resonate throughout the organization. Just as the success of organizations depends on empowering workers, giving individuals responsibility for independent thought and action, so does the effectiveness of their crisis programs. If the rank and file do not easily grasp the logic behind management's actions during a crisis, then they will most likely become part of the problem rather than part of the solution. Information makes or breaks empowered workforces. Withhold it, and a containable crisis will prove fatal. Share it forthrightly, and antibodies flourish to stop the disease.

If crisis were an economy, information would be the coin of its realm, and you would measure common crisis in nickels and dimes, unthinkable crisis in packets of bundled hundred dollar bills. A common crisis will not likely generate the same motivational level among employees as a fight to preserve the very existence of the organization and the jobs it provides. Therefore, management must take great care when communicating the severity of a given crisis.

Some organizations, particularly those in Japan, perpetuate a crisis myth, keeping their workers in a state of constant stress. While this can and does generate waves of motivational momentum, it also produces the organizational version of burnout. Since the end of World War II, Japanese management has motivated workers with the fear that less effort on their part would result in foreign domination of the international market and the decline of Japan. Lately, however, after 40 years of phenomenal effort, Japanese workers have begun to question the myth and demand such unheard-of concessions as a five-day work week, just as World War III, the trade war, is breaking out.

American management errs in the opposite direction. CEOs strive so feverishly to keep stock values high by painting rosy pictures for analysts that they keep their employees working in isolated pockets of contentment right up until the pink slips land on their desks. You cannot win the fight for survival of an organization by keeping employees in the dark about their future. You can only do so with open, honest, accurate communication of a practical and accessible program that even your mail room clerks can get behind. Of course, you must tailor your communication to your organization's character, adopting the style that works best with your people.

Mythology: Entertainment and Error

Frankly, we've gotten a kick out of writing the first section of the book, which has dealt with the five myths of crisis. It's not that the other sections interest us less, but even when we're deeply involved in a consulting engagement with clients, we see how much they, too, enjoy the sessions that address the myths. We think we know why.

Crisis is universal. Fly to a seminar attended by 100 different corporate managers from 100 different countries, representing 100 different products and services, and you will find that your audience shares two attributes: everyone thinks taxes are too high, and everyone experiences crisis, day in and day out. When we analyze crisis from the perspective of the five myths, we make the always distracting and sometimes deadly understandable to the whole audience. For example, we invariably see smiles of recognition on the faces of a board of directors dealing with a serious crisis, when we show them that their particular challenges do not flow from error or oversight but rather from a complex and ambitious vision. Suddenly, a light bulb goes on and their energy shifts from trying to find an offending decision or policy to making careful adjustments to their corporate vision. It's an electrifying experience for an executive, especially after having been cooped up in some corporate retreat for five consecutive days trying to resolve a crisis.

In addition to making crisis more understandable, a discussion of myths makes it more enjoyable. After we detail the myths, we sit back and watch managers open *The Wall Street Journal,* read about the latest-breaking corporate crisis, and identify a number cruncher, spin doctor, or white knight at work. While we were writing this section, Kodak fired its CEO and brought in George Fisher, who had done such a great job with Motorola. At the time, we were working with a group of CEOs from the Young Presidents Organization (YPO), who immediately eliminated the spin doctor label, citing press observations about the "soft-spoken" Fisher, hardly the hallmark of a center-stage crisis star. Another YPOer commented that "Fisher has never fired anyone in his life." Scratch the number cruncher label. By elimination, this group of CEOs identified Fisher as a white knight, a dedicated builder who would take all the potential languishing at Kodak and jump-start the company with a vision of what it could do with that potential. In addition, the group speculated that Fisher might actually bring about permanent solutions and get Kodak off of the crisis merry-go-round. Sure enough, a few weeks later Fisher announced that he was "transforming Kodak into a leader in the electronic multimedia age."

The fact that understanding the five myths tends to make crisis more user-friendly should not divert you from the fact that the myths play a major role in crisis management. By our definition, a myth means misinformation, and misinformation means mistakes. While believing in a myth may not appear to invite serious consequences in the beginning, the consequences rapidly multiply over time. Imagine that a straight horizontal line A represents a correct understanding of crisis, and that a parallel line B represents the misinformation and mistakes instigated by a belief in the crisis myths.

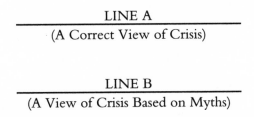

LINE A

(A Correct View of Crisis)

LINE B

(A View of Crisis Based on Myths)

The gap not only seems relatively small, it appears that it never widens. In fact, however, line B does not run parallel to line A, it actually aims downward, ever so slightly. If you magnify it by the power of 10, looking at it from a satellite's rather than a worm's eye view, you'll see that eventually, inexorably, line B takes you further and further away from line A:

LINE A

(A Correct View of Crisis)

LINE B

(A View of Crisis Based on Myths)

No matter how gradually or subtly or seemingly inoffensively the gap widens, the misinformation and mistakes caused by myths end up placing the organization further and further away from correct crisis solutions. At first the missteps are microscopic, but as the crisis develops the missteps become astronomical. When misinformation seeps into an organization's crisis thinking, then, more often than not, all attempts at effective crisis management will fail. Organizations who follow the path of line B commit these fatal errors: managing all crisis alike, placing image over substance, and traveling with too much baggage, the subject of the next section of this book.

Thinking about Crisis: Fighting the Errors of Crisis Management

Given the intensity that accompanies crisis, you must assume that errors will occur as your company struggles for survival. Faulty information may lead to unwise decisions or hampered communications might result in ill-timed implementation of solutions. But these expectable mistakes do not really worry us. Instead, our experience has convinced us that the most serious errors management can commit during crisis are fundamental flaws in crisis thinking that derail all attempts at effective crisis management from the very start. These errors literally sabotage sincere efforts to solve crises because they flow from the myths of crisis and result in outcomes as faulty as the myths themselves. In order to avoid these errors, you must identify what myth or combination of myths contribute the faulty logic that caused the error. Then, you need to weigh the negative consequences of the error so management can isolate that error and deal with it directly. Finally, you must replace the actions that contributed to the error with appropriate actions based on a proper understanding of crisis. Let's briefly examine each of these errors, which we will discuss in detail later in the book.

Error Number One:
Managing All Crises Alike

All crises can and should (for the sake of effective crisis management) be placed in one of two categories: common crisis and the unthinkable. A common crisis temporarily detours an organization from its intended course, while an unthinkable crisis threatens to derail an organization completely and fatally from its path toward a planned set of objectives. One crisis creates varying levels of distraction, while the other detonates a series of destructive consequences.

Once you correctly define your crisis, you can then apply one of two completely separate methodologies for addressing it. One method identifies the distraction and adjusts organizational activity to correct the problem, while the other forces a radical review of the organization, resulting in a literal restructuring.

Error Number Two:
Image over Substance

In addition to all the concrete challenges that normally accompany crisis, an added dimension has sprung up in this age of instantaneous, worldwide communications. Technology has turned crisis management into public performance. Handicams, satellite links, facsimile machines, computer data bases, and the print media, from *The Wall Street Journal* and CNN to the *National Enquirer* and "A Current Affair," have removed any chance of privacy during the management of crisis. Corporate and political leaders, captured and immortalized on videotape, or otherwise exposed to the world by authorized or unauthorized investigations, can no longer work quietly behind the scenes. Every organization with visibility or power finds itself center stage whenever crisis strikes.

Unfortunately this pressure causes many executives to commit the error of playing more to the lights and cameras than to the crisis itself. They divert their energy from actual crisis management and solution to a public relations strategy aimed at protecting the company image at all costs.

Error Number Three:
Too Much Baggage

Crisis tends to force a mental (and sometimes a physical) journey, jarring management from the comfort zone of activities, plans, and objectives they thought they could control, plunging them headfirst into a mire of confusion and disruption. The very real hazards of such a journey cause managers to embark on it cautiously, holding onto all the baggage of the past. Like the proverbial millstone, excess baggage weighs down anyone who must move forward toward a crisis solution.

Organizations, like middle-aged people, become collectors, holding onto precious snapshots, old letters, worn clothes, and used furniture and stashing them in every spare nook and cranny, basement and attic. This accumulation poses no problem at all until moving day, when you must, under great pressure, decide what to take and what to toss.

Organizations collect less tangible junk, but given the mental nature of a journey to the future, the intangibles can burden you just as much as a grand piano. Change is hard enough, but trying to change while dragging every procedure, policy, nuance, and tradition is nigh on impossible. Yet many organizations attempt to make crisis journeys, lugging four particularly heavy pieces of luggage: entrenched leadership, outmoded strategy, old rules and rites, and unnecessary assets.

CHAPTER 6

A Matter of Life and Death: Distinguishing the Common Crisis from the Unthinkable One

Cold or Cancer?

A winter cold and lung cancer both make you sick, but while the one makes you sniffle, the other can put you in your grave. And, of course, you wouldn't treat the sniffles with chemotherapy or radiation any more than you would try to cure a malignant tumor with a couple of aspirin.

Amazingly, however, organizations all too often make just that sort of mistake when prescribing medication for their crises. All crises present problems, but not all problems respond to the same cure. As a case in point, look at two crises that seemed identical on the surface but they, in fact, required two radically different crisis responses. The crises themselves struck over six years ago, but you can still see the symptoms today.

In 1987, the National Highway Traffic Safety Administration began investigating consumer complaints of "unintended acceleration" by Audi 5000 sedans with automatic transmissions. The combined complaints alleged 513 accidents, 271 injuries, and 5 deaths in cars that suddenly took off when shifted from "park" to "drive." While any investigation by a federal agency causes management to worry, Audi did not see the challenge to its premier model as more than a passing crisis, the type for which all auto companies cautiously create contingencies. Audi took further solace from the fact that the National Highway Traffic Safety Administration was at the same time investigating General Motors for complaints linked to 1,121 injuries and 31 deaths, an investigation which seemed statistically more serious. Both crises seemed quite similar on the surface until "Sixty Minutes" singled out the Audi as a "killer car" on national prime-time television. The next year, Audi sales in America dropped 60 percent, turning a common cold into a debilitating cancer. One moment Audi, like General Motors, was fighting to protect its market share, the next *unlike* General Motors, it was battling for its corporate life.

Clearly, the national publicity of the "Sixty Minutes" exposé propelled the Audi crisis into the realm of the unthinkable. Richard Mugg, the fourth executive charged with saving Audi, claimed the car company was "hijacked by the entertainment network." Later in the book we look more closely into those events that tend to transform a normal crisis into the unthinkable, but for now, we want to focus on Audi's response.

Up until the prime-time publicity, Audi treated the investigation as an unwelcomed, but anticipated aspect of operating a major automobile manufacturer. Audi dealt with the National Highway Traffic Safety Administration and the adverse publicity the same way its competitor, General Motors, did. But after the "Sixty Minutes" segment aired, that crisis management approach began to unravel. Defending against a slide in market share requires much less effort than fighting for your life. Audi's problems forced the company into a broader, bolder, all-or-nothing approach that would radically change its future or leave it with no future at all. Now, some six years later, the automobile industry still reels from the effects of Audi's change in crisis management. Rather than simply dealing with the National Traffic Safety Administration (and "Sixty Minutes"), Audi went directly to the consumer with a radically redesigned line of cars and a radical new approach to selling them, offering free service for the average life of the car (five years) and providing a guaranteed trade-in value to protect the consumer against rapid depreciation. These two innovations forced the entire automobile industry to rethink its sales and service programs, all to the benefit of the consumers. On the other hand, General Motors, facing a routine crisis, faced it routinely; and it passed, routinely.

Our point is that once Audi's crisis took on the characteristics of a life-or-death battle, it would have been futile for the company to simply continue with routine crisis management. Their approach needed to change in tandem with the changes that were transforming their crisis. It would not have been enough to merely increase the intensity or urgency of their original crisis actions. Doing so would amount to thinking that if a cold demands two days of bed rest, cancer requires 20 days. This kind of prescription on the part of a doctor would almost certainly result in a malpractice suit. Instead, Audi needed to take an altogether different crisis approach. What saved them was the realization that their crisis had become radically different than it originally appeared and that they would be committing a grave error if they tried to manage the new crisis the same old way.

Anticipation, Damage, and Recovery

In its simplest form, a common crisis afflicts an organization like a cold, while the unthinkable attacks it like a cancer. Even at this rudimentary level of differentiation, it becomes clear that the approach to combat a cancer should differ dramatically from the steps to overcome a cancer. With that in mind, let's look more specifically at exactly *why* the same approach does not work for both types of crisis. Getting specific involves looking at crisis from three vantage points: anticipation, damage, and recovery.

Anticipation

This vantage point involves expectation. It asks the question, "How often do I expect this type of crisis to strike?" In the course of your lives, you expect that you will come down with a cold. This expectation even includes newborn babies, so when six-month-old Junior comes down with a cough and a fever, you, as parents, do not radically alter your lives to address the illness. At most, you'll suffer three or four days of distracted sleep and perhaps a few days away from the office until Junior's illness passes. More importantly, you have undoubtedly prepared yourself for the cold, given your expectation that it will likely occur.

On the other hand, people rarely expect cancer. Only the most pessimistic parents (excluding those with strong genetic indicators) assume that their six-month-old baby will one day come down with cancer. Consequently, when cancer strikes, it creates a set of consequences more unsettling than those that attend the common cold. Lifestyles, in the form of

77

work schedules, vacations, and college dreams, change radically. However, going through life mentally preparing yourself that one day cancer will strike your child would make your life miserable and probably do little to ease your pain if and when the cancer does finally strike.

Damage

While anticipation is a mental issue, damage is a physical one. When we talk about viewing crisis from the vantage point of damage, we are talking about actual, literal, and painful harm. Following our cold vs. cancer illustration, you worry less about the physical consequences of a cold than about the physical harm of a cancer.

In fact, most people feel so relatively comfortable with the damage that a cold can cause, that millions ignore cold symptoms and continue to stay on the job, until they get too sick to ignore the rest and medication they need to overcome the physical problem. This same approach does not work for victims of cancer, who seldom ignore or postpone their treatment. Nor do they cavalierly maintain their current lifestyles at the expense of their very lives. Clearly, assumptions about what kind of damage a particular type of crisis will cause affects both your attitude toward, and the timing of, the cure.

Recovery

This last vantage point is crucial because it involves the assumptions you make about what life will be like in the wake of the crisis.

As with a common cold, recovery from a common crisis does not demand a major change from life before the illness. With rare exception, you basically get back to life as usual, except for a few lingering symptoms. Cancer, on the other hand, puts all your schedules, routines, goals, and dreams on hold. In extreme cases, life as usual gives way to a vastly different life. Recovery then becomes a series of sweeping and sometimes abrupt changes. Even the mildest cancer leaves its victim forever changed.

Viewing crisis from the three vantage points facilitates classifying various crises, differentiating one from another in terms of anticipation, damage, and recovery. Again, crises differ, and differences demand different crisis approaches.

Common Crisis

Continuing with our metaphor, you should be able to identify a common crisis as easily as a common cold. But what if the cold turns into pneumonia? Will you come down with a cold this winter? Probably. Will you discover a malignant tumor? Probably not. Will you get pneumonia? Maybe. The statistical chances lie somewhere between a cold and cancer, making it sensible to entertain the possibility of pneumonia.

The viewpoints of anticipation, damage, and recovery take on great significance when identifying a "pneumonia-level" crisis. Lots of common colds occur every day, fewer cases of cancer crop up, but pneumonia occurs frequently. In the same way, scores of crises fall in the middle of the spectrum. Do you not run a greater risk of mistreating a crisis that falls between a cold and cancer than one that clearly resides at one extreme or the other, leaving little doubt about its type? For this reason, you must diagnose every given crisis accurately. Let's look at the symptoms that span the spectrum.

Frequency

Murphy's Law—anything that can go wrong will go wrong—generally holds true. Only the most inexperienced or naive executive assumes that carefully thought-out strategies will work in real life as well as they do on paper.

All executives expect problems to crop up in their organizations, though they anticipate that certain problems will strike more frequently than others. You can usually classify a crisis as common when you expect it to occur rather frequently. No, a common crisis does not erupt every day. It might strike only once every two years or twice every five years, but it does tend to happen with some regularity.

In Greensboro, North Carolina, Ford truck owners noticed paint peeling from 2-year old vehicles. The malady occurred so regularly that television station WFMY invited all Ford owners with bad paint jobs to show up at the local coliseum. About 70 did. That attracted the attention of State Attorney General Mike Easly, who pressed Ford for some sort of solution. Attributing the faulty paint job to a change in the painting process in 1985, Ford agreed to repaint the trucks, news of which triggered a national flood of similar complaints. Rough calculations show that Ford could be looking at upwards of 25 million vehicles at about $1,000 each to repaint. That's $25 billion dollars in potential repair costs.

At first glance, a $25 billion crisis appears unthinkable. But, unfortunately for the consumer, it represents just another common crisis for the auto maker. Ford builds into its thinking the reality that it will inevitably recall millions of its cars for any one of a score of defects. Not only does the company view the recalls as inevitable, they also see them as frequent—a common, everyday occurrence.

The element of frequency that makes a crisis common provides the motivation to prepare for the crisis. A crisis you can anticipate with some regularity rarely catches you off guard. For example, American auto companies set aside financial reserves to deal with recalls, and they have grown so accustomed to recalls that a government investigation, while attention-grabbing, does not ordinarily throw a wrench into the routines, plans, and objectives of the Big Three in Detroit.

Distraction

All organizations encounter normal problems they must overcome on the path toward meeting their goals. When a challenge crops up that forces a detour off the planned path, that also signals a common crisis.

Common crises present more detours, distracting management from their intended course. By its very definition, a detour poses a temporary condition that may force a company either to stop momentarily its forward progress or put forth enough effort to go around the obstacle. But in either case, sooner or later, the organization will "get back on the road."

In 1992, the Federal Drug Administration (FDA) served notice that red dye number 3 would no longer be acceptable for use in food products. Tests on laboratory rats had concluded that the controversial dye might potentially cause cancer. This presented a particularly urgent crisis for Norm Correia, the CEO of S & W Fine Foods, Inc.

Companies like S & W used red dye number 3 in scores of applications, from making gelatin look attractive to kids to coloring the cherries in fruit cocktail a striking red even after they've been sitting in the can. Banning the dye, while important for consumer well-being, created a crisis S & W needed to solve in short order. Consumers would not stand for a bottle of bland yellow maraschino cherries. But the crisis itself created but a short-term roadblock. In less than 12 months, the food industry had developed a set of alternative food colorings to replace red dye number 3. San Francisco-based S & W played a key role in the development process, and the entire food industry soon got back on track with regular production.

When classifying a common crisis, remember that the same distraction or detour may look different to various organizations, even though the actual crisis remains the same. For example, in three of the more affluent sections of Southern California in 1993, brush fires destroyed over 700 homes. The prices of these homes averaged $500,000. To the larger insurance companies, the fires represented an expensive detour to their profit projections for the year, but for others, the fires literally scorched the insurers, forcing them out of business in California. The exact same crisis posed a detour to some and the end of the road for others.

Reality Check

At various times for different reasons, organizations do not stay in touch with change. The story is told of a rural voter who, during the 1992 presidential primaries, was asked if he thought taxes should be raised and if the President was doing a good job. The voter answered a definite "no" on taxes, but commented that he thought "Ike" was doing a damn good job under the circumstances. To a certain extent, all executives behave like that misinformed voter from time to time. Change occurs so quickly, that not even the most astute observer can keep up with it. Consequently, you just wait until circumstances come along and force you to conduct a reality check and catch up with the times.

Crisis, of course, does not respect inattention, and it seems to attack precisely when you have gotten a little out of touch with your customers or your competitors. Losing an account, a product advantage, or an entire market illustrates crises that jar you into updating your perspective as it did for Procter & Gamble Co.

For years, Procter & Gamble worked hard to develop binding relationships with the stores that sold their products. Their commitment to this strategy even caused them to station full-time employees near Wal-Mart's headquarters in Arkansas to work closely with the giant retailer. But the approach did not keep Wal-Mart from offering its consumers private label look-alike alternatives to Procter & Gamble products such as Tide detergent. The private-label detergent carried a price tag significantly lower than Tide, which attracted consumers, and the ire of Procter & Gamble.

The consumer trend toward acceptance of private-label alternatives to the brand names that have dominated retail shelves for years has become a source of deep worry to companies, from Coca-Cola to Ralston-Purina. The crisis has caused organizations like Philip Morris Co. to perform a careful reality check, resulting in their slashing the price of Marlboro cigarettes, which sparked a cigarette price war. Similar battles are being waged in soft drinks, diapers, shampoo, and pet food. No brand-name product, it seems, remains safe from competing private-label alternatives.

We classify a crisis that demands a reality check as a common crisis because in such a situation, you still enjoy a reality to check. Procter & Gamble faces stiffer competition from a consumer trend that values price over hype, but P & G products have by no means disappeared, nor is P & G fighting for its life as a producer of consumer products. In reality, private-label detergents accounted for only 3.2 percent of total U.S. laundry detergent sales for the 12 months ending in August 1993. This loss hardly poses a major threat to Procter & Gamble, where Tide accounts for only a fraction of the company's sales. But still, you must check reality. Ignore a trend long enough, and soap executives might themselves be all washed up, a victim of private-label growth gone unchecked.

Having categorized a common crisis as one that occurs relatively frequently and poses an annoying enough distraction to demand a reality check, we now must consider a crisis that breaks beyond these constraints into the realm of the unthinkable.

Unthinkable Crisis

Identifying an unthinkable crisis involves evaluating conditions using the same three criteria of anticipation, damage, and recovery, only in the case of unthinkable crisis, the evaluation results in vastly different conclusions on each point. While a common crisis strikes frequently, distracting management and forcing a reality check, the unthinkable occurs randomly, can be dangerously destructive, and demands that the organization make a radical paradigm shift or perish.

Randomness

Respecting Murphy's Law, all organizations plan for problems. Unfortunately, the problems executives anticipate tend to reflect what they think will probably occur, while downplaying the possible but highly unlikely occurrence. This approach works fine under normal conditions. Most corporate and government crises fall into the category of the probable. But as organizations journey through the '90s into the next century, improbable conditions are fast becoming the norm rather than the exception.

The emancipation of Eastern Europe; the decline of Communism in the former Soviet Union; the creation of a single economic trade zone between Canada, the United States, and Mexico; the disintegration of IBM; the on-again, off-again merger of Volvo and Renault; the creation of a U.S. national health-care system based on socialized medicine; Japan's importation of foreign rice; and Michael Jordan's early and abrupt retirement from basketball all represent improbable occurrences that became reality in the first three years of this decade. Peter Drucker warns that "every few hundred years in Western history there occurs a sharp transformation." That transformation has arrived.

When a crisis strikes randomly and without warning, beware. It may be serving notice that it will escalate to unthinkable proportions. A combination of improbability and randomness makes preparation for this type of crisis nearly impossible. Look closely at the mechanics. Say, for example, that a business traveler, a million-miler, believed that sooner or later his flight would crash crossing the Pacific Ocean to Japan. That's an improbable, but possible scenario. So, on every flight, the traveler dons a life jacket, inflates it, and wears it throughout the flight. Even though the plane might crash, the concerned executive cannot determine which flight will actually crash. Since the crash would be a random phenomenon, the traveler must wear the life jacket on every flight. Is there something wrong with this picture? Indeed, the traveler will not only spend half a day flying in discomfort, he won't get any important work done along the way. A whole set of business and global conditions akin to the potential for such a plane crash began to assemble, and Pepsi ran smack dab into one of them.

In a bizarre case of copycat tampering, consumers began reporting cans of Pepsi with hospital syringes *inside* the can. The company knew that the sabotage was not occurring at the bottling plant, but somewhere else. The company's suspicions proved correct when authorities eventually apprehended a suspect accused of planting syringes in the cans. Given the millions of cans of soft drinks sold every day, such tampering will possibly happen again. But Pepsi and the other soft drink manufacturers cannot spend each day wearing life jackets waiting for the plane to crash. They simply cannot defend each can against a random occurrence of tampering.

Consequently, random occurrences such as major oil spills (Exxon), chemical leaks (Union Carbide), nuclear plant malfunctions (Three Mile Island), fraud by executive officers (Charles Keating), major product disasters (Rely tampons), adverse legal judgments (Texaco), and even the loss of a key asset (the Chicago Bulls facing Jordan's retirement) qualify the crisis for classification in the category of the unthinkable.

Destructive

In 1993, a federal jury in Arkansas found DuPont Co. liable for over $10 million in a lawsuit alleging that a fungicide manufactured by the company damaged crops. The award does not seem particularly damaging to DuPont until you consider that this was the first of over 400 damage suits around the country involving Benlate, the fungicide in question. Now, let's put this in perspective.

DuPont looks like a well-run company with a great reputation in the industry and among consumers. It clearly did not intentionally manufacture Benlate to damage crops. Nor did it attempt to cover up the negative impact of its product when consumers began complaining. In fact, since DuPont voluntarily pulled its product in 1991, it has paid out about $500 million to settle claims with nearly 2,000 growers. Yet the company still faces over 400 lawsuits that, based on the outcome of the first court case, will cost the company dearly.

DuPont's disaster beautifully illustrates a case of bad things happening to good companies. And they happen all the time. When they do, they can destroy, obviously thrusting the crisis into the domain of the unthinkable. Ironically, a shady company pushing a shoddy product half expects the boom to be lowered sometime in the future. But a good company, marketing what it considers an excellent product, really gets clobbered by an unthinkable crisis.

When studies allegedly linked tampons to toxic shock syndrome, two companies, Procter & Gamble and Playtex (then a division of Esmark, Inc.), became embroiled in the recall and the numerous lawsuits that followed. As in DuPont's case, it stretches the imagination to conclude that Procter & Gamble and Playtex intentionally entered the market with a product they knew to be hazardous.

As with common crises, the damage caused by an unthinkable crisis can run the gamut from distraction to destruction. In the cases of DuPont, Proc-

84

ter & Gamble, and Playtex, you cannot fully measure the damage in financial terms. All three companies carry adequate product insurance. Rather, the damage comes in terms of shattered public trust and confidence. Each company sells products that demand that the consumer hold the company, and its product, in high regard. Lose that regard, and you may well lose your corporate life.

Paradigm Shift

Major changes in your life force major changes in your thinking, and genuine rethinking requires a paradigm shift. The word "paradigm" derives from the Greek word *paradigma,* which means "pattern." When you shift a paradigm, then you do not merely adjust a faulty assumption or make a small adjustment to accommodate an obstacle in the road, but you completely repattern your thinking. A paradigm shift is to a reality check what a hurricane is to good kite-flying weather. The state of affairs that confronted a U.S. business when it awoke from New Year's Eve celebrations on January 1, 1993 provides a compelling example.

At the stroke of midnight on December 31, 1992, 12 European nations combined to form a powerful confederation called the European Community (EC). Overnight, with one stroke of the clock and a swift swipe of the pen, the United States dropped from its perennial position as the world's number-one creator of gross national product and gross exports and imports to number two. The 12 European countries that once expended energy and effort competing against one another now turned that energy and effort toward a concerted attempt to dominate global competition.

Admittedly, it will take time before the impact of a newly unified Europe begins to reveal itself. But even before 1993 ended, the group had taken steps to create a single currency, a central bank, and a united European military force apart from NATO. The scope of these changes demands of U.S. business more than a simple reality check of modern geography. It requires a complete restructuring of all existing assumptions about global competition. For starters, Americans can stop wringing their hands over Japan and start wringing them over a more powerful Europe.

In 1989, Michael Silva toured Brazil on a lecture tour with futurists Al and Heidi Toffler. While eating Japanese food in a swank Sao Paulo suburb, the Tofflers listed one paradigm after another that would shift in the '90s. Software would come to dominate computer hardware, knowledge assets

85

would replace hard assets in calculating organizational value, consumer control would eclipse control by producers, nation-states (like France and Mexico) would give way to mega-states (the EC and NAFTA) and global corporations would become values-driven not profit-driven, and on and on. These kinds of changes force radical changes in thinking, but rarely do people change their thinking voluntarily. Rather it often takes an unthinkable crisis to blast you out of your complacency and into a whole new way of thinking.

Having defined an unthinkable crisis in terms of randomness, destructiveness, and paradigm shifting, we can now compare the two types of crisis to see exactly why they demand their own crisis management approaches.

The Right Stuff

Notice how the attributes of each type of crisis differ so completely:

Common Crisis	Unthinkable Crisis
Anticipated	Random
Distracting	Destructive
Reality Check	Paradigm Shift

The opposing nature of these characteristics of common and unthinkable crises prompts an obvious conclusion: the solutions to them should be equally opposing.

Managing all crises the same way creates one of two problems: either you apply too little or too much of the right stuff. Most thinking about different types of crises involves measurements of seriousness and intensity. Is this a crisis, a *serious* crisis, or maybe even a *mega*-crisis? As our classification of crises as common or unthinkable suggests, you should view every crisis as a serious one, just different in structure. Since any crisis challenges the course pursued by the organization, then it follows that, one by one, the organization must address and resolve every crisis, regardless of its type or severity. In this sense, you should take every crisis seriously. Further, the difference in intensity between a common and an unthinkable crisis does not always vary that dramatically. Interestingly, a simple crisis often wreaks as much management havoc as the most pressing problems.

In nature, crises stimulate animals to respond one of three ways: freeze, flee, or fight. The rabbit goes hopping along the trail until it runs into the fox. The organization goes merrily about its business until it encounters a threat to its existence. In both cases, the sight of danger sends signals to the brain: danger, danger, danger! And the body responds by freezing (maybe the fox or the crisis will not see me and leave me alone); fleeing (maybe I can outrun the fox or the crisis); or fighting (maybe I can bowl over the fox or crisis and scamper to safety). Interestingly, the mind and body responds the same way to a lesser threat. The rabbit meets a larger, more aggressive rabbit; the organization comes up against the bigger, bolder competition. Again, the body prepares itself to freeze, flee, or fight. In the former case, if you freeze, you may be eaten alive; if you flee, you will probably not escape; if you fight, you will lose. In the latter case, freezing or fleeing or fighting may well carry the day. Clearly, the correct response depends on the nature of the threat. In the long run, you should not deal with the fox or the unthinkable crisis the same way you would handle the larger rabbit or the more muscular competition, but when either condition arises, the same emotions erupt, causing all animals, whether rabbits or managers, to seethe with emotion that clouds the decision to freeze, flee, or fight.

In this way, even minor organizational crises tend to cast managers into a crisis mode, causing them to set aside daily routines to clear the agenda for concentration on the problem at hand. Special meetings are convened to gear up for the action required to meet the challenge. No matter the category of the crisis, initial activity often looks the same, and it takes the same emotional toll. Later on, as the intensity or seriousness of the crisis becomes more apparent, as it turns out to be either more or less than it at first appeared, only then do you stop and question the intensity of your initial response to the crisis. Only then do you think, "Hell, we overreached on this problem!" or "Damn, we didn't take this problem seriously enough!"

As a crisis unfolds, managers tend to treat seriousness and intensity as whipping posts. When your crisis approach doesn't get results, you tend to blame it on taking the crisis too seriously or not seriously enough. But doing so skirts the real issue. Take education, for example.

No one would argue that a crisis does not exist in U.S. education. The government knows it, the teachers know it, and the parents know it. While everyone shares the perception that the crisis has existed for 10 years or more, no one has developed a comprehensive solution that all parties can accept. Should the education establishment put forth a stronger effort to solve its problems? It could, and perhaps it should, but that alone won't solve the problem, as Hawaii learned the hard way.

The Board of Education in the state of Hawaii is mired in crisis. Along with the usual concerns over math, language, and science test scores, the board also deals with a diverse culture in which less than 27 percent of the population comes from any single racial background. In addition, it must grapple with socioeconomic issues, such as the fact that a growing percentage of the elementary students are latchkey kids whose working parents are not home when school ends at 3:00 P.M. This has forced some schools in Hawaii to become care centers from 3:00 P.M. to 5:00 P.M. Finally, Hawaii's acceptance and tolerance of immigrants creates the expensive condition in which English is not the first, or often, the second language. These conditions make it very difficult for the Board of Education to operate within the budget constraints imposed by the legislature.

Budget overruns ignite a groundswell of public opinion that Board Superintendent Charles Toguchi needs to work harder to solve the system's problems. Yet, our association with Superintendent Toguchi suggests anything but a manager lacking in motivation or effort. In addition, when we met with over 3,000 of his administrators and teachers, we found a group that worked above and beyond the call of duty, commonly bringing to the classroom their own teaching resources (such as paper, learning aids, and pencils) and personally dealing with non-classroom issues such as physical abuse and malnutrition. It would be difficult, with a clear conscience, to go along with the accusation that the entire system lacks sufficient effort. Instead, it could be concluded that the system needs not more effort, but a strong dose of the right stuff in the form of a modified approach.

The solution to any type of crisis stems less from the intensity of your effort than from selecting the right response. Organizations often do not get the results they think they should because they've chosen the wrong response, not because they did not work hard enough. Success hinges not on hard work but on implementing the right approach at the right time. In other words, during a crisis, effectiveness (doing the right thing) matters much more than efficiency (doing things well).

The ability to differentiate common crisis from the unthinkable and to avoid the error of treating both crises alike becomes important in Part Four, where we will discuss the most effective methods of managing crisis.

CHAPTER 7

Spin over Substance: When the Facts Aren't Friendly

Physician, Heal Thyself

In November 1991, the FDA revealed a startling fact: silicone gel, commonly used for breast implants, caused highly malignant cancers in more than 23 percent of test rats. The finding immediately ignited demands from consumer advocacy groups that the FDA ban all silicone gel implants. The initial headline and the consumer response caught the medical profession by surprise. Stunned by the potential impact of an all-out ban, the American Society of Plastic and Reconstructive Surgeons quickly hit the press with their version of the crisis. Attacking the FDA study, the doctors charged that the study had "little, if any, relevance to humans." The response, which struck consumer groups as a blatant attempt by the doctors to protect their business and sounded much like the rebuttal from the tobacco industry to charges that smoking causes lung cancer, only further alienated the public.

Stung by the negative reaction to their press release, the American Society of Plastic and Reconstructive Surgeons next tried a more subtle approach. While admitting that silicone breast implants carried some risk, the doctors argued that the benefits to women far outweighed the danger. The argument was sound. For women who have been affected by breast cancer, implants promised salvation in the form of near-normal appearance.

Unfortunately, the doctors extended the argument to apply to women who sought implants for cosmetic reasons, suggesting that a ban on implants would significantly affect the self-esteem of the underdeveloped woman. At this point, the consumer groups again saw red, and the crisis turned downright ugly.

In the midst of the implant controversy, politicians and the press were debating the larger issue of how and who would pay for basic medical care for millions of under- and uninsured Americans. In the middle of this debate, the American Association of Plastic and Reconstructive Surgeons' response to the implant issue sounded to a skeptical public nothing short of self-serving greed.

It is tempting during crisis, particularly for a high-profile organization, to worry more how a crisis looks, than to pinpoint its true nature. In light of the revolution in communications that can transform an ordinary crisis into a prime-time event, you sometimes feel you must, first and foremost, present your case to the media, even if you haven't fully developed your case. That's what the plastic surgeons did, and they paid for the mistake in terms of the very sort of bad press they wanted to short-circuit.

At one time, crisis was private property. An organization could confine its problems to the boardroom, choosing when and how to release glimpses of its struggles with those problems. This control over information insured that any public display would portray a desired image of the organization. But then crisis became public performance, as the technology of handicams, satellite links, facsimile machines, computer data bases, and the reports of "Sixty Minutes" and its host of copycat television exposés wormed their way into every nook and cranny of corporate and government life. These days, everything you say and do about crisis can be captured and immortalized on videotape or computer disk or in unauthorized biographies. As a result, any organization with responsibility or power sets foot on stage whenever crisis strikes. Faced with this reality, too many organizations, like the plastic surgeons, favor spin over substance.

In the public mind, the FDA study provoked a paradigm shift regarding the use of implants. Cancer in laboratory rats had convinced the media and consumers that implants indeed posed a danger. The damage was done. The spin on the crisis offered by the American Society of Plastic and Reconstructive Surgeons only pitted their opinion against that of the rats, and the rats won. A panel, specially formed by the FDA, recommended that implants only be allowed for surgery to reconstruct diseased breasts and be banned from all strictly cosmetic use until further testing, which may take years. The physicians were stunned. Breast enhancement for strictly cosmetic motives accounted for a whopping 80 percent of the silicone implant business. In the end, the physicians stung themselves with their own spin on the situation.

The decision to apply spin rather than deal with the substance of a crisis derives from the faulty assumption that an organization will incur less damage if it tries to manipulate the public image of its crisis struggle. The assumption may have worked at one time, when an organization could closely guard and control information. However, in our current communications environment, where information flows freely and invites daily public scrutiny, putting a self-serving spin on a crisis rarely works and often backfires. Just following the Gulf War, Charles Jackson, a physician at the Veterans Affairs Medical Center in Tuskegee, Alabama, diagnosed the ailments of a Gulf War veteran as having resulted from exposure to chemical weapons. His patient, a fireman from Columbus, Georgia, was one of over 8,000 veterans of the Gulf War who had officially registered complaints of symptoms possibly associated with chemical warfare. In response, the Pentagon emphatically denied the use of chemical weapons by either side during the war. The Pentagon's position, conjuring up memories of the military's denial that nuclear testing contaminated certain rural towns in Arizona, Utah, and Nevada (a position from which they were eventually forced to retreat) prompted great skepticism. However, proof did not exist to counter the government position until an independent study conducted by the Czech military detected trace amounts of mustard gas and the nerve agent sarin in Saudi Arabia during Desert Storm. The Czech finding forced the Pentagon to reverse itself, leaving an already skeptical public disgusted with what looked like a cover-up.

The Pentagon's preference for defending its image versus addressing the substance of the crisis not only proved unproductive as a crisis management approach, but it also intensified the initial problem by creating an additional crisis of credibility. A spin approach, in other words, tends to pay too little attention to the substance of a fiasco, doing nothing to fix it and even making it worse.

When an organization emphasizes protecting its image during a crisis, it usually does so with what we call damage control.

Damage Control

The military loves to talk about "damage control," a phrase that refers to the energy and efforts an organization puts forth to control an accident or some other unwelcome event that has harmed the organization. We like the phrase ourselves. If a fire breaks out on a naval warship, the vessel's personnel focus on the single objective of limiting the consequences of the fire as soon as possible. But imagine a scene where, as the fire blazes, the damage control team first meets to assess how the fire (and their efforts to contain it) will reflect on their service records and careers. Then picture the team writing a memo to be broadcast over the ship's public address system downplaying the danger of the fire, denying any responsibility for causing the fire, adding a philosophical note that "fires happen," and then suggesting that the team should not be held liable for any consequences that might occur while they fight the blaze. All this before anyone unrolls a single hose! The imagined scenario makes us laugh, but organizations play it out every day when fires break out, and often with dire results.

The concern over how the world perceives an organization during crisis often gets in the way of effectively managing the crisis itself, compromising and diluting real damage control to the point where it becomes "damaged control." The play on words suggests a situation in which the real crisis rages while the organization diverts its effort toward its image and the honor of its management. While many factors contribute to damaged control, two figure most prominently: playing the victim and legal wrangling. These two activities cause damage because they do absolutely nothing to address the crisis itself. When they come into play, the organization in crisis finds itself dealing with two unrelated issues at the same time, much like trying to read a book while peddling a bicycle down the highway. You might pull it off, but the book does not propel the bike and peddling the bike does not make the book any easier to comprehend. While each activity might benefit an individual, they do not benefit each other. Now, add the element of a pack of wolves chasing the bike. In this situation, not only do the activities not benefit each other, but one activity actually hinders the other. Continuing to read the book while trying to pedal for your life and skirt potholes would almost certainly turn you into wolf food. Warren Anderson knows from experience.

On December 3, 1984, while most of the impoverished residents of Bhopal, India, slept, a Union Carbide pesticide plant leaked poison gas into the air. Within hours, at least 2,000 residents had died and 200,000 lay injured. The number of dead and dying may have been grossly underestimated. No one knows the precise numbers even 10 years after the accident because entire villages were wiped out and many of the dead were burned in mass funeral pyres before officials could record the deaths. In addition, the extreme poverty of the area left many of the injured unreported as they simply migrated elsewhere. But even the conservative numbers suggest a crisis of tragic proportions. While helpless villagers suffered and died, Warren Anderson, then chairman and chief executive officer of Union Carbide, did an amazing thing. He boarded a plane for Bhopal. Now, in hindsight, many public relations professionals and lawyers criticize Anderson for that decision. Many have even taken to challenging his motives, pointing to his legal background and painting his journey as an attempt to head off lawsuits at the pass. Regardless of his motive, however, Anderson took a refreshingly different approach to the crisis. Instead of hiding in the corporate bunker headquarters at Danbury, Connecticut, with an army of public relations consultants and a legion of lawyers, he struck off alone to face the consequences of a tragedy his company had caused. Unfortunately, the journey ended poorly. Indian officials arrested Anderson almost immediately after his plane landed, then they released him and put him on a plane back to the United States. Sadly, Anderson's creative and courageous crisis management ended, and Union Carbide adopted the more common approach of damage control, playing the victim and resorting to legal wrangling.

Playing the Victim

During a crisis, an organization can easily succumb to the temptation to play the innocent victim of circumstances or someone else's malice. Union Carbide began assuming the role of victim shortly after Anderson returned from India, when he called the press conference and "launched a trial balloon" hinting at the possibility of sabotage. But the balloon popped. A number of investigations failed to produce a single shred of evidence to support the "deliberate act" Anderson had suggested to the press.

Union Carbide then tried out another victim role. At another press conference Anderson stated that "noncompliance with safety issues is a local issue." His line of thinking suggested that since Union Carbide India, Ltd., managed the plant, the local management, not Union Carbide, should accept accountability for the gas leak. But the press greeted this reasoning with great skepticism, especially in light of the failed sabotage story. *The New York Times* argued that Union Carbide retained "the authority to exercise financial and technical control over its affiliate, Union Carbide India, Ltd., and the American parent often used that right, according to former officials of the Indian company and others with knowledge of the concern." The Indian government agreed with the *Times'* assessment and found Union Carbide's attempt to "pass-the-rupee" to its local co-owners "unjustifiable and unacceptable."

Legal Wrangling

When the public refuses to see the organization as a victim, management passes the scepter of crisis management to the lawyers. This move represents an important change in crisis thinking because the lawyers come at crisis management with a single-minded intent on limiting liability. They concern themselves less with the long-term impact of their legal strategy than on the protection of immediate dollars. In the case of Union Carbide, limiting liability meant arguing that a life in Bhopal, India, was worth less than a life in Brooklyn, New York. If the argument held, the settlement for the dead and injured would amount to much less than the opposition lawyers had claimed. In addition, the legal juggling act of valuing a human life the same way a neighborhood would value a house, led Union Carbide to donate a scant $1.1 million toward initial relief, only to find itself ordered by U.S. courts to provide an additional $5 million for interim relief. Still, the total amount came to less than $20 per victim.

It might seem irrelevant to resurrect a tragedy that occurred over 10 years ago to make a point about emphasizing image over substance under crisis conditions, but, in reality, the Bhopal disaster actually represents a *current* crisis. How Union Carbide conducted itself during the tragedy resulted in three current issues that plagued the company long after the initial gas leak.

First, will the real Union Carbide please stand up? Warren Anderson's unsolicited and unprecedented passage to India presented such a stark contrast to his later tact of playing the victim and dragging the value of the dead through court that you must wonder which tactic represents the company's values. The question poses the sensitive economic question, "Would you like a Union Carbide plant in *your* town, given its response to Bhopal?" If, perchance, an accident occurred in a U.S. plant, would the company's lawyers argue that a life in the rust belt of the Northeast is worth less than a life in the sunbelt of the Southwest? Or would a Warren Anderson rush to the site and do whatever was required to right the wrong?

Second, did placing image over substance really pay off? After seven years of legal wrangling, Union Carbide settled for roughly $450 million in compensation to the victims of Bhopal. Almost a decade after the disaster, at a rally held in Jayaprakash Nagar, a Bhopal slum where the gas leak killed residents, Indian Prime Minister Vishwanath Pratap Singh announced that his government had decided to reject the $450 million settlement. "We have decided to do away with the settlement and pursue the $3 billion suit against the company and also the criminal suit against the Union Carbide officials," Singh declared. "We believe there can be no deal over human corpses."

While you might question the political and economic motives behind Singh's words, clearly Union Carbide's takeover battle with GAF, a chemical and roofing materials company, affected the Indian government's position. In an effort to fend off GAF's hostile takeover, Union Carbide bought back 55 percent of its stock for roughly $3 billion. Analysts commented that the amount spent by Union Carbide to defend itself against the takeover made the amount offered in settlement for the victims of the Bhopal disaster look paltry.

The attempts by the Indian government to pursue further compensation, coupled with the threat of criminal proceedings, suggests that Union Carbide's image strategy of playing the victim and limiting liability through protracted legal wrangling may not have been cost-effective in the long run. While we can only speculate in hindsight, it seems plausible that Warren Anderson's initial compassionate crisis approach coupled with a fair (not merely legal) settlement may have put the crisis to rest, once and for all. But for now, Bhopal remains an open-ended liability, hanging like a dark cloud over Union Carbide's future.

Third, did the emphasis on image address the possibility of another Bhopal-like disaster occurring in the future? Amazingly, just eight months and eight days after the Bhopal accident, a toxic gas leak at Union Carbide's Institute, West Virginia, plant sent 135 area residents to hospitals for treatment. Fortunately, no one died. But then, just two days later, another leak at a Union Carbide plant in South Charleston, West Virginia, spilled about 1,000 gallons of chemicals into the environment and sent four area residents to the hospital for eye irritation and nausea. Just two weeks later, at the same South Charleston plant, yet another spill spread hydrochloric acid into the area. Though this leak caused no injuries, it could have spelled a real disaster to

95

the 60,000 fans attending a Chubby Checker concert just one and a half miles upwind of the plant. The Environmental Protection Agency cited this particular plant for 16 toxic spills in 1984 alone. To top it off, in 1991 an explosion occurred at Union Carbide's Seadrift plant in Port Lavaca, Texas, killing one person and injuring 26 others. The company suspended operations at that plant, lopping off two-thirds of the company's polyethylene production.

A subtle but very real connection exists between Union Carbide's safety record in the United States and the 10-year-old disaster in Bhopal. Following the Bhopal accident, Union Carbide attempted to position itself as a victim of the improper management and safety procedures of local executives. This line of reasoning, while possibly producing short-term legal benefits, lulled Union Carbide's workers into believing in the safety of their own plants in the United States, even though they followed safety procedures and guidelines identical to those in place at Bhopal. While the Bhopal disaster should have forced an immediate rethinking of all Union Carbide's safety procedures, the company instead stuck to its story that Bhopal simply occurred as a by-product of doing business in Third World underdeveloped countries, a story that quickly proved false.

Seeing with a Different Set of Eyes

You can easily criticize a high-profile company like Union Carbide struck by a high-profile disaster like Bhopal, but you should pause to view the crisis through the eyes of Union Carbide. Since every business and government organization at one time or another faces the same sort of dilemmas encountered by Union Carbide, you can gain some insight into crisis management by seeking some common denominators. Three, in particular, stand out.

Risky Products

Union Carbide, the fourth-largest chemical company in the United States, deals with some truly dangerous stuff. While the public may disdain the accidents and loss of life that chemical plant mishaps can cause, neither will the public tolerate life without ziplock bags, nylon carpet, brightly painted cars, colorful wallpaper, computer keyboards, and Mont Blanc pens, all of which owe their existence to the chemical industry. Whether a company

makes cars, toys, Christmas tree lights, or even information, its activities usually incur a dangerous downside risk of creating a crisis. On some scales,
every organization can meet its own version of Bhopal.

Legal Eagles

When crisis strikes, some form of legal action inevitably follows in its wake.
Managers in every quarter accept without question that legal risk accompanies every organizational activity, a risk exemplified by John P. Coale, a
personal injury lawyer in Washington, D.C.

Dan Kurzman, author of *A Killing Wind: Inside Union Carbide and the
Bhopal Catastrophe,* recounts that Coale was riding in a taxi when the news
of Bhopal came over the radio. Although Coale had never heard of Bhopal,
he immediately realized that it could turn into the biggest legal case in history. Within days he formed a legal team, including Ted Dickenson, an assis-
tant, and Arthur Lowy, an independent lawyer who worked with Coale in a
suit against Iran on behalf of 11 former hostages. Since none of the team
knew anything about India, Coale prevailed upon his tailor, C.S. Sastry, who
hailed from Bangalore, India, to join the team. Sastry "stopped work in mid-
stitch," and the team headed for India on December 7, arriving in India
only one day after Union Carbide's Chairman Warren Anderson landed in
Bombay. While at a stop in Frankfurt, Germany, Coale learned that Melvin
Belli, the famous San Francisco tort lawyer, had already filed a $15 billion
suit against Union Carbide on behalf of the gas victims, even though Belli
had not yet met a single Indian client. By December 14, Coale's team had
signed up 20,000 clients, obtained a letter from the mayor of Bhopal assign-
ing to Coale the right to represent the city of Bhopal in the suit, and had
boarded a plane back to the United States. As they left, another legal team,
representing the Los Angeles firm of Gould and Sayre, arrived in Bhopal to
snare their share of the potential clients. The speed of Belli in filing the suit,
the creativity of Coale in getting clients, and the persistence of Gould and
Sayre suggest that any crisis will attract the legal eagles faster than carrion
attracts buzzards.

Public Scrutiny

It's hard enough managing a crisis, but dealing with the press in your face
spells double trouble. The press itself doesn't pose the problem so much as

the reality that a crisis occurs in real time, with the cameras catching it all and eliminating any second chance to create a first impression. Take, for example, a press conference Union Carbide convened three and a half months after the accident. During the conference, Warren Anderson said that the Bhopal plant followed such inferior safety procedures that the plant "shouldn't have been operating." This statement contradicted an earlier statement, uttered shortly after the disaster, that Union Carbide owned 50.9 percent of the Bhopal operation and thus shouldered the majority of the responsibility for the accident. The new strategy to distance Union Carbide from the Indian operation backfired. The damage was done. The company appeared uncertain and perhaps even deceptive, a sorry image for a company of Union Carbide's stature.

Every organization, regardless of size, faces the same three issues at varying levels of intensity during its life. Despite the strong temptation to address them with image over substance, the wise organization realizes that not even an all-out effort to protect its image will produce the most beneficial results, even with the yardstick of raw dollars.

Where Image and Substance Meet

In three specific areas—goodwill, organizational culture, and crisis prevention—an organization can defend and even enhance its image, while actually concentrating on the substance of the crisis. In these areas, emphasizing one aspect of crisis management (image) does not detract from the other vital consideration (substance).

Goodwill

The megabillion-dollar industry of buying goodwill includes activities as diverse as advertising and corporate charity. In the advertising sector alone, the top 15 holding companies in the world racked up just over $111 *billion* in billings in 1993. Companies spend all these dollars trying to create positive images of their activities and products. Let's assume that company XYZ has spent $10 in fiscal year 1993 building goodwill on a national level. A crisis strikes in which the lawyers propose a "non-responsibility" strategy that might limit potential losses to $3. However, management wants to take full and immediate responsibility and do whatever it takes to correct the situation. The management alternative will end up doubling the cost to the company, from the $3 proposed by the legal eagles to $6.

Now comes the tricky math. While the legal solution may appear cheaper, it actually costs more. The communications approach required to limit losses to $3—shifting responsibility, identifying scapegoats, stonewalling the press, and linking immediate financial assistance for victims waiving their rights to conduct future legal action—literally negates the $10 already spent trying to build a positive public image. This raises the potential loss to $13 (the $3 of limited loss plus the $10 of negated advertising, public relations, and community service dollars already invested). The management alternative does just the opposite. The estimated $6 cost to implement management's plan adds to the $10 the company has already spent on goodwill because the efforts of the organization to take full responsibility, go the second mile in seeking a quick solution, and worry more about the victims than their own legal liability contribute directly toward their goodwill, and often on prime-time television for the duration of the crisis. This amounts to spending $16 on building a positive image— more than the original budget, but certainly better than *losing* $13. The best examples of this math in action can be found in the accidents that *we never even hear about.*

Have you ever wondered why you don't hear about personal injury suits against Disney? To put the question in perspective, consider that the Magic Kingdom, EPCOT Center, and the MGM Studios theme park in Orlando, Florida, serve over 26 million visitors per year, each of whom could fall off a ride, slip on a wet ice cream wrapper or get hit by a car in the parking lot. Given Disney's high profile and fat bank account, you can envision the parade of ambulance chasers (also known as personal injury lawyers) walking through the gates. Since accidents do happen in the best-run theme parks, why do we hear so little about Disney in this regard? The answer lies in the attitude the organization takes toward its image. Michael Eisner, Disney's chairman, sees one of his primary responsibilities as "protecting the Disney image." But Disney protects its image by focusing on substance rather than spin. For example, in 1990, ABC's "Prime Time" television show aired a highly unfavorable 12-minute segment entitled "Tragic Kingdom?" In the show, correspondent Chris Wallace criticized the Disney organization for disregarding environmental considerations and construction rules in their quest to expand the Magic Kingdom in Anaheim, California. "I don't think Walt Disney would be happy with it at all," Orange

County Commissioner Vera Carter said on camera. "They are simply and purely a profit making machine."

Just three weeks later, one Vera Carter also appeared on television, this time on the NBC "Today Show," which presented a similar exposé on Disney. The telecast exposed such issues as congestion on Orlando's streets, and all the tacky souvenir shops and sleazy hotels that had sprung up on streets outside the gates of the Magic Kingdom in Anaheim, California. Disney responded swiftly. Instead of seeking to distance itself from the problems, find a scapegoat, or ignore the criticism, it attacked the substance of the crisis.

The day after the Wallace report aired, Tom Elrod, head of marketing at Walt Disney World, drafted a four-page memo dealing with each point raised on the show. Disney then offered to work with Orange County (home of the Magic Kingdom) on the refinancing of a 1980 housing loan, with the goal of making available $80 million in new funds for low-income housing. Disney later donated the proceeds from a golf tournament held at Walt Disney World (Orlando) to an organization working for the homeless. While you might argue that Disney could have avoided any of the costs associated with the crisis by taking a hard legal stand, forcing their critics into a courtroom, consider the wisdom of simply attacking the substance of the crisis, adding to the goodwill account, and further enhancing a public image. The company handles personal injuries at any of its theme parks in much the same way. Instead of taking a hard legal stand, the company offers to cover all expenses and immediately provides a generous settlement to end the matter as soon as possible.

When considering the costs of compromising goodwill in the effort to limit legal liability, remember that the judicial system may function on points of hard law and deliberate intent, but the court of public opinion does not. Further, public opinion can bite with even sharper teeth in the form of regulatory agencies and government scrutiny. In the case of Union Carbide's handling of the Bhopal incident, Congressman Henry Waxman publicly stated that it had "come to a point where I don't think I can take Union Carbide's word for what's happened." Now, the company has Congress on its back.

Even if an organization successfully wins the battle of limiting its short-term legal liability, it may still lose the war in terms of long-term cost in hard dollars. These costs come in the form of increased regulations, surcharges, and higher taxes. The added costs accrue as the government reacts to a company's handling of a crisis, which in turn depends on how the public reacts to that handling. So, in a sense, during a crisis, the public plays judge and jury—a judge and jury swayed less by points of law than by demonstrations of responsibility, repentance, and restitution. Unfortunately, a belligerent CEO, perceived by the public as irresponsible, unrepentant, and greedy, blaming everyone but the organization for a crisis—say, a toxic chemical spill—does not get off with a light sentence in the people's court. On the other hand, the CEO who offers a forthright apology, makes sincere attempts to alleviate the suffering of the victims, and takes positive steps to prevent the same type of crisis from happening again, gets a sympathetic ear. P.T. Barnum once said, "You can never go broke underestimating the intelligence of the American public." We would amend that to read, "You can go broke underestimating the power of public opinion."

Organizational Culture

The battle for image and goodwill goes beyond the public-at-large. In an age where productivity and quality make or break companies, you must wage the same battle for the hearts and minds of the workforce.

During crisis, employees listen intently to all the company's communications—more intently, in fact, than people whose paychecks do not depend on how the company will weather the crisis. Unlike the public at large, employees know the details of the crisis, and, more importantly, they know the history that led up to it. How management handles the situation tells workers how management will treat them. For example, if management misleads the public, will it not also mislead its own workforce? When tragedy strikes and management seeks to limit the organization's liability, should workers expect any different treatment when an industrial accident strikes an employee? Or if a product—say, a gas tank in an automobile—turns out to pose a danger to the public, but the company refuses to redesign it because the cost would affect the bottom line, what signal does this send the workforce about the company's attitude toward plant and equipment safety?

Unlike the court of public opinion, this judge and jury possesses a good deal of inside information, possibly even more than management, which makes them particularly sensitive to the spin that the organization puts on the crisis, especially when communications play fast and loose with unfriendly facts. Imagine how Union Carbide's workers felt as their chairman tried to convince the press that the standards of plant operation in

Bhopal, India, differed markedly from those at the Institute, Virginia, plant. They could reach only two conclusions. Either Warren Anderson had so lost touch with his own company that he really believed that the standards differed, or he was deliberately misleading the public. Either conclusion severely damages management's credibility. Enlightened management, however, can enhance its credibility during a crisis, as in the case of Chez Michelle, an exclusive beachfront restaurant in Waikiki, proves.

For over twenty years, the owners, chefs, and staff of Chez Michelle have excelled at providing both unique and time-proven culinary experiences. One particular evening, however, a customer hated the way a certain dish had been prepared, and he made his dissatisfaction known not just to the waiter, but to every patron within earshot. Instantly, the unhappy and vocal customer became the center of everyone's attention. To address the crisis, Chez Michelle convened a miniconference including the dissatisfied customer, the waiter, the head chef, and the maître d'. The customer demanded that the chef recook the dish. Did the head chef bristle at this demand, blame the crisis on poor suppliers, a junior cook, or the worried waiter? No. He offered a sincere apology that the dish had offended the customer and immediately retreated to the kitchen. A few moments later he emerged in full sight of all the customers with a junior chef and a platter full of ingredients. He then explained that Chez Michelle used only the very best and freshest food available on the island, and he offered the platter as proof. Further, he introduced the flustered junior chef who had prepared the dish and cited his experience and qualifications, adding that he himself admired his subordinate's skill and could not cook the same dish any better. Consequently, since the best chef at Chez Michelle had used the best ingredients to prepare the dish, the kitchen staff could not possibly improve the quality of this particular dish, so perhaps the customer would like to order a different entrée, on the house.

The actions of the head chef sent two messages reverberating throughout the restaurant's culture. The first stressed that the staff's best efforts go into every dish and that management stands firmly behind those efforts, which accounts for the fierce loyalty of the restaurant's employees. Second, Chez Michelle values all customers, even the most obnoxious, and will treat everyone with the utmost courtesy and respect, without compromising the integrity of the product. The Chez Michelle management neither anticipated nor welcomed the customer crisis, but when it struck, they used it to encourage and empower their employees to higher levels of service, not to mention the gawking customers they impressed (among them, one of the authors).

Crisis Prevention

On June 10, 1991, telephone customers of Pacific Telesis experienced a "crash" that disrupted phone service for a short period of time. Instead of blaming the equipment or software manufacturer, Telesis executives accepted responsibility for the mishap, publicly apologized, and immediately conducted extensive diagnostic procedures in an effort to isolate the cause of the service interruption and prevent a future incident. Ironically, they traced the cause of the crisis to faulty software from one of their major suppliers. As the company initiated corrective procedures on the software, the system went down again in Los Angeles, and simultaneously in Washington, D.C., Virginia, West Virginia, and Maryland, this time with equipment operated by Bell Atlantic Corporation's Chesapeake and Potomac Telephone Companies. Fortunately, the corrective measures from the previous crash in Los Angeles quickly led investigators to the same software glitch in a mere three lines of code in a software program millions of lines long. The necessary corrections were already underway when systems went down in Pennsylvania on July 1 and 2, and in San Francisco on July 3. However, Pacific Telesis' decision to begin immediate corrective measures, rather than blame its suppliers and wait for them to take action, prevented extensive shutdowns of service nationally.

Effective crisis prevention begins when an organization takes full responsibility for an existing crisis. Only with full responsibility will the organization feel the full necessity of finding corrective measures before the same type of crisis strikes again. Would a credible management team tell the public and the press that they accept absolutely no responsibility for a crisis and then expect to motivate its own employees to correct the very problems that the front office claims do not exist?

Tracking with the Truth

When, on June 25, 1993, Ashland Oil, Inc., the nation's second-largest independent oil refiner, spilled 759,000 gallons of diesel fuel into the Monongahela and Ohio Rivers, the company reacted with a response all too rare in the world of corporate public victims: complete candor! Within 48 hours of the spill, the oil slick had spread over 100 miles into the Ohio River basin, threatening to contaminate the drinking water of 1,000,000 people in four states. Did those people form a lynch mob and march on corporate headquarters? No, because Ashland's Chairman John R. Hall faced a skeptical press with blunt honesty, admitting up front, "Hey guys, we've made a mess here. We've got to clean this thing up and we've got to try to do anything we can to help all the people who have been inconvenienced, to try to minimize the impact." Brushing aside the advice of cautious corporate lawyers, Hall made a public apology, accepting full blame for the company's error. In addition, he hired Battelle Institute to conduct an independent investigation, then called a press conference to announce the findings, *before* knowing the results of the investigation. When the crisis passed, *The New York Times* wrote that Hall had turned the public perception of Ashland from that of a "rotten oil company" to a bunch of "pretty good guys." But Hall didn't stop when the perception of Ashland turned positive. After the crisis, the company bestowed a grant on the University of Pittsburgh to fund a study of the long-term environmental impact of the spill on the waterways. Researchers concluded that the spill would create no significant long-term effects on the river, but recommended additional monitoring of select areas. Ashland provided the funds for that further observation.

Hall's novel approach of *tracking with the truth* achieved the enviable result of both enhancing the image of his company (not to mention his own reputation) and intensely addressing the substance of crisis in an effort to deal decisively with the spill and take the steps to prevent the same sort of accident in the future. Hall wisely trounced the temptation to put the image of Ashland Oil ahead of the quest to solve the crisis. All organizations must do the same before they implement the solutions suggested in Part Four.

CHAPTER 8

Moving from Your Comfort Zone: Travel Light and Travel Fast

The Accidental Tourist

Eighty years ago, an unusual migration took place in Cortland, New York, when a local steel company, under pressure from workers for higher wages and better working conditions, hit upon an unpopular solution. Rather than cave in to local demands, the company "imported" hundreds of workers from Southern Italy and the Ukraine. In the 1990s, Cortland once again made headlines when the town experienced another migration, only this time in reverse. Instead of importing workers, typewriter manufacturer Smith Corona decided to "export" its entire production facility to Mexico, a move that would lay off 875 of the company's 1,300 workers in Cortland. To defend this less than popular decision, Smith Corona executives argued that the very survival of the company depended on its traveling to Mexico.

As in the case of Smith Corona, crisis tends to force a mental (and sometimes a physical) journey, jarring an organization from its comfort zone of controllable activities, plans, and objectives and plunging it onto a path through unchartered territory where danger lurks around every curve. When management loses its control at the helm, confusion reigns, and the greater the crisis, the further the organization journeys into a land of chaos and danger. Until such a forced journey commences, an organization's problems have not yet become a crisis. Movement from your comfort zone, from your planned and anticipated world, signals that a certain event (or series of events) has turned into a true crisis.

Of course, it's often a matter of interpretation. While a naturally clumsy person might consider hanging upside down from a bar 100 feet above the ground a crisis, a professional trapeze artist would relish that act as a performance. Jumping out of airplanes spells crisis, but paratroopers do it for a living, and skydivers do it just for the thrill. Swimming with sharks petrifies most people, but shark expert Eugeny Clark routinely entices 10-foot blue sharks to bite her arms and legs to test a new shark-resistant wet suit. Living on the financial edge mortifies Fortune 500 CFOs, but during the '80s, investment bankers flourished on the exhila-ration of one leveraged buyout after another. In all of these examples, the circumstances remain the same, but the perspectives of individuals differ greatly.

Circumstances themselves define crisis less than your interpretation of those circumstances. Will an event push you off your chosen path? When a test pilot intentionally places an aircraft in a position of jeopardy, she has *cho-sen* that desired destination and hardly considers it a crisis. However, when a recreational pilot finds herself plunging into a flat spin, she finds herself caught in a true crisis.

Perception and interpretation play a central role in exercising good crisis judgment. While *every* crisis forces a journey, not all crises force the same type of travel. One crisis may require minor course adjustments, while another may demand a major disruption in direction. Mere detours require minor adjustments: make a few left-hand and right-hand turns, ease back a bit on the throttle, and you're back on your chosen path. But major disruptions cut off all routes to preferred destinations: all adjustments fail to get you back on course, and you find yourself propelled on a per-ilous journey.

To manage in crisis, though, a manager must fully understand the scope of the journey, and a manager invites disaster if she or he never fully under-stands the journey, and the organization playing the role of the accidental tourist finds itself "on the road again," lugging too much baggage. In order to fully appreciate the danger of this error, you must first consider the dif-ferent types of trips organizations take.

Detours and Dead Ends

The journey forced by crisis confronts both detours and dead ends. A closer look at both can prepare you to "pack" appropriately, taking along just the right kind of luggage.

Detours

Most of the daily crises that afflict organizations simply *sidetrack* efforts to achieve objectives. As we said earlier, we classify such crises as common. Although common crises range considerably in severity, they do not threaten an organization's basic ability to accomplish its goals. Rather, they temporarily place an organization off-track until it can solve its problems and once again proceed on its intended way. Common crises incur both delay and expense.

Delay. This is as straightforward as it sounds. In the course of pursuing organizational goals, you will always encounter unanticipated events that stall progress. While your overall objective does not change, your timing may suffer a lot.

Millicom, a successful telecommunications company, watched as its stock nosedived from $25 to $7⅞ during a particularly difficult expansion period. The company provides cellular telephone service, primarily to underdeveloped countries such as Costa Rica, Ghana, Pakistan, Paraguay, and the Philippines, and it has scheduled at least 20 other countries, including India and Turkey, for service in the near future. As you would guess, starting and operating cellular service in these countries entails a few more obstacles than establishing similar service in Dallas or Des Moines. Each obstacle brings with it delay, but the primary objective of the company remains attainable. Millicom owners and management accept the inevitable delays, because results will come sooner or later. Cellular service in the Third World makes a lot more money than it does in the United States. Millicom customers average 270 minutes per month (versus about 160 minutes in the United States), with an average monthly bill of $115 (versus about $85 in the United States). Finally, with about 25,000 subscribers, Millicom achieved a breakthrough with a public offering of its European-based joint venture. At the time, however, dropping stock price presented a detour for the company, albeit one that did not permanently push Millicom off its path.

107

Expense. Not all detours create delays. Some simply increase the costs of staying on course, as has happened to major players in the airline industry, especially American Airlines.

Although American appears financially strong enough to weather considerable challenges to its market supremacy, the 1992 fare wars put a real dent in the company's revenues and made it much more costly for it to stay at the top of the industry. Then, just two days before the 1993 Thanksgiving rush of travelers began, American's flight attendants initiated an 11-day strike which cost the company millions in lost revenue per day. Having weathered the strike, the airline then faced another fare war, this one occurring over the 1993 Christmas season. In addition to increased internal operating costs and the loss of revenues during its fare war with its established competitors—Delta, United, and NorthWest—American also faces a market challenge from smaller, more flexible airlines that *habitually* undercut their fares by a whopping 50 percent, but again, as with Millicom, the company should weather this storm and will not likely lose its dominance of the passenger market.

Dead End

Unlike those that run into detours, some companies find themselves rushing down dead-end streets. Far from temporary distractions, dead ends threaten to destroy the entire quest. Instead of delaying progress, this type of crisis destroys progress altogether, and its destructive potential makes it unthinkable. The fact that the whole future may ride on the single solution of a particular set of problems only adds to the unthinkable. Reckoning with a dead end requires that the organization weigh both its options and the ratio between cost and benefit.

Options. The lack of options often signals impending doom. When a crisis defies any effective response, then the destination of the organization lies in real jeopardy. Look at TransWorld Airlines, for example.

TWA got caught up in the same crisis as American, but in its case, the fare wars, while great for the consumer, became an unthinkable crisis for Carl Ichan, the company's controlling shareholder. For Ichan, what amounted to increased expense for bigger competitors became an almost insurmountable obstacle, one which literally threatened to eliminate the airline from competition. Ichan's destination, that TWA remain a healthy competitor (under his ownership) positioned for sale or merger, became, for all practical purposes, unobtainable. Here the fare wars did not pose a common crisis, as it did to American, but rather the last untenable crisis TWA would face under Ichan's direct control. To keep TWA flying, Ichan was forced to relinquish his control of the airline.

Cost vs. Benefit.   Not every unthinkable crisis lacks viable options. Sometimes options exist—perhaps lots of them—but each would cost so much that they make the destination no longer viable.

The first half of this decade witnessed a record number of catastrophes, both natural and man-made. Rioting in Los Angeles, flooding in Chicago, and a rash of tornadoes in the Midwest and Southeast escalated insurance claims to $3.7 billion in a three-month period alone. Hurricane Andrew slammed into Florida, adding another $7 billion in claims, followed by Hurricane Iniki, which leveled the island of Kauai. Without Andrew and Iniki, claims had already increased a whopping 66 percent over the year before. Then flooding ravaged the entire Mississippi plain, and fires claimed over 1,000 of California's most expensive homes. This concentration of calamities did not leave the insurance industry without options, but those astonishingly expensive options forced companies to take a hard look at whether they could afford to play in, much less dominate, the casualty insurance market. Deciding that the road had come to a dead end, Transamerica Corp., no rookie or lightweight in the insurance industry, decided to halt its journey and rid itself entirely of its property-casualty insurance operation.

With this basic understanding of the difference between a detour and a dead end, you can now more fully appreciate the danger of traveling with too much baggage.

Stuck with Samsonite

Sprinting for the gate with only two minutes before the plane will depart creates stressful experience. Imagine making the dash carting a 200-pound carry-on bag!

Maturing organizations, like middle-aged people, become collectors, holding onto precious snapshots, old letters, worn clothes, and used furniture, and stashing everything in every spare nook and cranny in the basement and attic. This accumulation of *stuff* poses no problem at all—until moving day. Then comes the reckoning and the choice to part with once-cherished items or risk perishing under the burden of moving every last artifact and knickknack.

Organizations collect less tangible *stuff,* but given the mental nature of the travel caused by crisis, the intangibles become every bit as much of a burden as an old grand piano, long since out of tune. Four common pieces of organizational baggage deserve note.

Entrenched Leadership

During the waning days of the Cold War, it turned out that Toshiba had sold illegal technology to the Soviet Union, which allowed the Soviets to produce superior submarine propellers. When the transaction came to light, the top leadership of the Japanese company resigned, even though they knew nothing of the transaction and did not and would not authorize such a transaction. The actual transfer of technology had been conducted by an autonomous joint venture of which Toshiba owned only 50.01 percent. In a similar case, the chairman of Japan Airlines resigned after a packed Boeing 747 slammed into a mountainside, killing all aboard. The crash occurred due to a structural problem in the manufacture of the aircraft, hardly the fault of the resigned chairman.

You might consider such Japanese resignations extreme. However, we applaud the Japanese sensitivity to the relationship between leadership and crisis. When you delve into any organization's crisis, you can usually find some degree of faulty leadership. Yet in most organizations, leadership entrenches itself and refuses to let go no matter how severe the crisis. Worse still, boards of directors only reluctantly pry them loose.

In Chapter 1, we argued that crisis often results from conditions not related to executive errors or shortcomings. Specifically, we pointed out that changing technology, shifting trends, organizational aging, and global capitalism create much of the crisis surrounding organizations today. To hold management responsible for crisis caused by these conditions would amount to little more than shooting the messenger. However, we also pointed out that, in many situations, executive's error, negligence, or sheer incompetence exacerbates rather than solves a crisis. When this occurs, a management change may seem necessary, but the change tends to drag on, eroding the organization's ability to deal with its situation effectively.

110

Take, for example, the case of Senator Bob Packwood of Oregon. Shortly after his reelection to a second term, accusations surfaced that he had sexually harassed a number of women. His accusers numbered more than 10, each with credible allegations and successful backgrounds that made their stories hard to dispute. The senator apologized for conduct that voters might construe as sexually harassing, but he refused to step down from his office. This recalcitrance created a serious problem for the Senate, which itself was caught in a crisis of confidence with the American people. How could the public support and respect a body of elected officials that could sanction the improper conduct of one of its most powerful members?

We hesitate to include a private sector example of a stubborn leader who refuses to leave because an elected official willingly subjects his or her conduct to public scrutiny. But should a company manager deserve any greater protection of privacy when his or her actions have weakened or destroyed a company? Still, we shall not name names in our next example.

In 1993, one of the nation's most powerful unions faced a staggering 25 percent unemployment rate among its 140,000 members. In addition, the union operated with a deficit, despite the fact that the union charged the highest dues of any union in its particular trade. In the midst of these crisis conditions, the president of the union *admitted* during a national meeting that he had used the $2.5 million union jet for personal travel and that he had paid hundreds of thousands of dollars to his secretary to decorate a $1.9 million "conference center" mansion that became his home. Yet, despite these actions, he refused to resign, forcing the board of directors to hold a three-day internal hearing to consider his ouster. The internal hearing brought to light the facts that, while unionism battled for its life in early 90s, this particular union's management held annual "think tanks" in Honolulu, Acapulco, and Lisbon, where attendees received $500 in "walking-around" money. Union funds had also paid for the president's personal dermatologist, a party for his housekeeper to celebrate her winning U.S. citizenship, and a plane ticket for his wife to fly the supersonic Concorde to attend a meeting in Europe. While none of these actions proved illegal, they certainly appeared improper, given the economic straits suffered by the blue-collar workers whose dues supported the lavish management style.

In the case of both Senator Packwood and the eventually ousted union leader, their attempts to hang on became another burden to their organizations, adding a crisis of confidence to an already dire situation.

111

While an organization can fairly easily dispense with leaders who admit their shortcomings but fail to step aside, they find it much harder to deal with less offensive behavior. In fact, when the faltering leader is smart, experienced, values-driven, sincere, and puts forth an all-out effort to solve the crisis, the board of directors quite often refuses to address any other shortcomings. This happened at Westinghouse with Paul Lego.

Founded in 1886 by George Westinghouse, Westinghouse Electric teetered on the brink of bankruptcy almost 100 years later. Ranked high on the Fortune 500, the company was nevertheless bleeding red ink from its credit operation, Westinghouse Credit Corporation. Having already written off a billion dollars in bad loans, the company entered the 1990s with over $3 billion in problem loans and bad real estate investments. Lego tried to sell the troubled lending operation for 37 cents on the dollar, but failed. The company then posted staggering losses in 1992 and 1993, which prompted the board to remove Lego after only two and one-half years at the helm. An otherwise admirable man, the CEO had failed his organization. Entrenched capable leadership causes more problems during crisis than entrenched incompetents. In the case of Westinghouse, the company retained the wrong leadership for almost three years, sapping valuable time and energy desperately needed to engineer a turnaround. When the board of directors finally realized that they were carting the wrong luggage, the company had already traveled far down the path of decline.

Outmoded Strategy

If crisis forces a journey, then organizational strategy must go along for the ride, with adjustments or complete overhaul. Clinging dutifully to an element of existing strategy, no matter how well it worked in less troubled times, makes absolutely no sense during crisis because doing so forces the organization to lug Arctic gear to the Gobi Desert, or vice versa.

This common mistake usually stems from entrenched leadership. Even under the best circumstances, it's hard to manage well, but under crisis conditions, it's infinitely harder. When crisis erupts, a company's existing strategy should perhaps go to the scrap heap, but many midlevel managers simply can't do that because they have based all their effort and their very careers on a specific course of action. This applies especially to megacorporations that have dominated their markets for decades, where any sort of change, especially a massive one, befuddles and even paralyzes managers.

Naturally, then, most managers conduct business as usual during crisis, even though doing so got them into the current mess in the first place. High-tech giant, Atari, provides an unfortunate case in point.

Only ten years ago, Atari ranked just behind Coca-Cola in name recognition and, at its peak, the company generated sales of $2 billion with 10,000 employees. Then a rash of poor-quality computer games sent sales plummeting to a dismal $250 million. Atari owner Warner Communications sold or, more accurately, *gave* the company away to Jack Tramiel, founder of Commodore International, for $240 million in promissory notes. Tramiel built sales back to $500 million, but the situation completely unraveled as sales dropped back to $250 million and losses skyrocketed. Twenty-seven executives left the company over a 30-month period, and stock that once sold for $16 a share in 1987 went for 1⅝ in late 1992. What went wrong? Tramiel made a fatal mistake by taking over a company mired in crisis and trying to save it with the same old strategy.

Earlier in his career, Tramiel had triumphed by undercutting the competition with such cheap computers that he needed to spend little on marketing, promotion, or overhead. The cheap strategy worked so beautifully that Commodore's stock value surged, propelling Tramiel to the "Forbes 400." When he took over Atari, Tramiel naturally tried the proven approach, this time through his son, Sam, whom he appointed chief executive officer. Together they put out cheap computers as an alternative to games, but doing so did not address Atari's central problem—namely, that every major competitor was also putting out cheap computers, all of them perceived as better machines than Atari's. Making matters worse, new electronic game competitors such as Nintendo were taking the game genre to new heights of sophistication, effectively differentiating games from computers. The old strategy just wouldn't work in the new war for consumer dollars.

Old Rules and Rites

In most organizations, practice does not make perfect, it makes permanent. Do something long enough, you forget why you started doing it in the first place, and you even develop a fear of ever stopping. When this happens, an organization turns its old rules and rites into liturgy, a nearly religious drive to maintain the status quo. During crisis, the organization worships its established rituals, even though they have long since lost their power.

Health care, immersed in a genuinely unthinkable crisis, has been struggling to change its strategy piece by piece. The modern birthing center, aka the maternity ward, provides a prime example of a valiant effort to change. Gone are the days when fathers paced in the waiting room, passing time until informed by a matronly nurse that a son or daughter had arrived. Now the delivery rooms look like hotel suites, replete with king-size beds, a TV and VCR for recording and replaying the event, a reclining chair for the dad, and an interior motif that resembles a stylish suburban bedroom. Hospitals have designed the environment to make everyone feel comfortably at home, albeit within the safety zone of a fully staffed and equipped care center. The new delivery room does not deliver more patient safety—baby and mother always enjoyed plenty of safety—but it does represent an innovative marketing move. Attracting expectant postyuppie and baby-boom mothers has become big business since the days of doctors determining hospital policies have fallen by the wayside. Thus, health-care providers, seeing themselves as deliverers of consumer products, have fashioned birthing centers to match the Regency Floor of the Hyatt.

But there's a hitch to this plan. Many senior nurses, the professionals who have worked in the field a long time and really know what they are doing, can't fully let go of the old system. Oh, they tolerate the facade of birthing as a pleasant family experience, at least during the early stages of labor, but when the going gets rough, they go right back to the old days of harsh orders, bright lights, and advice to dad to "stay the hell out of our way." To their minds, bright lights, rather than muted pastels, make for healthy babies, and they will pay lip service to the newfangled environment only until doing so violates the time-honored liturgy. Then the liturgy of tradition wins out.

During crisis, even with new strategies in place, few leaders reassess the old rules, falsely assuming that employees will automatically decide which rules and rites should survive the change and which should fall by the wayside. Ironically, this penchant for naturally deciding which rules to keep or discard gets people fired during periods of non-crisis. Demanding the sanctity of rules during stability trains workers not to violate those rules under any circumstances, so when management changes the strategy but retains the old rules, the employees end up lugging along each rule in an over-packed duffle bag to the new destination.

Unnecessary Assets

New strategies and new rules should alter the valuation of organizational assets, especially the most important organizational asset: people. This places management in the difficult position to having to hurt some to save others. On a personal level, this type of decision, while brutal, captured the attention of the nation when an isolated logger trapped his leg under a three-ton tree. Unable to pull his leg out and bleeding profusely, the logger saw only one desperate option. Using an ordinary pocket knife, he methodically amputated his own leg, first cutting away the skin and muscle, then carving right through the bone. He accomplished all this without painkillers. He then dragged his body two miles to a country road where a passing driver spotted him.

Unfortunately, many organizations face the logger's dilemma. They can make the necessary cuts, or they can slowly bleed to death. Changes in technology that eliminate jobs, competition from Asia and Mexico that pays workers less in a day than American unionized workers make in an hour, and an explosion of government rules and regulations such as employer-paid mandatory health-care insurance, provide incentives to shrink employee ranks. Some companies, like IBM, have valiantly tried to do so by retraining and reassigning people, but this once moral solution ultimately became immoral because attempting to hold on to all its workers undermined the chance of survival for the rest of IBM's workforce. This dilemma hit Roger Stempel, former CEO of General Motors, hard. Faced with declining earnings, Stempel, who knew that he had to cut 120,000 workers, tried to compromise at displacing only 75,000. The internal surgery did not save the patient and it eventually cost Stempel his job.

Corporate America now faces the troublesome fact that a portion of America's workers has become baggage. These workers weigh down their companies at precisely the time that global competition requires speed and agility and when no company wins points for loyalty to the workforce. Like the logger, many companies must choose to lose a leg or lose a life.

Organizational Size

Goliath learned the hard way that big is not always better, but that lesson gets lost on most CEOs. When hard times strike a big company, it usually responds by trying to hold the organization together. This attitude forces management to attempt a crisis solution built on the assumption that the organization will survive in its entirety, when that may, in fact, be impossible. Consider the case of Tektronix Inc.

Tektronix, a leading maker of television equipment and oscilloscopes, headquartered in Wilsonville, Oregon, has experienced flat sales despite the valiant efforts of Jerome J. Meyer, who came aboard as chief executive officer in 1990. Profits tumbled 59 percent in 1992, an event that attracted the attention of George Soros, the manager of Quantum Fund Inc. In 1993, Soros' company bought 13.9 percent of Tektronix, took two seats on the board, and boldly suggested that Tektronix, with a market value of $685 million, might be worth as much as $1 billion if it broke up and sold its operating units. Not surprisingly, Meyer strongly resisted the suggestion, arguing that "financially and strategically, it makes sense to keep Tek as a whole." However, with sales and profits in decline, the Soros group asks: "Can the company push ahead in three disparate areas and be successful?" The answer is probably "no."

Jack Welch, Jr., Chairman of General Electric, preaches, "Speed is really the driver that everyone is after. And there's no question that the smaller one is . . . the faster one gets." Yet, despite the dawning realization that size alone can't win the battle, holding things together remains the corporate gospel. Even IBM's new CEO, Louis Gerstner, bristles at the thought of breaking up Big Blue, although each separate unit could become a global powerhouse in its own right. That resistance turns the road to crisis recovery into a quest to carry 28 fat pieces of luggage on one big cart, when perhaps you only need seven smaller carts loaded with four suitcases each. Sadly, the perception persists that a big cart moving slowly accomplishes more than several smaller ones moving swiftly.

Traveling Light, Traveling Fast

Some leaders understand the importance of traveling light and fast during turbulent times. Not merely slash-and-trash artists who chop organizations down to nothing in order to survive, they work more like surgeons, slicing away unhealthy parts of the organization in order to bring it back to health. Like the patient of a skilled heart surgeon, the organization will probably feel better than it has for years. And like medical surgeons, these organizational leaders specialize. Four specialists deserve mention here.

The Enlightened Leader

The board of directors does not shoulder all the responsibility for knowing "when to hold them and when to fold them." Enlightened leaders know that the strong organization makes that decision itself. John Akers, former chairman of IBM, illustrates the point.

When IBM announced the biggest loss in American corporate history and its stock sunk to a 17-year low, Akers went to IBM's director James Burke (the retired chairman of Johnson & Johnson) and expressed his willingness to step aside because "the company would be better off." Three considerations make the Akers example noteworthy. First, John Akers possesses considerable talent, ability, and integrity. He has never displayed obvious shortcomings. Second, he knew the depth of IBM's problems and acted quickly when he realized that he alone couldn't turn the company around. At the time of his resignation, Akers had *already* cut over 100,000 jobs, drastically reorganized the company, and split the personal-computer division into a separate unit. Third, and most important, he voluntarily departed. Contrary to many leaders who force their organizations through debilitating divorce procedures, Akers cared enough about his company and its employees that he personally paved the way for a smooth rather than a bumpy transition to new leadership.

Akers' enlightened self-evaluation not only allowed IBM to avoid the trap of entrenched leadership, but also pointed out an important aspect of effective crisis management. Even the most astute executive cannot necessarily adopt the management style that a crisis might demand. In the case of Akers, a career of building and maintaining a corporation did not train him for the downsizing and radical corporate restructuring the IBM crisis required. His stepping aside, rather than an act of admitting failure, represented the move of a CEO who understood the workings of crisis more than most, certainly more than those who continue to cling to power even when they can no longer contribute crisis solutions.

The Strategy Doctor

When leadership changes, the organization's strategy must also change. Otherwise, the new regime can make the same mistakes as an entrenched one.

Chase Manhattan Bank, once one of the two biggest banks in the world, had dwindled by 1992 to only the sixth-largest bank in the United

States. While nearly all American banks ran into trouble in the early 1990s, Chase Manhattan clearly got sicker than most. Its return on assets went negative, its stock price dropped to under $10 from $44 in 1989, and it failed in its attempt to create a nationwide branch banking system. The bank's crisis forced then-chairman Willard Butcher to resign, paving the way for Tom Labrecque to impose a new strategy on the ailing organization.

Labrecque, a Chase employee since 1964, joined the company right out of the navy and never left. An organization man who had spent almost 30 years with the company, Labrecque seemed, on the surface, more a part of the problem than the solution, but after only three years at the helm, every one of Chase's vital signs points positive, the result of a radical change in strategy. First, while banks raced to go global, Labrecque sold most of Chase's branch banking subsidiaries abroad, including those in Spain, Belgium, Brazil, Chile, Taiwan, Singapore, and the Netherlands. Second, while the bank continues to operate internationally, it focuses on fee-based investment banking, foreign exchange trading, and debt underwriting, ignoring loans and collecting deposits from local consumers. Third, it has limited its national presence to two major operations, consumer credit cards and mortgage banking. Finally, it continues its only full-service, all-inclusive banking operations in the New York area, where Chase operates like a large regional bank. The modified strategy has allowed the bank to focus on just three types of operations, eliminating all other drains of capital, energy, and effort that do not fit the new approach, resulting in a radical improvement in its efficiency (non-interest expenses divided by revenues) from 75 percent down to 60 percent.

Perhaps the most impressive facet of Labrecque's leadership stems from the fact that his new strategic direction goes so much against the grain of the traditional strategy pursued by the competition. During a period when most power-lunching bankers can't utter three words without saying, "off-shore," Tom Labrecque calmly understates, "ours is not a global strategy."

The Corporate Surgeon

Of course, results may require more than a new leader and a new strategy. Some painful surgery may be in order. In just five years, Percy Barnevik has made over 60 acquisitions on five continents to build Asea Brown Boveri (ABB) into an international powerhouse. As CEO, Barnevik carries with him a belief that strikes fear in the hearts of the newly acquired: that within 12 months, administrative staff must be cut by 90 percent.

ABB is no small operation in which cutting staff by 10 percent involves a mere few hundred employees. The company posts revenues of over $32 *billion* dollars and operates with an army of 25,000 individual and autonomous profit centers. While Barnevik's dictums may look like slash and burn on a global scale, that's not really the case. ABB doesn't just prune away corporate deadwood, it motivates and drives the survivors to new heights. In other words, Barnevik operates like a corporate surgeon with a clear vision of what a healthy patient will look like after the surgery. Most importantly, he runs his strategy on a tight schedule. When ABB operations in Germany asked for six years to phase in changes demanded by Barnevik, he gave them two. And while other CEOs wring their hands and spend countless hours worrying about cutting back a single plant in response to a sluggish global economy, Barnevik closed 15 plants in 1993 alone.

Percy Barnevik seems to possess an innate sense of just how lean a business can become without suffering operational anemia. During crisis, most organizations respond to suggested cutbacks by pleading that the downsizing will destroy operational effectiveness. This places CEOs in the unenviable position of having to make the call themselves. They alone must decide, and they alone must live with the second-guessing of the media and the financial community. Few organizations in transition eagerly step up to the plate when cutbacks must occur. Rather, they prepare every excuse and reason why further cuts will cause great harm. Barnevik not only makes the right decisions under these conditions, but he thrives on the conditions themselves, driven to create the most productive organization possible.

The Less-Is-More Prescription

The right leader, the right strategy, and the right surgery might not do the trick unless you get over the American romance with sheer size. Robert Crandall, CEO of AMR Corporation (American Airlines), does not win popularity contests. Faced with unreasonable demands from the flight attendants' union during the 1993 Thanksgiving holiday, Crandall accepted a strike rather than make concessions that would hamper American Airlines' competitiveness. It took President Bill Clinton's threat that the U.S. government would force an end to the strike to convince Crandall to enter into binding arbitration with the union, ending wthe strike just two days before Thanksgiving. However, Crandall's unpopularity derives less from his refusal to meet union demands than from his desire to shrink the company.

119

In the atmosphere of deregulation, United, Delta, and American Airlines have grown to dominate global air travel, with one slight hitch. They can't turn a profit! Regional hubs, sprawling international routes and large fleets of aircraft look impressive, but they don't make money. In fact, only the small regional carriers consistently turn a profit by flying crowded routes with efficient aircraft and more reasonable labor costs. Crandall therefore reasons: do we want to be big, impressive, and earning-poor, or do we want to scale down and drive a less impressive airline all the way to the bank? Obviously, smaller also means fewer jobs, lower salaries, and more work per person. For example, Crandall wants the flight attendants to pitch in and clean up the inside of the aircraft after each use. The flight attendants hate the idea.

Crandall has joined a growing number of corporate leaders who no longer love sheer size. This new breed prefers smaller, more flexible, more controllable, and more profitable organizations. By not joining this movement, Pan American, once the flagship of world air carriers, remained impressive right down to the day it closed its doors for good.

John Akers, Tom Labrecque, Percy Barnevik, and Robert Crandall, each in his own way, demonstrate the understanding that carrying excess baggage can not only exhaust you, it can kill you. Without this realization, an organization cannot hope to implement the third rule of effective crisis management, which suggests that a leader in crisis must change it *all* and change it *fast*.

Managing the Dangers
of Crisis

The two dangers inherent in every crisis exist in the dimension of crisis management that emphasizes *how* an organization resolves any crisis, regardless of the particular solution the organization uses to solve a particular crisis. This makes for a sticky situation because management must not only solve a given crisis itself, it must develop a process that positions the organization positively long after that crisis has passed. The two specific dangers which flow from the crisis process rather than the actual crisis itself are the twin facts that crisis puts organizational values and management skills on public display.

Values on Display

While the public readily associates a company or government agency with its product or service, it does not so easily match up an organization with its values. Since values are an intangible collection of beliefs and commitments, you can't see, touch, or hear them. For all practical purposes, values are invisible, particularly to the public, until crisis shines a bright light on them.

Because, crisis is a condensed period of rapid and very intense activity, often played out in the public eye, any and all actions you perform during a

121

crisis send signals to the world about your values. If management remains unaware of this phenomenon, it can make deadly mistakes.

Skills on Display

Like values, the true skills of the management group go on display during crisis, recorded instantly and indelibly by the media industry. Given this type of exposure, solving a crisis is one thing, solving it with style or élan is something else.

To thwart this danger, a management team must prepare itself to handle any and all crisis. You can't just look the part, because crisis will eventually strip away any pretense toward crisis management that does not truly exist. Proper preparation demands three skills: *cutting-edge thinking,* which offers some hope for a bright future beyond the current chaos; a *crisis-oriented culture,* that does not become ruffled, panicked, or depressed over distasteful events; and, finally, a *willingness* to do whatever it takes to put the company on a positive postcrisis path.

CHAPTER 9

Insight, Decision Making, Communication, and Focus: The Four Skills for Managing Crisis

Illuminated by Crisis

The Eastman Kodak Company, after five restructurings in less than 10 years and one disappointing new product after another, fired its chairman and CEO and reached out for a savior in the form of George Fisher. Fisher, in a stunning move, forsook the security of high-flying and stable Motorola, where he had doubled sales in a five-year period, for the danger of troubled and turbulent Kodak. At Motorola, the largest supplier of semiconductors in the United States (fourth-biggest supplier in the world) and a leading manufacturer of cellular telephones, Fisher had posted a record as an extremely effective, yet largely faceless, chief executive. Now at crisis-ridden Kodak, his every move came under scrutiny, with his competence and credibility always on the line. Like Fisher, any executive courts a lethal danger when taking over an organization in crisis, because his or her skills will now come under a very bright spotlight.

Every crisis creates dangers directly associated with the crisis itself. For example, a batch of improperly canned tomatoes might result in consumer lawsuits, a loss of public confidence in the product, and a dip in the trading price of the company's stock. These consequences arise directly as a result of the crisis itself in a cause-effect relationship. The cause, spoiled tomatoes, results in an effect, such as bad publicity. However, many other more indirect dangers attend crisis, and the chief one relates to how management performs during the crisis. Suppose, while in the course of a press conference, the executives of the tomato company appear unsure, indecisive, or perhaps unwilling to accept responsibility for the flawed product, blaming it on nature or an unreliable distributor. The media and the public will surely brand these behaviors as inappropriate, and their perceptions will remain long after the actual crisis has come and gone. In this sense, you might say that the hard results of crisis management affect companies, while the *means* of crisis management affect careers. Take the example of Teledyne.

The creation of Henry Singleton, Teledyne once flew high as a collection of over 100 companies generating over $4 billion in annual sales. But then a recession trimmed the company's earnings and created losses on fixed-rate government contracts, while at the same time the U.S. government suspended purchases from a Teledyne operation because of product performance failures. As a final blow, the company became a target of an investigation by the FBI looking into allegations of fraud by defense contractors, and Teledyne ended up paying over $40 million in fines. To combat the crisis, the company turned to William Rutledge and Donald Rice for leadership. Rutledge, who came to Teledyne from FMC Corp., and Rice, a former defense analyst who had turned around the Rand Corporation, immediately set about righting the company's problems, consolidating companies, imposing centralized controls, and slashing the workforce from 43,000 to 22,000. Interestingly, while the company faced a serious set of crises, it had not incurred a single unprofitable year since 1960! However, under the glare of the spotlight, the skills of the management team got tagged with labels that included loose, inflexible, and disrespectful of the rules that govern other defense contractors. Now, even though the hard crisis has passed, the reputation hangs on, forcing Rutledge and Rice to axe three subsidiary presidents, three vice-presidents, and nine senior managers in an attempt to restore the credibility of the organization. Fortunately, the problems associated with *how* an organization manages crisis also offer an opportunity, because in the midst of a crisis a manager (or an entire team) can develop positive consequences from its crisis management style even though they may not actually resolve the crisis itself successfully. This happened to Peter Ueberroth.

Following successful stints as the organizer of the 1984 Summer Olympic games in Los Angeles and as commissioner of professional baseball in the United States, Ueberroth took on the turnaround of HAL Inc., the parent of Hawaiian Airlines, one of two carriers that ply the interisland route serving tourists and residents of the state of Hawaii. With high maintenance costs, escalating fuel prices, and a heavy debt load, the airline floundered in red ink, a condition that even the capable Ueberroth could not remedy. Finally, in 1993, the state government stepped in, granting the company what amounted to low-cost loans so it could remain solvent. Ueberroth had failed. However, despite his inability to turn the airline around, his method of crisis management continued to impress onlookers, and Adidas A.G., the German sporting-goods maker that was getting trounced by dueling sportswear giants Nike and Reebok, picked him to fix their situation.

The fact that Teledyne suffered even though it solved its crisis and Ueberroth prospered even though he did not suggests that the dangers, and, on the flip side, the potential opportunities that come about when the spotlight shines on your skills deserve serious attention. In our own experience, four skills in particular can make or break a career illuminated by crisis: insight, decision making, communication, and focus. Not coincidentally, they happen to be the same skills management always needs, not only during times of crisis. However, during crisis, each skill takes on a slightly different emphasis, a subtle twist in application. If you lack them, then you, and perhaps your entire team will come across as inept and overwhelmed by the crisis you face, but if you display them during a bout with crisis, you and your team can emerge with a reputation for sound crisis thinking and the ability to confront serious challenges. Bear in mind that even the mildest crisis attracts an audience, if only a single co-worker. Magnitude doesn't matter. Whether a co-worker or a national audience of prime-time television viewers, someone is watching you, weighing your every word and action in terms of your management skills. More importantly, a manager (with a career at stake) never gets a second chance to make a first impression.

Let's take a closer look at the skills of insight, decision making, communication, and focus. Since none of these skills is unique to crisis, we won't explore each in great depth. Rather, we simply want to point out how each skill makes a difference during the management of a crisis, pointing out the slight twists you can give each during a crisis.

Insight: Isolating the Symptoms from the Disease

Insight enables you to see past the symptoms of a problem and precisely identify the problem itself. Doing so is crucial during crisis because under pressure you can easily mistake the effects of crisis for its causes. For example, during the OPEC oil embargo of 1972, sales of Japanese cars soared while Detroit's models sat on showroom floors. The U.S. auto executives falsely saw the root cause of their crisis as gas mileage and proceeded to manufacture more economical American cars. However, when fuel prices dropped, American consumers continued to buy Japanese alternatives. It took Detroit another 10 years to realize that a lack of quality rather than a lack of fuel efficiency had caused their problem. Today, 20 years after the initial crisis brought on by the embargo, America's auto manufacturers have finally begun holding their own against Japanese imports by selling cars that meet much higher quality standards. Detroit's lack of insight into the true crisis of consumer confidence wasted years of playing with stopgap political and economic fixes. Lack of insight invited danger.

Danger

Executives who lack insight during a crisis invariably misapply scarce resources. Rather than working to solve the core of the crisis, they apply all efforts to the fringes, creating a false perception that they are dealing with the crisis when, in fact, they have skirted the important issues and the crisis lives on. This particular danger plagues Exxon a full five years after its tanker, the *Valdez,* spilled 11 million gallons of oil into Prince William Sound. To put the danger in perspective, consider a bit of comparative history.

Eleven years before the spill of the *Exxon Valdez,* the *Amoco Cadiz* broke up off the coast of France, dumping six times as much oil into the ocean as the *Valdez* did, making it the largest oil spill in history. But according to John S. Herold Inc., a petroleum research firm in Connecticut, the cleanup cost for the *Cadiz* spill totalled $72 per barrel spilled. So far, the cleanup in Alaska has cost Exxon almost $8,000 per barrel, more than all the profits made by every Exxon oil well, refinery, and service station in the United States the year after the Alaskan spill. Yet, despite Exxon's cleanup expenses, the crisis persists well into the 1990s with no sign of final closure. During the initial stages of the crisis, Exxon failed to see a nation sincerely

126

concerned about the environment and not merely annoyed by the economic impact of one big spill. For years, environmental issues preoccupied special interest groups, often extreme in their beliefs. Companies like Exxon could openly flaunt their power against such groups without fomenting the ire of a general public that had historically turned an indifferent ear to environmental issues. Somewhere along the way, however, the environment became a pressing national, not merely a special interest, issue. With this change in public concern, Exxon's giving $180 million to local fishermen to compensate for a lost harvest and scrubbing rocks one by one did not address the public worry that Exxon remained unconcerned that it might happen again. Even *Fortune,* usually a staunch supporter of big business, expressed amazement that Exxon's CEO Lawrence Rawl "didn't rush to the site." It quoted Rawl as saying that he "had too many other things to do." Lack of insight? You bet, in spades.

The real crisis for Exxon *is* (not was) the fact that, as the nation's largest oil company and one of the top 10 biggest companies in America, it *cannot* be trusted to protect, not merely clean up, the environment. According to *The Wall Street Journal,* even Exxon's own employees feel "confused, embarrassed, and betrayed" by the company's attitude toward the *Valdez* spill. With this reputation firmly entrenched in the public mind, the crisis of the *Valdez* spill will continue for as long as Exxon pumps oil and not merely until Alaska's beaches regain their pristine beauty. Clearly, Exxon failed to seize an opportunity inherent in the *Valdez* problem.

Opportunity

Faced with the exact same crisis of credibility in terms of the environment, the Dow Chemical Company used its insight to fashion a change in its corporate values from a company that ignored environmental issues to one that paid close attention to them. Again, a brief bit of history puts Dow's efforts into perspective.

The Dow Chemical Company manufactured Agent Orange to defoliate Vietnam so that American troops could more easily spot enemy movements. Dow also produced napalm for that war. Who can forget the Pulitzer Prize-winning photo of a Vietnamese child, horribly burned by misdirected napalm, running naked down a desolate road? Other newspaper stories at the time told how a Dow Chemical executive was rescued from angry antiwar college students by a Hell's Angels chapter armed with chains. Finally, a national headline blamed Dow for dumping a "Stream of Dioxin in Midland, Michigan." Despite these sorts of crises, the company amazingly gained insight into the environmental mood of the country.

At the height of their difficulties, Dow formed a 12-member task force to evaluate its reputation with seven key groups: customers, employees, competitors, the news media, regulators, customers, and scientists. By interviewing key representatives from each of these constituencies, the company learned that most of them viewed Dow as "an insular and sometimes arrogant company that shunned compromise" when it faced environmental issues. In addition, several polls commissioned by Dow placed the company only "one notch below the tobacco industry" in terms of its concern for consumer well-being. This rating stunned Dow's management because they did not perceive themselves as negatively as did the public. Rather than turn their backs on the problem, however, they embarked on an ambitious plan, not to change public opinion, but to change their own practices in an effort to create greater company concern over the environment. To do so they installed a 24-hour hotline to answer questions about the chemical industry, started a Visible Scientist Program to communicate the company's concerns to schools and citizens groups in 30 cities across the United States, and they regularly mailed out Public Interest Reports explaining Dow's attempts to reduce hazardous wastes and address other environmental concerns. In addition, the company joined forces with the League of Women Voters (on hazardous household waste education) and the National Wildlife Federation (on wetlands protection). Finally, Dow contributed funds to a national education program publicizing the importance of organ and marrow donation. A mere two years after the company initiated these programs, an independent study showed a 60 percent gain in favorable attitudes toward Dow on the part of customers, scientists, employees, and the media.

A cynic might say that Dow's actions merely reflected a desire to enhance its image, changing the leopard's spots without really changing the leopard. Even if they did amount to little more than public relations gimmicks, you still must admit that Dow's leaders displayed insight. For whatever reason, Dow's leadership sensed a shift toward the "greening of America" whereby the entire nation was becoming more sensitive to and more involved in the quest for a better environment. With this insight, they transformed their crisis into an opportunity to bring their organization more in line with national thinking on environmental issues. Any executive can do likewise.

Developing Insight

Insight basically arises from asking never-ending questions in a constant quest to separate vitally important issues from merely urgent problems. An executive seeking to develop greater insight must avoid getting caught "in the thick of thin things," addressing symptoms rather than causes of a crisis.

Developing organizational insight demands a faithful adherence to two rules. First, you must hold no rule, policy, structure, product, procedure, department, plan, budget, or philosophy sacred. During crisis, you must ruthlessly question your activities and attitudes. Second, you must never let a turf-defending, status-quo-protecting manager or management team get in the way of rule number one.

Decision Making:
Finding the Pivotal Options

Don't executives, by definition, possess this skill? To an extent, yes, every executive makes decisions, but the skill of *deciding* encompasses a complex process in which the need to know meets the need to act. For example, consider the simple task of buying a computer as a Christmas gift for a spouse or a friend. Should you consider an Apple Macintosh or an IBM pc? Desktop or laptop? Internal or external fax modem? Color or grayscale monitor? A 40-megabyte hard drive or a 120-megabyte hard drive? What about CD-ROM? Will a 3086 processor be fast enough, or should the system sport a 4086? What about the printer? Should it be color or just black ink? Impact, thermal, or jet? Dot matrix or laser? Anyone recently choosing a computer from the array of possibilities knows that this list represents just the beginning. Fortunately, you can answer each question with a little research, analysis, and deliberation. For instance, assume your husband needs only simple word processing for personal letters and maybe a basic program for balancing a checkbook and keeping track of expenses. He'll put the machine in a small alcove in the kitchen, though he may also want to use it out by the pool. Finally, since the recipient of the gift can't type, the computer must be easy to use. Assume further, however, that it is 5:45 P.M. on Christmas Eve and the store closes at 6:00. Suddenly you face a crisis and a relatively straightforward decision becomes an emergency, with insufficient time to weigh all the variables. The time to research, analyze, and deliberate always runs short in a crisis.

Danger

Fear of making the wrong move always hampers decision making during crisis. This applies particularly to a high-profile crisis in which chaos reigns and everyone is looking over your shoulder. In reality, however, a stalled decision during a serious crisis poses a greater danger than a wrong decision. To appreciate this fact, imagine a lost hiker facing a fork in the trail. Should she go right or left? Sundown approaches quickly, and with it, lower visibility and plummeting temperatures. Facing the choice, the hiker lingers, unable to choose. Time passes, and so does the daylight, placing the hiker in great peril. Now, imagine the hiker quickly making the best choice possible but proceeding down the wrong trail. Thirty minutes later, she realizes that she made a poor choice and corrects the error. She may have lost some time, but at least her walking has kept her warm, and she now knows exactly what choice to make.

We've oversimplified this story to make a point. Certainly a delayed but still timely decision beats a shoot-from-the-hip approach, yet, surprisingly often, highly skilled managers balk at critical decisions so long that they end up freezing to death.

Little more than a decade ago, computer companies were debating whether the computer would make the transition from the boardroom to the family den. The fork in the road preoccupied the entire industry, for although IBM clearly remained number one in business applications, a dog fight had broken out to determine second, third, and fourth places. During this industry crisis, Digital Equipment Corporation president Ken Olsen felt unsure that personal computing would evolve into a real industry. Consequently, Olsen opted to wait and see. When he finally decided to move in the right direction, time had run out. Today DEC makes little impact on the personal computer market, an odd situation for the second-largest information systems supplier in the world.

Had DEC made a quicker decision to embark down the path of personal computing, like our hiker, it could have retreated from an original course when it determined it had been traveling down the wrong path. Doing so would have smeared some proverbial egg on its face, but the $13 billion company could have absorbed that problem fairly easily and taken the heat. However, by delaying, Olsen missed the market completely and now remains near the rear of the pack. Hindsight tells us that DEC failed to seize a major opportunity.

Opportunity

Just as the commotion of crisis creates danger for the indecisive, it also generates opportunity for those willing and courageous enough to act. Consider tiny Morris Air.

Founded by June Morris in Salt Lake City, Utah, Morris Air grew an upstart charter operation out of a thriving travel agency business. Like most small-time charters, the airline contracted with established air carriers to run a flight to Hawaii for a set price. Morris then assumed the risk of selling enough seats to cover the cost of chartering a plane for the run. However, June Morris thought beyond vacation charters, seeing an opportunity in short-haul flights to destinations that drew both business and vacationing passengers. As a result, Morris's itinerary read like a Greyhound Bus schedule: Salt Lake City to San Francisco, Los Angeles, San Jose, San Diego, Las Vegas, Denver, and Seattle. Most flights lasted less than 90 minutes. Within eight years, the charter operation achieved revenues of $116 million, profits of over $5 million, and the attention of Delta Air Lines, which dropped its fare a whopping 500 percent in order to compete. Inevitably, Morris Air's success attracted attention and fear.

In 1992, Alaska Airlines complained to the federal government that Morris operated more like a scheduled airline than a charter service. After investigation, the government agreed and fined Morris $200,000. Crisis? Not for June Morris, who again saw an opportunity to make a smart decision. Despite the fact that the combined airline industry had not turned a net profit in 10 years, she transformed her charter operation into a scheduled carrier, sort of a mini-Delta Air Lines. Expanding to 22 Western cities, Morris Air became *the* high-volume, low-fare carrier in the Rocky Mountain region, operating out of Delta's Salt Lake City hub. In 1993, Southwest Air bought Morris Air for $129 million, boosting June Morris not only into the decision-making Hall of Fame, but into the ranks of America's multimillionaires.

The success of Morris Air, in addition to illustrating the benefits of decisiveness, underscores the role that indecisiveness plays in creating the very opportunity that more action-oriented individuals can exploit. The success of Morris Air flowed from its ability to make a profit from fares that were not only competitive but seemed almost in another cosmos from those charged by more established air carriers such as Delta. The company turned a profit on lean fares because its expense structure amounted to roughly 7 cents per passenger mile, compared to almost 10 cents for Delta, its major competitor. Morris Air kept expenses down by flying a fleet of identical aircraft, using non-union labor, offering absolutely no frills, and serving meals that amounted to tossing passengers a muffin when they boarded. Now mighty United Airlines has chosen to do the same in an innovative project it calls U-2.

U-2 amounts to setting up an airline within an airline to fly routes of less than 750 miles. Pilots who fly for U-2 will take home 20 percent less than other United pilots, and they will fly seven hours more per month. However, while U-2 looks like a great crisis solution to the raging fare wars, it comes late. While American, Delta, and United fiddled with the concept but could not or would not come to a decision, upstarts like Morris seized the opportunity and prospered. While the big guys fiddled, the little guys assembled more musical bands. Anyone can do likewise.

Developing Decision Making

Good decisions obviously depend on more than decisiveness. Consequently, the topic of decision making fills volumes of management self-help books and academic texts. We can't add much to that literature, but we can stress that decision making under crisis conditions requires the sense to know when to stop asking questions and to start taking action.

While insight requires asking the right questions, questions alone do not produce products or deliver services. Sooner or later the questions must translate into action. That may seem painfully obvious, but, in fact, it's not so easy in an information-glutted business environment. Quite literally, all the right questions and all the right research and analysis relating to a crisis could preoccupy a management team for years, but crisis does not afford you that luxury. Thus, the key decision-making skill during crisis involves isolating *pivotal* pieces of data that prompt rapid decision making and swift action. You can find an example of this type of pivotal data in a survey of frequent fliers, corporate travel directors, and vacationers. When queried as to the most important elements in their choice of airline, the respondents agreed on two major ones: schedule and fare. No other factors even came close. Meals, leg room, entertainment options, lounges, and the like, while desirable, scored far below concerns for a timely flight at a competitive price. While the airline giants and the unions that provide them labor struggle to find a solution to the crisis of declining profitability, their decision-making needs really account for only two really critical factors. Doing so might involve restructuring, renegotiating union contracts, backtracking from the hub system, flying fewer types of aircraft, reducing the frills offered passengers, and any number of other moves in the quest to turn a profit and lower fares. Asking a million other questions that do not address this central goal only delays action and courts disaster.

We have found that the solutions to most crises hinge on only a few pivotal options. Most everything else usually hinders the search for crisis solutions. We'll talk more about this topic in the next section on the rules of effective crisis management.

Communication:
Understanding What's Different

We hesitate bringing up this skill because other organizational consultants have abused it so much. The admonition to communicate more quickly, more fully, and more clearly has been bandied about corporate training rooms for the last twenty years, until good communication has become enshrined for whatever ails an organization. Unfortunately, too little of the advice on the subject addresses the specific issue of *difference*.

If you follow the progress from insight to decision making to communication during the effective management of a crisis, you will find that crisis communication stresses *differences*. Now think about this carefully. A lot of corporate crisis communication involves either cheerleading, cover-up, or both. The cheerleading comes in the form of shouting "We will beat this thing" or "When the going gets tough, the tough get going." The cover-up is not nearly as malicious as it sounds, because it usually amounts to defending a system, structure, or activity against the jaws of crisis, proclaiming such stances as "We will not let this oil spill get in the way of our long-term plans" or "Space exploration is vital to our quality of life." While this type of communication and the intent behind it matters to some extent, it does not account for what's *different* now.

133

Effective crisis communication tells the organization and the world what it will do *differently* in order to resolve the crisis. In the end, only this aspect of crisis communication matters. Take the simple example of a flat tire. The instruction manual (a communication) doesn't offer much help if it tells you that you will *soon* be on the road again or that you have been driving on the *best* tires even though they have gone flat. You want to know precisely how to change the damned tire. Since flat tires represent an abnormal situation, the instructions communicated by the manual stress the difference between this situation and the normal activities associated with driving the car.

Even the smallest crisis forces an organization to veer from what it does normally to what it must do abnormally, if only for a very short period of time. Consequently, to assess how well an organization responds to crisis, you can simply measure what it has chosen to do differently. If it continues to do what it did before the crisis, then how will it ever resolve the crisis? Acting normal in an abnormal situation does nothing to reduce danger.

Danger

We cannot overstate the need for highly specific and pointed internal communications during crises. Swiss drug company F. Hoffmann-La Roche learned this lesson the hard way. According to a July 4, 1991, story in *The New York Times,* the U.S. affiliate of the drug company warned the parent company in 1980 about potential problems with the new sedative, Versed. However, despite the internal concerns, distribution of the drug went forward as scheduled, resulting in 46 deaths and 40 other serious adverse reactions within 18 months of the product's introduction to the market. F. Hoffmann-La Roche denies any problems with the drug, a fairly standard, legally cautious response. However, the question remains, why did the company ignore the warnings of its affiliate?

Given a frequently anti-business environment, you might assume that the parent simply allowed its greed to overrule the warnings. But unlike what you see in movies, real-life corporate executives rarely operate without conscience or scruples. More likely, the affiliate's crisis message somehow did not adequately communicate the intensity or urgency of the danger—in short, the difference between Versed and other proven drugs. In a large company, which monitors multiple projects and faces numerous crises, any given crisis message concerning one sedative can easily get lost or seem not serious enough to require action. According to this scenario, F. Hoffmann-La Roche did not intentionally do wrong, but rather it did not communicate in a way that the message signaled a clear and present danger. Again, by not seeing a danger clearly, a company missed an opportunity.

Opportunity

Most times, crisis communication allows management to emphasize certain characteristics of the organization that can become positive forces in solving a crisis. Lynn Wesbrok, a local United Way director, turned a national crisis for United Way into a positive opportunity for her local chapter.

Crisis struck United Way when investigators reported that the CEO of the nation's largest charity had "developed a taste—if not a habit—for a lavish lifestyle and all of its trappings," frequently financed by small donors who thought their money went to impoverished families. Among the offending trappings were a half-million-dollar yearly salary, $92,265 for limousine services, $40,762 for Concord flights to Europe, $37,894 for 29 trips to Las Vegas for the CEO and his associates, and $33,650 for trips to Gainesville, Florida, home of a special female friend. William Aramony, 22 years the CEO of United Way, angrily denied the allegations, arguing that he always acted in the best interests of the organization. But the board responded quickly, essentially sacking its CEO. As with most corporate cultures, the example of senior management, especially the CEO, sets the level of conduct for all who work for the organization. Consequently, excesses at the top usually result in the same excesses at lower management levels. The executive director of United Way in New York City resided in a $4,700-a-month apartment, paid for by United Way, and enjoyed a $1,700 annual membership at a swank lunch club, also funded by the charity. While most United Way activities come under local control and boast modest accommodations, the organization's headquarters occupied a lush and ostentatious Park Avenue address where the rent exceeds the entire income of a poor Appalachian township.

United Way's national crisis sharply undermined the credibility of the local chapters that did not reflect Aramony's example of excess. But how do you convince a small community that *its* United Way chapter differs from the national image? Facing this crisis, Lynn Wesbrok came up with a simple, yet effective, form of crisis communication. She posted her W-2s, declaring a salary of $57,000 a year, on public bulletin boards throughout her community. This bold action set her, and her organization, apart from the rumors of sky-high salaries and excess expense accounts. It literally saved her chapter, and the local poor who depend on it, from a year of depressed contributions. The wise executive does what Wesbrok did.

Developing Communication

The key to developing effective crisis communication lies in stopping *bull-
----*! Strong words? Yes, but let's be honest about the problem. Too often, organizations communicate with their own rank and file the same way that they do with the public, issuing overly cautious half-truths, defending the status quo, and favoring the image of the organization over the substance of solutions. Since this approach doesn't work with the public, why should it fare any better with employees?

Employees, unlike the public at large, know a lot about the details and dynamics of a crisis. It doesn't do much good for leaders to paint a picture of a crisis that differs from the reality, because the employees know the reality. Since the crisis surrounds them, only a food doesn't level with them. Can you imagine Washington, D.C., police officers arguing that the press has overstated the scope of crime in the nation's capital? A U.S. senator who lives in plush Alexandria might, but not the cop on the beat who must wear a bullet-proof vest in hundred-degree July weather.

You must not only communicate honestly with employees, you must communicate what's different in a troubling situation. Only then will employees know what to do to move the organization beyond its crisis.

Focus: Controlling Activities with Concepts

It takes focus to direct individual or organizational energy and resources toward a crisis solution, and focus requires concentration on one or a few concepts at a time. This skill comes especially into play during crisis, where every organization seems critically important and cries out for individual attention.

Don't confuse our emphasis on focus as a key skill with tactical considerations such as prioritization or management by objectives. You need these tools, too, but they address *activities*, while our notion of focus emphasizes *concepts*.

During crisis, all actions should unite behind a common concept or set of concepts. For example, take the cost-cutting rage currently rampant in corporations throughout the world. Streamlining provides a useful tactic during a crisis, but you must do it according to a guiding concept, such as increased quality, quicker distribution, or a faster research and development cycle. To cut costs for their own sake or just to boost next quarter's bottom line leads potentially to two extreme errors: either cutting too little or lopping off too much. For an organization to cut costs to the right level, it must measure a cost-cutting *activity,* such as downsizing the workforce, against the bench mark of a *concept,* such as higher-quality services. Let's apply the relationship of activity to concept to another example.

Some 10 years ago, when the information revolution struck the retail industry, Radio Shack chose to convert from basic cash registers to point-of-sale computers in all its stores. The new system required that all sales people record the name, address, and phone number of each purchaser. This new activity meant that a customer, whether buying two AA batteries or a complete computer system, provides the same amount of information. It also meant that it took the same amount of time to buy a set of batteries as it did to buy the computer—a fact that, 10 years later, created frustratingly long and slow lines at Radio Shack retail outlets. Now, the *activity* of gathering more information about customers can make good sense, but if the activity does not promote a guiding principle of better customer service or consumer follow-up to generate future sales, the activity exists only because the technology to perform it exists. In other words, Radio Shack automated for automation's sake, rather than to accomplish an important corporate goal.

Unfortunately, during a crisis, executives implement all sorts of activities for their own sake. Knee-jerk budget cutting, rushed dictatorial meetings, arbitrary objectives assigned to employees, and the like, may feel and look to executives like tackling a crisis head-on, but without the focus of guiding concepts, they just squander scarce energy during a time when every ounce of energy should be directed to resolving the crisis. Wasting time is always dangerous.

Danger

During any crisis, management should focus everyone's energy on the concepts that will make or break the organization. Otherwise, all the crisis-combatting activities in the world will do nothing to turn the crisis around. Such occurred at Borden, Inc.

Based in New York City, Borden is a leading diversified food company best known for its dairy products, popularized by Elsie the Cow. The company also provides more of the world's largest pasta than any other company, and it holds a dominant market position with such products as Cracker Jacks and Cremora. In the early 1990s, like most major food companies, Borden faced withering competition, the increased popularity of non-brand, private-label products, consumer skepticism, declining margins, and increasing production costs. However, Borden did not sit idly by, watching its profits decline. CEO Anthony D'Amato implemented a two-year streamlining program that reshuffled assets and restructured everything in sight. Nevertheless, the company still posted a loss of almost a half-billion dollars in 1992. D'Amato resigned to avoid being fired.

Sadly, D'Amato's efforts lacked the focus of a guiding concept. Had Borden restructured around the concept of higher quality such as Motorola did, or around the quest of becoming either number one or number two in each product category like General Electric did, things might have turned out differently. What, really, did the company wish to accomplish? Did it want to dominate a high-volume, relatively low margin industry such as dairy products or a lower-volume, higher value-added product category such as snack foods, where they rank as the second-largest salty snacks maker in North America, just after Frito-Lay? Should it shift into more non-food items, adding to existing product lines such as Elmer's, Krazy Glue, Wall-Tex, and Wonder Bond? What, exactly, should drive any restructuring activities? Concepts such as product grouping, production costs, global expansion (less than 30 percent of sales came from outside the United States in 1992), pristine quality, consumer health niches, distribution dominance, or a score of others could have provided the bench marks by which Borden could have measured all its crisis-solving activities, but without guiding concepts, the measure of executive performance came down to a "bet-your-career" program, in which a single measurement at the end would reveal whether the CEO wins or loses. D'Amato lost because he did not incorporate any bench-marking interim steps where he could envision crisis activities against a concept-driven focus established at the beginning of all the activity. A wiser executive would have created that focus.

Developing Focus

The development of focus under crisis conditions hinges on constant *assessment,* an ongoing evaluation of each activity in terms of its consistency with a guiding concept. Nowhere does focus make more of a difference than in the cockpit of a commercial jetliner.

Amazingly, few people die traveling on airplanes. While the occasional plane crash can kill hundreds in an instant, the death toll is a tiny fraction of the total number of people who fly every day on every airline worldwide. It all boils down to constant assessment of a constant threat.

Although technology plays an important role in the safety record of air transportation, flight routines and rituals that make up a liturgy for the aviation industry play an even bigger role. From the most experienced Delta Air Lines captain to the shadiest drug runner aboard a single-engine Cessna, pilots hold sacred all the checks and rechecks designed to ensure flight safety. The guiding concept? Aircraft safety. Not surprisingly, the activities that ensure safety in the air also figure heavily in the cost and time involved in running an airline. A lot of money could flow to the bottom line if the industry cut corners and scrapped time-consuming assessment routines. Profits would soar, at least until planes began falling out of the sky.

Organizations need to adopt a similar attitude toward their actions during crisis. Each major crisis-solving activity must stand up to two questions. First, exactly how will this activity contribute toward a crisis solution? Second, is this activity consistent with the concepts guiding all crisis management efforts? By asking these two questions, you can make certain that you never confuse well-intentioned but relatively unimportant efforts with those that mean life or death. Look again at the cockpit. A smart pilot should brush up on the latest tech reports on fuel consumption, but he or she should not engage in that activity during landing and takeoff. Likewise, during a crisis, the management team must separate the important from the crucial. A smart executive conducts an annual budget review for a regional office, but he or she should not perform that same review during a major oil spill off the Alaskan coast.

In the Thick of Thin Things

The skills of insight, decision making, communication, and focus combine to combat an interesting characteristic of crisis: organizational overload. Simply put, organizational overload occurs when a company fails to put together enough of the right stuff to solve a crisis. Consider the crisis of the South American rugby team made famous by the book *Alive*. Stranded by a plane crash high in the Andean Alps, the survivors' concerns boiled down to three main issues: food, warmth, and rescue. Only limited options existed for each issue. The only food consisted of a few candy bars, several unbroken bottles of wine, and the flesh of dead teammates. The crisis decision, although startling, came down to cannibalize or die. They ate human flesh and lived to tell about it. Had they worried instead about the length of their hair, shaving, collecting mementos, or what the world would think of their desperate solution, all would have perished.

Many organizations experiencing crisis overload themselves with unimportant worries, gathering too much information and not sifting the life-sustaining from the less important data. Too many options cloud decision making and forestall decisive action. Too much rumor and conflicting communication obscure the message needed to unify organizational efforts. Finally, too many departments and too many people sincerely, yet ineffectively, running in different directions prevent genuine crisis solutions. In this type of overload environment, characterized by too much of everything, the organization fails to do the right things. The four skills we've discussed help correct the problem, because they enable you to weed out and eliminate those issues and activities that bring little to bear to the task of combatting crisis. In summary, they keep the organization from getting bogged down in the "thick of thin things."

Crisis thrusts these skills into the spotlight. For those managers who possess and effectively deploy these skills, crisis, although unwelcome, at least provides the opportunity to demonstrate competence—competence the world will remember long after the crisis has passed. Those who lack these skills also invite scrutiny, but such that they would rather forget. Their detractors rarely do.

CHAPTER 10

What You See Is What You Get: How Corporate Values Undermine Action During Crisis

Like people, no two organizations, no matter how close the resemblance, look exactly alike. Some academicians and consultants attribute an organization's uniqueness to its distinctive culture. We prefer to see it in much simpler terms: Every organization possesses its own unique personality.

To get a feel for how corporate personalities evolve quite differently, even in the same industry, consider two organizations in the business of professional basketball. The Detroit Pistons, playing "in your face" defense and blue-collar, nothing-fancy offense, have earned a reputation as the bad boys of basketball. In contrast, the Los Angeles Lakers use quickness on defense and finesse on offense to create an image sportswriters have labeled "show time." Both teams win their share of games, both display world championship honors in their arenas, and both play awe-inspiring basketball. But they look different because they *play* the game with unique styles. In the competitive world of personal computing, IBM and Apple display equally distinctive traits. One wears button-down white shirts, maintains vertical management, and moves cautiously in the marketplace. The other favors Levi-Strauss to Brooks Brothers, project management over hierarchy, and bold marketing moves such as the Newton, the latest high-tech, hand-held toy. Again, like the Pistons and Lakers, both computer companies play the PC game well, but they play it quite differently.

141

All sorts of qualities and attributes join to create an organization's personality, from dress codes to the location and style of company headquarters, but none shapes the corporate persona more than values.

Corporate values consist of standards of behavior which an organization *believes* are important. You cannot see, touch, or smell them. In fact, they possess no material properties whatsoever. Consequently, you can recognize that a value exists in either a person or an organization *only* when an action reflects the existence of that value. For example, we might strenuously proclaim our honesty, but until we commit honest actions, you cannot know for sure whether we are really honest or not. Similarly, you cannot detect an organization's values in what it says or writes down in a cleverly worded mission statement, but rather by observing what it does. Take Ford Motor Company's slogan that "quality is job one." The slogan would lead you to assume that Ford cherishes quality production as a deeply ingrained value. However, every year, Ford recalls hundreds of thousands of cars and trucks to repair everything from paint jobs to brakes. Between 1986 and 1993, Ford recalled an unbelievable 45 percent of all of the Tauruses, Mercury Sables, and Lincoln Continentals the company sold during that period. Can you imagine Sony having to take back one out of every two televisions that it sells or Motorola replacing half of the cellular telephones it manufactured in the last seven years? Ford's tendency to release shoddy products into the marketplace and then mass-repair them later demonstrates that quality does not really represent a deep-seated value at Ford. Lest you think we've unfairly singled out Ford, let's put automobile recalls in perspective. Every automobile company suffers from recalls, even the Japanese and the Germans, though only U.S. car producers, like Ford, recall their products *consistently* year after year.

While a company should base its values on deeply held beliefs about which standards it reveres and which it does not, those beliefs do not spring from religious or philosophical concepts of right or wrong. Unlike truth or beauty, which most people cannot clearly define, abstract notions of corporate values represent tangible activities. The Lakers play a showy up-tempo game because it works for them. No one can say they have chosen an inherently right or wrong style of play. They've simply chosen a style that enables them to accomplish their goals on the court. Similarly, when weighing the dress codes of IBM and Apple, you can't judge the rightness or wrongness of the choice the organization has made, you can only weigh whether it works or not. Such preferences not only influence a company's success, they play vital roles in how well, or badly, that company manages crisis.

Just as individuals feel attracted to certain personalities and put off by others, so, too, does the public feel attracted to and repulsed by certain types of corporate vales. Even though corporate values may reflect mere preferences, certain values accomplish more than others at any given time, especially in the minds of the group most important to any organization: its consumers.

We have identified four corporate values that seem both to work well and to invite public acceptance in the current business environment—four values that the environment *outside* of the organization (the public and consumers) prefer to see resident *inside* an organization. They are stewardship, environmental concern, respect for employees, and horizontal guidance. Essentially, these values relate to the social costs of doing business in the next century, not the way a company produces a product or delivers a service. Unlike values such as quality, customer service, or innovation, these social-cost values reflect how an organization conducts itself as a community citizen. Consider two former heavyweight boxing champions, Mike Tyson and George Foreman. In terms of their actual product (boxing), both personified values of quality and innovation. As professional boxers, both also provided a service in the form of mass entertainment, which they delivered with a stress on premium customer service. But when it came to values not directly related to their specific product and service, their paths diverged. Tyson demonstrated a flagrant disregard for his role as a community citizen and, as a result, ultimately ended up being sentenced to a prison term for rape. Foreman, on the other hand, demonstrated again and again a high level of social responsibility, culminating in his religious ministry dedicated to minority youth. While Tyson sits idly in a jail cell, Foreman stars in commercials and appears in prime-time situation comedies. Both boxers demonstrated their values in no uncertain terms, but the public clearly preferred one set of values over the other. In the corporate ring, consider the corporate values of A.H. Robbins, which suppressed its *own* research findings in order to deny the allegations of infection resulting from the use of its contraceptive, the Dalkon Shield. Then contrast Robbins' values with Johnson & Johnson, who in the famous Tylenol scare, recited the first paragraph of its mission statement, which stressed its responsibilities to mothers and fathers who use it products, and pulled Tylenol capsules from store shelves, *despite* protests from the FDA. In the long run, which set of social values did the public prefer?

The values of stewardship, environmental concern, respect for employees and horizontal guidance separate the good companies from the bad. Pick up any business periodical or recently published business book, and you'll see these values mentioned as prerequisites for corporate prosperity in the future. To be sure, scores of other values will fuel a company's success, but we believe these four will matter most because they link directly to crisis. As crises flourish in the future, they will illuminate these four corporate values the same way they do the four skills we mentioned in the previous chapter.

WYSIWYG

Exploring the four social-cost values in depth, we'd like to elaborate on the computer concept WYSIWYG, which translates to "what you see is what you get." In the computer world, this means that how a document looks on the screen shows exactly how it will look when it comes off the printer. In the context of crisis management, it means that an organization's values determine *how* an organization acts during crisis. When crisis erupts, an organization's actions show the organization's true personality, its real values. Furthermore, the values you see displayed during crisis show exactly what you can expect from the organization long after the crisis has passed.

During times of relative calm, a company can carefully orchestrate its actions to create the image that certain values exist, but when the hurricane of crisis hits, the harmony between values and actions becomes harder to maintain, especially if the values did not really drive the company in the first place. During crisis, WYSIWYG. For example, in the previous chapter, we talked about the expense excesses of United Way's former chief executive officer. The exposure of swank headquarters, first-class flights to exotic conferences, and lavish galas provided the public with a glimpse of activities that did not square with the notion of United Way as the protector of the downtrodden. Under the pressure of crisis, the nation's largest charity could not manipulate its actions to create the perception of values it did not, in fact, possess. Instead the public saw values that suggested United Way operates like any other business whose principal product happened to be fundraising for the poor, but whose main purpose had become protecting the lifestyles of its executives. At the top, United Way's actions told the public that the organization did not really concern itself with the plight of people lacking enough food, adequate shelter, or proper health care. The United Way case reveals another aspect of the relationship between crisis and values. While it takes a constant flow of actions to demonstrate a positive value, only a few missteps

144

can fashion the perception of a negative value. It takes years for a person to develop a reputation for telling the truth, but someone catches you in a *single* lie, your entire reputation can crumble as quickly as it did at Rohr, Inc.

The major defense contractor, Rohr, admitted that it had improperly tested certain parts that attach the engines to the wings of Air Force C-5 transport planes. In some instances, the company didn't perform mandatory tests at all. While admitting the offenses, the company also insisted that its actions did not pose any safety hazards for aircraft crews. The government fined Rohr and required that it plead guilty to fraud, but the settlement did not prohibit the company from pursuing future government contracts. This meant a lot to Rohr, which had already laid off half its workforce as defense department budgets dwindled with the end of the Cold War. In a highly competitive market, with the same number of companies chasing after fewer contracts, why would the government award a contract to a company that had confessed to fraud? Unfortunately, the government forgot WYSIWYG and rehired a baby-sitter who had confessed to child abuse. That may represent a noble gesture of forgiveness, but did it keep the interests of the child at heart?

The inevitable display of one or all of the four social-cost values under difficult circumstances makes crisis a dangerous time for any company. Just as management's skills go on display, so does crisis illuminate an organization's values, creating a volatile factor as threatening as the crisis itself. On the other hand, crisis also provides the opportunity for an organization to demonstrate strong community values that might otherwise go unnoticed.

Stewardship

By definition, a steward accepts responsibility for a certain domain. The steward protects the interests of everyone and everything associated with his or her domain and, more and more, the public expects organizations to behave like stewards, holding them responsible for voluntarily conducting their activities in a way that protects all the elements of their particular domains. While this may sound like a pretty straightforward concept, stewardship requires long-term vision and deep commitment. Take the pharmaceutical industry, for example.

Under the concept of stewardship, drug manufacturers should accept responsibility for all aspects of their industry: development, testing, packaging, labeling, pricing, monitoring, and correction. As a steward, a pharmaceutical company should protect the interests of the public throughout each and every activity, accepting the negative consequences of manufacturing and marketing a certain drug as well and the positive profits that accrue from a successful drug that causes no harmful effects. However, if the industry truly practiced stewardship, society would not need the host of agencies government has created to control the activities of drug manufacturers from development to distribution. The very fact that the agencies exist suggests that the industry has not embraced the concept. If it had, testing of prospective drugs would meet internally rigid standards rather than those demanded by the government. Pricing would reflect long-term profitability rather than short-term benefits to the bottom line. And, a drug gone awry would not require a legion of attorneys to deal with victim's claims. Sadly, most pharmaceutical companies haven't got the slightest idea of what stewardship entails and would prefer minimum testing, the highest prices, and ducking blame for any negative consequences.

Does stewardship run against the principles of free enterprise and profit? Not at all. Pharmaceuticals play a vital role in the quality of life. People need them, even when they pose certain dangers. It follows that the public should award the privilege of making a profit in this industry to those organizations that best display the value of stewardship. The award should not come from some bureaucrat's stamp of approval, but rather from the natural selection of a skeptical and informed public that will not buy products from a company that does not see its role as a steward of the public's health and welfare. Those who shun stewardship do so at their peril; those who willingly accept it do so to their advantage and to the advantage of their consumers.

Downside

The pressure of crisis can illuminate a seemingly total disregard for any social responsibility not legally mandated. This unwelcomed display of values occurred during the conflict between Wes McKinley and the U.S. government.

The conflict between McKinley and the Department of Justice began with allegations that defense contractor Rockwell International had allowed toxic chemicals to pollute soil and groundwater near its nuclear weapons plant at Rocky Flats, 15 miles northwest of Denver. In addition, the government alleged that the plant site itself had become contaminated with radioactive plutonium. The government, faced with the crisis of a potential corporate polluter, forced a special federal grand jury to investigate the charges. Chaired by rancher Wes McKinley, the jury voted to indict Rockwell, five of its employees, and three people who worked for the Department of Energy. The deliberations and subsequent actions of the grand jury indicated that they felt that the actions of Rockwell constituted a major infraction with significant repercussions to the environment. However, the prosecutor assigned to the case settled for an $18.5 million fine against Rockwell and filed no charges against the company or the individuals involved. Case closed.

Against global sales of over $12 billion, the fine amounted to roughly .001 percent of Rockwell's annual revenue. Put in perspective, if Rockwell were an individual making $100,000 a year, the fine for dumping hazardous waste would have amounted to $100—less than the price of a business dinner in New York, a mere slap on the wrist for wrecking the environment.

To the jurors' minds, and particularly to Wes McKinley's, the Rocky Flats issue exposed the true values of the Department of Justice regarding their stewardship of the environment, so they pursued the case on their own time and with their own money. First, some of the jurors told their story on national television. Then they retained a high-profile environmental-law expert from George Washington University, who charged that "the deal Rockwell cut in Rocky Flats would make John Gotti blush." Finally, they got the attention of the House Committee on Science, Space and Technology, whose subcommittee chairman Harold Wolpe, of Michigan (not Colorado), observed that, "the most important thing that federal prosecutors bargained away in negotiations with Rockwell was the truth." Furthermore, the House Committee's report chided the government for reneging on its stewardship of the land when it decried "the Justice Department's tendency to treat environmental crimes as unimportant." Although the government did not cause the original crisis, the dynamics of the crisis resulted in exposure of the government's apparent disregard for environmental crime. This perception will not die easily.

Upside

A crisis also provides the opportunity for an organization to act like a steward, taking full responsibility and doing all that it can to protect the public welfare during a difficult situation. This certainly occurred at McDonald's.

Somewhere in the transition from the 1980s to the 1990s, public awareness about environmental issues skyrocketed and concern over all sorts of issues, from ozone depletion to hazardous waste management, became the focus of public scrutiny. One of the most offending products was polystyrene, the stuff that fast food firms use to package almost every product. Since more than 20 million people visit a McDonald's restaurant every day, with a new McDonald's opening its doors every 18 hours, polystyrene packaging and Big Macs became a lethal social issue. To its credit, the burger giant responded far beyond the call of duty. Without the threat of government sanctions or global boycotts, McDonald's announced a long-term plan to eliminate polystyrene packaging, introduce recycled paper bags and sandwich containers, and develop a massive program of waste composting.

The company received a huge amount of favorable publicity for its actions, and that is precisely our point. The crisis, while not directly aimed at McDonald's, did put the values of the company on the line, with millions of consumers looking on. McDonald's could have stalled, argued that the concerns over polystyrene were scientifically unfounded or premature, funded counterstudies to sway public opinion, or admitted to the problem but whined about the immensity of the solution. However, it did not, choosing instead to behave in a way fully consistent with other actions for which McDonald's does not get nearly as much global attention but that suggest its motives flow from deeply held values. For instance, the company has also displayed its sense of stewardship by establishing Ronald McDonald Houses near major children's hospitals in communities across the nation. These hospice-like bed and breakfasts provide lodging and limited cooking facilities for families with seriously ill children who cannot afford local hotel rates. In addition, McDonald's has become the largest U.S. employer of minority youth. Since 1990, over 65 percent of the franchisees who trained to become owner/operators represented minorities or women. Finally, the company has established the largest employee stock-option program in the history of U.S. business. These actions, when considered in conjunction with McDonald's response to the polystyrene crisis, suggest a company self-motivated to address all of the socially sensitive facets of its business. Consequently, when a crisis calls McDonald's values into question, the company always answers positively.

While both the McDonald's and the Rocky Flats examples involve specific environmental issues, they relate more closely to our discussion of stewardship. In both cases, the specifics regarding the environment matter

148

less than a fraction of the overall attitude toward social responsibility. In the case of McDonald's, its movement toward recycled paper products provided just *another* indicator, among many, of a strong social conscience. Unfortunately, the same holds true for the Department of Justice. Rockwell International, a major defense contractor, participated in both the space shuttle and the B-1B bomber projects. The record suggests that whenever a major defense contractor gets caught committing criminal activities such as kickbacks and bribes, they incur little more than a relatively lenient corporate fine and rarely a jail sentence for the executives involved. Amazingly, the government *continues* to grant contracts to the companies at fault, strongly suggesting values that favor the defense industry and prompt looking the other way in the effort to protect the industry from its own errors. Again, that is precisely our point. It took the Rocky Flats incident to flush out the government's values regarding its stewardship (in this case over the environment), and the public clearly found the values lacking.

Environmental Values

Although stewardship often involves environmental concerns, the environment itself deserves special emphasis. Consider again the example of McDonald's and Rocky Flats. In both cases, the environment played a supporting role not related directly to either organization's core activities. Neither McDonald's nor Rockwell International work primarily as environmental organizations. However, Exxon, U.S. Steel, Union Carbide, and Archer-Daniels-Midland do because their operations not only affect the environment, they make their living directly from the land.

While every company bears a stewardship responsibility toward the environment, oil, mining, chemical, agricultural, and real estate development companies shoulder unique responsibilities. In exchange for the privilege of *intentionally* exploiting the environment for the sake of the products and services the public needs or wants, the public holds these companies responsible for keeping any damage to acceptable levels and for restoring the environment to its original condition whenever possible. Since tremendous competition characterizes these industries, sooner or later consumers will support those companies that seem most sensitive to the resources that drive their corporate engines and will select out those that take from, but return nothing to, the environment. Consider two oil companies that charge (to the penny) the same price for gas at the pump, but Company A displays a record of active environmental concern, while Company B seems insensitive, even arrogant, when it encounters environmental issues. With no price differentiation in the marketplace, the public loses nothing and gains everything by voting with their dollars for the company that delivers its product with a sincere interest in protecting national resources. The boycott of Exxon gas stations after the *Valdez* spill may represent just the tip of an iceberg for a company the public perceives as insensitive to the welfare of the planet.

While companies may trumpet their environmental values in cleverly worded annual reports, nothing proves or disproves their true concerns like a crisis. If a company's actions disprove its concerns, it will pay dearly; if its actions prove its concerns, it will benefit immensely.

Downside

A stunning example of crisis exposing a lack of environmental values involves a company that had supposedly dedicated itself to protecting the environment, Martech USA, Inc.

Estimates indicate that government and private industry will spend more than $200 *billion* on environmental cleanup over the next 20 years, an expenditure from which Martech could benefit enormously. The company struck it rich sopping up the sludge from the Prince William Sound when the *Valdez* spilled its cargo of oil. It also helped keep crude oil out of Saudi Arabia's desalinization plants during the Persian Gulf War. Finally, it was one of the first U.S. cleanup operations to tackle Eastern Europe's decades of toxic pollution. By all rights, Martech should be oozing environmental concern, but instead, the company finds itself flooded by a steady stream of allegations.

Martech's initial crisis did not come from the environment at all, but began when the Securities and Exchange Commission opened an investigation into the company's alleged accounting irregularities. The non-environmental crisis called increased attention to Martech and, after the press caught wind of what looked like a disturbing trend of allegations, its scrutiny ultimately came back to the environment. *The Wall Street Journal* discovered that the Environmental Protection Agency was suing the company for botching an asbestos cleanup. In addition, it turned out that several state agencies, the Naval Criminal Investigative Service, the Army Criminal

Investigation Department, other military agencies, and at least two U.S. Attorney's offices were probing allegations of fraud and illegal dumping of hazardous wastes. Overnight, the scrutiny of Martech turned into a full-blown expose. In Louisiana, the state's Department of Environmental Quality shut down Martech operations at a Chevron Corp. oil-pit cleanup site. Chevron engineers claimed that Martech spread contaminated waste over an area more than twice the size of the original cleanup site. At Edward's Air Force Base in California, officials accused Martech of handling a jet fuel spill "in an unsafe and environmentally unsound manner." In Hawaii, Vernon Hoo, an industrial hygienist Martech had hired to oversee environmental and safety compliance, said he witnessed the company "run roughshod" over environmental laws and regulations on contracts at Pearl Harbor and Barber's Point. However, the most damaging allegations came from Puerto Rico. In 1990, GE Caribe, a General Electric Co. unit, had hired Martech to clean out waste ponds that contained cyanide, among other toxins. The waste ended up at a disposal facility in South Carolina. Although a review of Martech's documentation indicated that the waste did not contain any levels of cyanide, officials of the state of South Carolina commenced a thorough investigation.

The track record of environmental litigation suggests that the allegations may remain unresolved after the turn of the century, but legal resolution may pose the least of Martech's problems. For a company whose mission involves the protection of the environment, any questions raised about its actions generate serious concerns about its professed values regarding the environment. Even if Martech settles the various legal actions successfully, it will have lost a lot of public confidence. Martech's actions simply don't reflect the values you would expect from a company that owes it very existence to the environment.

In the oil industry, the profits pumped up in the form of liquid gold have tempted certain players to ignore environmental corners, as evidenced by the conflict between Chuck Hamel and the Alyeska Pipeline Service Co.

In 1990, Chuck Hamel tipped off regulators and Congress to alleged environmental wrongdoing along the Trans-Alaska pipeline, claiming that all of his information came from workers inside Alyeska, a jointly-owned company that runs the pipeline for Exxon Co., British Petroleum Ltd., and Atlantic Richfield Co. Instead of investigating the charges and making a full public disclosure, officers of Alyeska ordered Hamel's phone calls taped, rifled through his mail and garbage, researched his phone bills and sorted through his credit card charges. Worse, Alyeska hired Wakenhut Corp., the Miami-based security firm, to set up a bogus environmental organization called Ecolit, which offered Hamel its assistance in pursuing litigation against the oil industry. The real intent? To gather evidence against Hamel for use in the same litigation. The fraudulent environmental company operated for seven months before Alyeska finally shut it down. However, the crisis didn't end until Alyeska settled with Hamel, agreeing to pay millions of dollars in exchange for his dropping charges alleging invasion of privacy. The questions about Alyeska's values linger long after the settlement. For example, why did the organization panic over the allegations of environmental wrongdoing, even when the information came from inside sources? Why didn't it investigate the allegations and fix them if true, and publicly refute them if false? What difference does it make if the information originates from employees, as long as the allegations prove false, unless, of course, Alyeska really lacks true environmental concern. In the latter case, inside information regularly leaked to outside sources would create tremendous embarrassment and huge legal liability. Why didn't Alyeska learn a lesson from the *Exxon Valdez* catastrophe and avoid a growing public perception of wrongdoing?

Upside

Although slow and subtle, a measurable change has been taking place in the relationship between corporations and the environment. Unfortunately, the stereotypes of greed-driven executives blatantly wreaking havoc on the environment have distracted the public from the companies that have been making real and, more importantly, sincere strides to behave with an environmental conscience. In 1991, a global summit convened to review environmental practices and develop strategies for protecting earth's resources. Among those attending were senior executives from DuPont, BASF, Browning-Ferris, Ciba-Geigy, and Kodak. All signed a charter pledging themselves to a sustained emphasis on environmental preservation. A poll of the signatory companies found that they expected to spend 50 percent more money on pollution reduction in the next 10 years and cut their emissions by half during that same period. Interestingly, the global conference also coined a new phrase to describe industry's efforts to regulate itself with respect to environmental issues. That phrase, "sustainable development," has become the watchword to define balancing economic development with natural resource preservation. Again, skeptics may decry the phrase as "all talk and no show," but doing so ignores a number of specific examples in which organizations are backing their environmental values with action. These examples respond directly to crisis conditions.

In 1989, consumers protesting the slaughter of thousands of dolphins trapped in the nets designed to catch tuna launched a boycott of StarKist tuna products. The nets, nicknamed "walls of death" by marine conservationists, run hundreds of miles long, passively floating in the open ocean. In the quest for larger tuna harvests, commercial fishermen were each year killing millions of fish, whales, dolphins, seals, sea birds, and turtles. When the crisis of the boycott struck, StarKist used the opportunity to transform the industry, offering "dolphin-free tuna" and moving beyond mere PR by signing a contract with Earthtrust, an independent marine conservation group which monitors StarKist's fishing methods and provides a seal of approval on all catches that meet dolphin-free guidelines.

Utility companies in New York also turned crisis into a springboard for demonstrating their since interest in protecting the environment by providing an economic incentive to conserve energy. In an era of gouging prices, they developed and pushed through the regulatory agencies and the New York state courts a pricing program that set electricity prices based on *power saved,* rather than on power used. Instead of coupling profits to rising sales, the new rate system couples profits to reduced demand. The strategy, called *demand-side management,* calls for utility companies to subsidize the cost of efficiency improvements for customers and recover the expense over time.

In the food industry, Ben & Jerry's Homemade Inc., an ice cream packing company in Vermont, also addressed the crisis of environmental concern in a way that left little doubt about the company's values regarding natural resources. The company sponsored "One World, One Heart" festivals in Chicago, San Francisco, and Stowe, Vermont, each of which attracted over 100,000 people eager to hear live music and learn about environmental issues. Attendees received postcards on which they could write their elected representatives, and at each event they planted over a *billion* seeds of grass to restore festival grounds.

Perhaps the most impressive statement of environmental concern comes from 3M, the first major company to apply the concept of preventing pollution rather than cleaning it up back in 1975, long before the environment become a mainstream public concern. Starting with the slogan "Pollution Prevention Pays," 3M implemented over 2,500 changes between 1975 and 1993, all designed to eliminate toxic materials and bulk waste.

All of these companies in some way have managed to communicate that they have chosen the road to greater environmental sensitivity, and they did so against the backdrop of assorted crises that thrust their corporate values to the forefront of public attention.

As an aside, consider how both action and inaction with respect to environmental concern during crisis underscore the deeply ingrained nature of values. All companies must heed certain environmental guidelines enforced by the federal and state governments, but the government tends to enforce its guidelines statistically, making it hard to differentiate those firms that really care about environmental preservation from those that see environmental sensitivity as a necessary evil to placate a whimpering collection of oddball special interest groups. Measured statistically during times of calm, the values of 3M and Alyeska might appear equally grounded in sincere environmental concern, but the advent of a crisis exposed a totally different reality, illuminating one company's true commitment and the other's disdain.

Respect for Employees

Organizations once considered how they treat their employees a strictly internal concern. Since management valued workers rather narrowly as a company asset, the issue of employee relationships seemed of little consequence. After all, management did not maintain relationships with its production machinery or delivery trucks, so why bother relating to the rank-and-file workers?

But now, a company's treatment of its employees has attracted great social attention that invites considerable consequences. Take, for example, Frank Lorenzo's attempt to start a new airline. When he ran Eastern Airlines and Continental, Lorenzo fashioned a reputation for flagrantly disregarding his workforces. Subsequent documentation suggests that Lorenzo had not actually disregarded both airlines' human resources as much as the unions had claimed and that at least some of his reputation was undeserved. However, when a group headed by Lorenzo applied for permission to start a new airline, the government denied his request, citing its concern that Lorenzo lacked managerial fitness. The government's decision made no secret of its position that Lorenzo's values in terms of employee relations argued against his case. Like the value of environmental concern, the value of respect for employees falls under a host of rules and regulations that tend to make all organizations appear statistically to hold the well-being of their employees in high regard. OSHA, mandatory health-insurance options, minimum wage, and overtime rules apply equally to most companies, from the top of the Fortune 500 to the nearest corner mom-and-pop grocery. But again, crisis has a way of slicing through the statistics and showing who really cares and who does not.

Downside

In the closing days of 1993, Wall Street powerhouse Goldman, Sachs & Co. faced the crisis of a 10-day civil trial where it stood accused of intentionally discriminating against a female employee. While the trial passed without attracting much attention, an unwelcomed illustration of the company's values emerged. Although women make up over 40 percent of the company's workforce, they represented only four percent of Goldman's partners, not a pretty disclosure in an era where women control more and more investment dollars. As a private partnership, Goldman need not report internal information such as earnings or executive pay. Consequently, its court crisis afforded a rare glimpse into the company's promotion practices that otherwise would never have come under public scrutiny.

Even IBM, long venerated for its sensitivity toward employees, has come under attack. Like Goldman, the attack arises out of a crisis. Experiencing the largest loss in U.S. corporate history, IBM found itself under intense scrutiny from all quarters. One of the criticisms leveled against the company centered on lavish spending under difficult financial conditions. In May of 1993, the company hosted an internal party featuring entertainment by Bob Newhart and Liza Minnelli and a mock talk show on current events hosted by Larry King. A five-act circus capped off the festivities. While originally exposed by disgruntled investors, the gala has drawn the ire of 180,000 IBM employees, to whom the company giant once promised lifetime employment, but who were now being forced into early retirement. Those employees still on IBM's payroll, many only a heartbeat away from losing their own jobs, bristled at the spending, arguing that the money should go toward protecting jobs not entertaining an elite few. What started as a single issue regarding a specific bash then escalated to an attack on IBM's system of private golf courses, beach resorts, and its fleet of executive aircraft, all of which brought into question IBM's true feelings toward the rank and file who do not make it into the elite corps at the top.

155

The experiences of Goldman, Sachs and IBM also illustrate how quickly public exposure of a single issue can mushroom into a bigger display of corporate values. The explosion of exposure turns even more troublesome when it occurs during the crisis that prompted the exposure in the first place. IBM, locked in a raging battle with tough competitors, and suffering shrinking markets and unprecedented losses, faces yet another major problem, the discontent of its besieged and worried workers, irritated by the insensitive displays of senior management. As IBM staggers, the cameras zoom in on it relentlessly, uncovering every nook and cranny of insensitivity.

Upside

When Nordstrom, the Seattle-based department store chain, was breaking one annual sales record after another, crisis struck in the form a report on CBS's "60 Minutes." Following allegations by the United Food and Commercial Workers, a union that had organized Nordstrom back in 1931, Morley Safer reported that Nordstrom exploited its workers, forcing them to provide additional customer services, such as home delivery and personal thank-you notes, all on employee time. This type of crisis could certainly damage a company that supposedly prided itself on its employee relationships, but, in fact, the crisis actually ended up exposing some very impressive values. Interestingly, the employees themselves, the very ones "60 Minutes" called exploited, used the crisis as a platform to set the record straight. After the report, "pep rallies" supporting the company spontaneously sprung up in Nordstrom stores. In city after city, Nordstrom employees chipped in their own money to purchase ads to proclaim their happiness with the organization, and in the summer of 1991, some 60 years after the United Food and Commercial Workers had organized Nordstrom, employees at the five Seattle stores voted *overwhelmingly* to decertify the union as their bargaining agent. In the Nordstrom's case, the public would not have learned how much loyalty existed between the company and its employees had the union not instigated a crisis which motivated employees to make their loyalty plainly visible.

Delta Airlines offers another example of a company using crisis as an opportunity to display positive values. For the last 10 years, the airline industry has suffered from oversaturation of carriers and poor earnings. Continental went in and out of bankruptcy on two separate occasions, while Eastern and Pan American went out of business altogether. The financial crisis drew a lot of attention to all of the major carriers, including Delta, particularly because both American and United were experiencing extremely tense relationships with their employees. The public assumed that the same conditions existed at Delta. Not so. Against the backdrop of layoffs and tough union negotiations troubling the airline industry, Delta made it known that it had not laid off any permanent workers since 1951. In 1992, when the airline posted huge losses, Delta announced that it was reducing its workforce by 5 percent, but, true to its word, it avoided laying off any permanent workers by cutting only temporary staff and allowing normal attrition to reduce other positions.

Neither Nordstrom nor Delta pretend to have created perfect working environments. Nor do their management teams apply Pollyanna attitudes to the task of balancing company performance with paternalistic treatment of the workforce. In fact, both organizations have built reputations for ruthlessness when it comes to competition and employee performance, but both companies, when faced with a potential employee relations crisis, seized the opportunity to display their deeply held values, which the public will remember long after the crises have passed.

Horizontal Guidance

By horizontal guidance, we mean flat organizational forms that differ markedly from traditional hierarchial forms that resemble a pyramid. At first glance, some would argue that horizontal guidance reflects management skill and style rather than a value. On the surface, that may be true, but we have included it as a value because horizontally guided organizations tend to feel about their choice of management style much the way a devout Islamic feels about a *jihad* or holy war. Far more than a choice of style, it ignites a religious fervor.

In our experience, those organizations that strive to flatten their layers of traditional hierarchy rarely do so in isolation from other progressive management choices. In other words, a flattened organization has also gone global while others contentedly remain regional, has also become assertive in the care of its workforce while some barely honor the mandated rules, and has also broken new ground with innovative products and services while others stodgily protect the status quo. Not only does horizontal guidance rarely stand alone, it most often runs along the cutting edge. Thus,

157

where you find this kind of thinking, you will most often find a management team pushing the envelope and doing so with fiery passion. Yes, an organization's structure really boils down to an issue of style, but those who opt for this style usually do so because they believe so deeply in it. Deep beliefs, of course, represent values. More to the point, the public has begun to believe in this style as well. The old pyramid structure increasingly invites scorn as the symbol of all that corporate America did wrong and that allowed Japan and Germany to make mincemeat of our corporations in our own marketplace. Consider the old military establishment as an example.

Edward Luttwak of Georgetown University made a remarkable observation about the military style of guidance. At the close of World War II, the U.S. military consisted of 12 million active-duty personnel engaged in the task of warfare. At their head stood 17,000 officers, ranked at colonel, navy captain, or higher. Of these 17,000, 101 were three-star generals or admirals. By 1983, during a period free of global warfare, slightly more than 2 million soldiers (including thousands of officers under the rank of colonel) served on active duty, but at their head stood over 15,000 officers ranked at the equivalent of colonel or higher. This number included 118 three-star generals or admirals, 17 more than existed at the conclusion of World War II. While the military "workforce" had decreased by 60 percent, senior management numbers declined by only 11 percent, and executive management ranks actually increased. This amounted to one manager for almost 800 workers during World War II to a single manager for every 133 workers in 1983. Industry by industry, America has duplicated this same type of structural imbalance. In 1950, companies employed 46 staff workers for every 100 production employees. By 1980, the ratio had increased to 56 staff jobs for every 100 workers. For example, in 1976, AT&T maintained an incredible 99 staff jobs for every 100 production jobs. This type of structural imbalance explains why the World Bank could dismiss all 6,500 staff members and replace them with a scant several hundred, and not lose an ounce of productivity.

Given the widespread negative perception of the traditional pyramid structure, the public has come to judge the quality of organizations in terms of their management layers. They admire leaner and flatter companies that appear more innovative, quality-conscious, and customer-driven, while they ridicule hierarchies that seem slow, bloated, and self-serving. A quick scan of *Fortune, Forbes, Business Week,* and *The Economist* over the last five years will not turn up a single instance of a major organization *adding* management layers as an example of cutting-edge leadership. The judgments may not be fair or even true, but public perception rarely is.

The negative or positive image that an organization's structure creates, again, makes crisis a dangerous period. For the most part, the public cares little about how an organization guides itself, but when a crisis strikes, it exposes a company's structure like a CAT scan.

Downside

Reeling from the consequences of its poison gas leak in Bhopal, India, Union Carbide found itself constantly under public scrutiny, and one of those watching very closely was GAF, a chemicals and roofing materials company. In Union Carbide, GAF saw a weak company with poor controls, a bulging pyramid, and a very big problem with the Indian government. Sensing an opportunity, GAF tried what ended up as an unsuccessful hostile takeover of Union Carbide, but even though unsuccessful, the attempted takeover forced Union Carbide to increase debt by $3 billion, carve back 15 percent of its staff, and divest itself of several operating units. A leaner non-crisis organization might have spared Union Carbide both attention and a forced reaction.

Similarly, IBM, once *the* example of organizational excellence, found its hierarchy exposed by a financial crisis which prompted a change in senior management, including its CEO. Some of the attention brought on by the company's monumental losses focused on the company's vast vertical management structure. Ironically, only 10 years earlier most experts held up that same structure as an enviable model for corporate America in its battle against Japan. This fact underscores how quickly a value can descend from public preference to public disdain.

In the cases of Union Carbide and IBM, note that the central crisis did not involve structure at all. Only during the process of fighting the crisis did the issue of structure float to the surface of public perception and then become a crisis itself, one totally separate from the initial crisis which had first aroused the public's attention.

Upside

Fortunately, a crisis can also provide the means for displaying a belief in the value of horizontal guidance. Again, consider the U.S. military establishment. In contrast to the steep pyramid documented in 1983, the military establishment has undergone a profound change in values and structure. Somewhere along the way, far from public attention, the pentagon turned progressive, and it took a nasty crisis to draw attention to the change.

When Bill Clinton became President, he honored a campaign promise by moving to end discrimination against gays in the military. With great fanfare, the Commander in Chief ordered the Chief of Staff to implement the guidelines necessary to end all bias against homosexuals. In a traditional hierarchy characterized by a control-and-command pyramid, an executive order should immediately go into effect. All those on the pyramid below the point of decision must obey the order. In this case, they didn't. The military, it turned out, had ceased to be a traditional pyramid. Particularly under the direction of Colin Powell, military units now operate with more independence, self-governance, and field decision making than ever before. The officers boast better education, particularly in liberal arts and cutting-edge management theory, and the enlisted men had often joined the service en route to a college degree. Blind obedience, not to be confused with loyalty to country and president, no longer carried the day. Thus, when the President's order did not sit well with all levels of the military, the organization skillfully rejected the command, without being insubordinate, but acting very much like an empowered entity. Certainly, the military has not become the structural equivalent of Microsoft Corporation or Nike, Inc., both very progressive and horizontally guided organizations, but neither does the military of the 1980s operate in the old rigidly managed way. Ironically, it took a specific crisis, itself pertaining to values, to expose the Pentagon's movement toward the preferred value of horizontal guidance.

Believing Is Seeing

If society prefers certain values, then it logically follows that astute organizations should want to develop those values. Logic, however, does not always rule. In a strict sense, an organization cannot develop values the way it does a product or service because values do not lend themselves to a series of steps that culminate in success. Nor can training seminars teach participants to practice a specific value. Instead, individuals evolve values, and when a critical mass of individuals share the same ones, then they automatically become corporate values. In a company, the CEO must accept responsibility for sowing the seeds of belief that can flourish into widely shared values.

Basically, values take hold in an organization when actions consistently indicate some level of belief in a particular standard. Since companies, particularly large organizations, cannot easily sustain actions over long periods of time that run contrary to deeply held beliefs, the more consistent and frequent the actions, the deeper the belief. When it comes to values, believing is seeing. In other words, the fundamental standards in which an organization sincerely believes will eventually come to light in its actions.

During crisis, you can reverse the relationship between actions and beliefs. If the WYSIWYG principle applies during crisis, then the actions you witness reflect true corporate values, good or bad. Imagine an organizational game called the Wheel of Corporate Morality: A crisis spins the company round and round, and the wheel stops at true values.

The Three Rules
of Crisis Management

Vision: See It All, See It Fast.   A crisis always violates an organization's vision. While a common crisis violates vision in a relatively minor way, an unthinkable crisis all but murders it. We have found that behind those companies that fail to manage crisis effectively lies a boneyard of failed vision.

To solve a crisis you must embrace a vision that includes three fundamental activities: crisis *prevention,* crisis *identification,* and crisis *solution.* Since each activity flows from an organization's vision, a weak vision will result in weak crisis management.

Values: Say It All, Say It Fast.   Martin Luther King, Jr., observed that "The ultimate measure of a man is not where he stands in moments of comfort and convenience, but where he stands at times of challenge and controversy."

Surprisingly few management teams recognize the relationship between values and effective crisis management. It seems so obvious that under pressure the entire organization must achieve consistency between what it believes and says and what it does. When words and actions do not harmonize, crisis management becomes cacophonous: a lot of noise, but no music.

Versatility: Change It All, Change It Fast.   If a crisis forces change on the organization, then you may as well get on with it. Getting on with it requires, first and foremost, the right mind-set.

Crisis-imposed change initiates a literal migration away from the old vision and all the carefully formulated plans of the past. When the journey begins, you must keep three directives in mind: travel *light,* travel *fast,* and travel *straight.*

CHAPTER 11

Vision—See It All, See It Fast: The Five-Minute Audit

The Violation of Vision

Essentially, vision involves a mental journey from the present to the future, during the entire course of which, you make choices from the montage of current facts, hopes, dreams, dangers, and opportunities. In even simpler terms, a vision represents what you want to be when you grow up. Vision has become one of the hottest issues in any discussion of organizational performance, but here we are limiting our discussion to those aspects of vision that relate directly to crisis. In so doing, we do not at all mean to suggest that other aspects of vision are unimportant. Rather, we simply wish to concentrate on those aspects of vision that come into play during crisis conditions. Every organization possesses a vision. The more complex that vision, the more frequently an organization will experience crisis. Consequently, the better an organization articulates its vision, the more effectively it will manage its inevitable crises.

Without exception, every crisis violates organizational vision. If a company's vision represents a crystal ball picture of a future when things go right, then when things go wrong, that vision gets clouded or even shattered. Just as the concept of *up* helps you comprehend the meaning of *down*, *fat* sheds light on *thin*, *hot* helps put *cold* in perspective, so also can things going *wrong* illuminate things going *right*. How can you hold a clear vision without an understanding of its opposite?

When an attacker struck international figure skater Nancy Kerrigan's knee during the 1994 U.S. figure skating championships, he did not inflict a debilitating injury. Kerrigan suffered no broken bones, no severed tendons, no lacerations. Thousands of kids across hundreds of playgrounds suffer worse injuries every day, but for Kerrigan to turn in a world-class performance at the 1994 Winter Olympics, she needed to be in perfect shape. Even this relatively slight injury could potentially violate her vision of Olympic gold. Similarly, even a mild crisis violates corporate vision. WQED, the first community-sponsored public television station in the United States envisioned a future of innovative changes that would keep the spark of public television alive. WQED's staff justifiably believed in its vision. The station had not only given America its first glimpse of Mr. Roger's Neighborhood, but it had also teamed up with *National Geographic* to produce stunning documentaries, 12 of which rank among the 25 most watched programs in the history of public broadcasting. Its record of 28 Emmy awards seemed to assure that WQED would lead public television into the next century. But a "United Way"-like crisis struck the station. While the station's fundraisers urged individual viewers in telethon after telethon to pitch in $10 here and $15 there, reports surfaced that the station's executives were making as much as $325,000 in salaries and benefits, including car allowances ranging from $15,000 to $22,000 a year. While not particularly excessive, even for a company in the lower echelons of the Fortune 500, the compensation did not seem proper in an organization that basically lived off of community donations. When it became known that the station was running a $4.8 million deficit, suggesting that it was living beyond its means, all the while appealing to households with average incomes less than $32,000 per year to support its cause, the public reacted harshly to the disclosures. Unfortunately, this crisis erupted at a time when the federal government and large corporations were cutting back on public television funding, forcing member stations to rely more and more on community support, and it quickly violated WQED's vision of leading the public television pack.

In both the Kerrigan and WQED crises, the scope and depth of the problems caused less harm to the victims' health than it did to their visions. Neither Kerrigan's knee injury nor WQED's spending disclosures spelled total disaster. Within a week, Kerrigan was skating again and WQED remained on the air. However, both crises posed major challenges to vision.

The linkage between vision and crisis suggests that effective crisis management must begin with an organization's vision, not with its specific crisis.

Every Organization Pursues a Vision

An organization cannot possibly sustain even 10 minutes of activity without *some idea* of what purpose or goal the activity serves. Even a lack of activity stems from a vision, some expectation of how *not doing* something will shape the future, even a future that lies just 60 seconds ahead of the present. Every individual and organization must understand this concept of vision as a universal component of activity. Individuals would not plant grass seed unless they expected that a lawn would result. You would never venture into intersections on a green light unless you anticipated that cars coming from opposite directions would stop for a red light. And, at the beginning of the new year, you would not desperately diet without counting on shedding at least a few pounds. Every action entails some sense of what will flow from the act. Even if your expectations are totally unwarranted, they still provide the basis upon which you act in the first place. Similarly, all organizational activities commence with some expectation of results. The sum total of the results an organization expects from its choices and activities comprise its vision, even when its vision involves no more than selling one product to one customer one time only. Vision guides thousands of kids who set up summer lemonade stands who expect no more results than that their parents will exchange a quarter for a paper cup of diluted sugar-water.

While a multinational service company and a street-corner lemonade concession differ greatly in many respects, they both pursue a vision. Not every company, however, pursues its vision aggressively. John Young, president of Hewlett-Packard Company, uses vision as "a kind of glue, the basic philosophy, the basic sense of direction, sort of a value set, that draws everyone together." The views of executives like Young have led management psychologist Warren Bennis to conclude that the best organizations create compelling visions and feel equally compelled to act them out.

Unlike Hewlett-Packard, not every organization possesses a compelling vision, nor does every organization carry out its vision with vigor. Such organizations do not *lack* vision, they simply lack an appreciation of the importance that vision plays in the performance of their organization.

A crisis occurs when circumstances attack vision, when something, someone, some event, or any obstruction blocks the forward progress mentally anticipated by the organization. When this occurs, the future formally detailed in written form or informally structured in the minds of management, comes under fire. Then, the organization must act decisively or it will no longer control its own destiny. Of course, that's more easily said than done, for two reasons.

The More Complex the Vision, the More Frequent the Crisis

While even the most basic organization pursues a vision, not all visions are equally basic. Think again of the lemonade stand. The simple nature of the vision—to sell a single cup to one parent—leaves little room for things to go wrong. You can count the potential crises on one hand: no lemonade, no ice, no cups, or no parents with whom to conclude the transaction. Any one of these factors, or more precisely any lack of these factors, obstructs vision, and therefore creates a crisis. Now, push the lemonade stand to a new level of vision, assuming that initial success in selling to parents sparks a marketing quest for additional customers. The entrepreneur goes mobile, carting the product on a red wagon to the front yard and expanding the market to passing motorists. Unfortunately, not all commuters feel as compelled to buy as parents, and sales don't materialize. There you are sitting with two dozen cups, two quarts of lemonade, a carefully crafted sign, and a violated vision.

Spectrum Information Technologies looks a lot like a lemonade stand when compared to giants such as IBM and AT&T. The tiny New York company engages in the basic business of transmitting data over wireless communications networks, but the organization greatly complicated its vision when it hired John Sculley, former Apple CEO, to run its fledgling operation. Within 90 days of Sculley's arrival, rumors circulated that he had fallen out with Spectrum President Peter Caserta. Although the media rarely pays much attention to the management conflicts inside companies that rack up less than $50 million dollars in annual sales, when Spectrum expanded its vision to include Sculley, it also increased the number of factors that might negatively affect the organization, especially in terms of publicity. Thus, when stock analyst Dan Dorfman commented about the rumor of Sculley's departure, the value of Spectrum's shares plummeted almost 40 percent in a single day. Ironically, the small company had originally sought out Sculley to enhance its image in the financial marketplace.

In Chapter 2, where we talked about the myth that all crises flow from ineffective management, we pointed out that three dynamics contribute directly to the frequency of crisis. First, as visions become more complex, they demand greater cooperation of others; second, competition increases as a vision comes in direct conflict with other similar visions dependent on the same customer base; and finally, timing becomes more crucial as a vision becomes more comprehensive. These three dynamics create an inevitable relationship between vision and crisis.

An Articulated Vision Results in More Effective Crisis Management

An interesting story, not widely told, involves the senior executives of Johnson & Johnson, as they battled the extortion crisis surrounding the painkiller, Tylenol. After seven unsuspecting consumers died from taking Tylenol Extra-Strength capsules laced with cyanide, William Webster, the director of the FBI, and Arthur Hayes, the commissioner of the FDA, personally appealed to Johnson & Johnson *not* to recall Tylenol capsules from retail shelves across America. They reasoned, not illogically, that if J & J withdrew Tylenol, it would send a signal to would-be terrorists around the world that they could bring American business to its knees by tampering with a few products. The story goes that James Burke, J & J's chairman and CEO, and David Clare, chairman of the company's executive committee, pulled out a written copy of the company's vision statement and dropped quickly to item number six, which explicitly stated Johnson & Johnson's commitment to the well-being of its customers. They immediately pulled the product, costing the company hundreds of millions of dollars.

In order for a vision to drive an organization, at least two people must perceive and understand it identically. If only one person perceives it, it amounts to a personal, not an organizational, vision. When a crisis violates a vision, the extent of the violation depends on how commonly the entire management team perceives and understands it. Take, for example, two managers from Acme Motors Inc. One perceives the vision to emphasize, in no uncertain terms, that product quality overrules all else. The other sees quality as important but not essential to the accomplishment of the company's goals. When a critical piece of machinery becomes misaligned, resulting in a tiny flaw in the steering mechanism of the hottest-selling car the company manufactures, the first manager wants to replace the part before the company ships any cars. She cannot imagine shipping a product with a known flaw, no matter how small. The second manager feels badly about the flaw, but not so badly that he would expend the time and costs necessary to correct it. Consequently, he overrules the other manager and ships the car, avoiding a crisis, at least for the time being. Now, both managers hold the same vision, but each interpreted it differently. For one, the problem greatly violated the vision, while for the other, it didn't. As a result, differing perceptions of the vision led to different crisis responses. A hypothetical example? Yes, but we can't help wondering why Chrysler shipped 115,000 1993 Jeep Grand Cherokees and Grand Wagoneers, with a defective part that could cause the steering column to separate into two pieces, when prompt correction could have prevented an expensive recall.

The extent to which people in an organization accurately perceive a crisis and *coordinate* their response depends on how similarly its management perceives its vision. Widely held views about an organization's vision result in widely held interpretations about the extent of a crisis, and, perhaps more importantly, about how to deal with it. Misperceptions in either regard can create massive problems in the midst of an actual crisis. During the initial hours of the *Exxon Valdez* spill, the local manager responsible for spill containment reportedly went back to bed when notified of the disaster. For whatever reason, his interpretation of the spill did not sufficiently violate his vision to warrant losing further sleep. In all fairness, this action may have resulted from faulty communication, but the fact remains, the problem didn't appear significant enough to warrant immediate action. While he slept, his crews were frantically mobilizing to meet the disaster because they did perceive its enormity.

The fact that all crises violate vision and that vision and crisis link in the three crucial ways makes vision itself an effective tool in the management of any crisis. In our experience, all effective management activities begin and end with vision.

The Value of Vision

In order to tap the power of vision during a crisis, you must understand the link between vision and crisis. Understanding that link will enable you to take the right steps in the very early stages of the crisis. Delay results in false starts, misallocation of energy and resources, and the perception that the crisis has overwhelmed or paralyzed the organization. The responsive organization, on the other hand, follows the rule: *see it all, see it fast.* Seeing the full extent of the crisis and seeing it immediately hinges on using vision to illuminate two important facets of the crisis: first, its type of crisis, and second, its intensity.

Type A or Type B?

Everyone bleeds red, but the blood loss depends on the severity of the injury. A paper cut requires a Band-Aid, a gunshot wound to the chest demands emergency surgery. Similarly, every crisis violates vision, but the extent of the damage depends on the intensity of the wound. In an emergency room, treatment begins with blood typing. During organizational crisis, effective treatment begins with an accurate assessment of the type of crisis that has struck.

Crises generally fall into one of two distinct categories, and you can differentiate between them by applying the yardstick of your organization's vision. If a crisis poses a detour along the path specified by the vision, then you're dealing with a *common* crisis. As the name suggests, common crises occur most frequently and are the easiest to identify and address. When managers find themselves "up to their waistbands in alligators," they are usually facing a common crisis. Such common crises come in an infinite variety of shapes and sizes, but most center on producing and delivering products and services. When the system goes down and financial information waits on software modifications, you've encountered a common crisis. If your company washes, sorts, peels, and halves a load of peaches, but the cans have not yet arrived, you've also gotten mired in a common crisis. When the high-priced model for Victoria's Secret, the lingerie chain, discovers that she is pregnant, she has created a common crisis for the company's advertising campaign.

If the American Airlines flight to Los Angeles from Dallas develops a mechanical problem at the departure gate, the company is merely experiencing a common crisis, and when a truckload of FedEx packages misses the promised 10:30 A.M. delivery time, the driver faces no more than a common crisis. Our list can obviously go on indefinitely, encompassing the endless possibilities of run-of-the-mill business problems. Although rather routine and expectable, the common crisis should not, however, lull you into complacency. An organization that does not manage the endless vari-

171

ety of common crises will soon find its vision stalled, the victim of too many detours management could have easily circumvented. In a sense, dealing with a common crisis is like dealing with termites. In a single day, those insects cause relatively little damage. But let them keep chomping away, and pretty soon the foundation of the house begins to crumble.

At the turn of the century, and well into the 1960s, most of America could not shop at Nordstroms, Ernst Home Center, Toys-R-Us, or Florsheim Shoes. Consumers, often isolated in rural communities, could not, or would not, travel to cities to do their shopping but, instead, depended on the Sears catalog to fulfill all their wishes and needs. From the Sears catalog you could buy anything sold in big city stores, and you could receive your order quickly at home or at a nearby catalog outlet. The Sears system not only won the company financial success, it provided what amounted to a public service, bringing the latest in convenience, innovation, and style into the homes of every community in America. The trusty Sears catalog represented a powerful vision, but somewhere in the last 20 years the vision crumbled, a victim of countless "termites." Department stores, specialty shops, and malls sprang up everywhere, one by one violating the vision of home shopping. But perhaps nothing violated Sears' vision more than home shopping itself. At some point, catalog shopping ceased being a matter of necessity and became a form of suburban recreation. This change spawned thousands of competitors, each vying for customers with more colorful, more specialized, more entertaining, and more frequent (monthly rather than annual) catalogs. Eventually, shopping from the Sears catalog felt like kissing your great Aunt Mary on her deathbed, something no one really yearned to do. Like Mary, the catalog would not survive for long.

The decline of the Sears catalog paralleled the company's failure to manage scores of common crises. Sears' vision, like its market share, did not suffer a single massive assault. Rather, it experienced a string of violations time and time again over the years until the entire dream finally died. The cumulative effect of common crises makes managing even the most ordinary one important. By the same token, if an organization does not adroitly handle all the little problems that crop up along the way, then it will get clobbered when an *unthinkable* crisis occurs.

The unthinkable crisis is to a common crisis what a hurricane is to a spring shower. Unlike a detour, the unthinkable crisis can not only block an organization's path toward accomplishment of its vision, but it can eradicate the path altogether. Fortunately, one of the characteristics that differentiates a common from an unthinkable crisis is frequency. The unthinkable doesn't happen often, but then, it only needs to strike once to kill you.

In January 1993, the Jack-in-the-Box fast-food chain faced the unthinkable when a number of outlets in Washington and Idaho served meat tainted with *E. coli* bacteria. Two hundred customers fell ill, including several children who suffered permanent kidney damage. One died. Quickly implementing a crisis management approach that perfectly matched the seriousness of the crisis, Jack-in-the-Box did for its burgers what Johnson & Johnson did for Tylenol. Although the company traced the contaminated meat back to a specific slaughterhouse of one of its suppliers, Jack-in-the-Box nevertheless decided to replace *all* the meat in *all* its outlets nationwide. Next, even though it replaced the entire stock and eliminated the *E. coli* danger, the company ordered employees to cook burgers 15 seconds longer than the two minutes ordinarily required by the company's policy manual. Finally, Jack-in-the-Box set up a toll-free number for worried customers, publicly assumed responsibility, backed its words with money, and expressed sincere regret. While the poisonings dropped the stock of the parent firm, Foodmaker, 2½ points during the three days following the poisonings, the stock climbed back to normal levels within seven days. However, mismanagement of the same crisis might have done irreparable damage to the company's market share in light of the national publicity created by the poisonings.

Not all unthinkable crises come packaged with the drama of a lethal lunch at a fast-food outlet. Quite often an unthinkable crisis will sneak up on an unsuspecting organization. Bruce Christensen, CEO of the Public Broadcasting Service (PBS), created an unthinkable crisis for his organization, not because he ignored a string of common crises or faced a major challenge like Jack-in-the-Box, but rather because he performed *too well*.

During PBS's early years, the public viewed it as a source of alternative programming. If someone did not want to watch prime-time sex, violence, shallow sitcoms, or commercially controlled children's cartoons, it could find a suitable alternative on PBS. Although only a fraction of viewers tuned in to documentaries on the mating habits of butterflies or shows on which cuddly puppets taught children to count, over the years Bruce Christensen fine-tuned the format and improved programming, until PBS itself became prime time. With the "McNeil-Lehrer News Hour," "Masterpiece Theater," "Nova," and "Barney and Friends," the federally funded upstart for alternative programming became an international leader in mainstream programming. The success of PBS prompted two unthinkable crises at the same time. First, cable and network television began to compete in the market with the same type of shows that once only aired on PBS. With Nickelodeon, The Disney Channel, and Discovery offering much the same quality of children's and nature programming that once only flowed from public television, the viewership of PBS declined. Second, and most important, Congress began to rethink its financial commitment to the project. After 20 years, public television was no longer an upstart alternative to network programming but became legitimate competition for the networks and cable operators. Congress naturally asked, "Why are we funding prime-time television when so many other projects are crying out for tax dollars?"

Increased competition and Congress's question violated the vision of PBS, and neither posed the mere detours of common crisis, but rather represented an all-out assault on the very existence of PBS itself. No longer the idealistic underdog in a quagmire of media greed, no longer a challenge to the establishment, PBS had itself become the establishment. Fortunately, as we will see in a later chapter, Bruce Christensen accurately identified the crisis as unthinkable and implemented equally unthinkable changes to the vision of PBS, which underscores the importance of accurately typing a given crisis. To solve a common crisis, management needs to modify the activities that translate a vision into practical reality. In contrast, unthinkable crisis demands a radical overhaul of the vision itself. Let's look again at Sears for a vivid example, but this time with a happy ending.

In the 1930s, Sears Roebuck CEO Robert E. Wood preached that "business must account for its stewardship not only on the balance sheet, but also in matters of social responsibility." Some 60 years later, Sears Chairman Edward Brennan sounded a similar note: "Sears wants you to know that we would never intentionally violate the trust customers have shown in our company over 105 years." Unfortunately, Brennan uttered his words in response to charges by California's Consumer Affairs Department and New Jersey's Department of Consumer Affairs that Sears had been *systematically* overcharging customers at its auto repair centers.

The overcharging and recommendations for unnecessary repairs stemmed from the company's compensation policy, which rewarded Sears managers for the volume of repairs authorized by customers. This resulted in a great deal of pressure on customers, most of whom lacked sufficient automotive expertise to second-guess the sales pitch. Further, the Sears policy set strict quotas the company expected each facility to meet or exceed. Aside from the actual crisis of pressuring customers into unneeded repairs, the unthinkable crisis of Sears being caught "cheating" created a far more hazardous problem. While the general public has always felt itself at the mercy of unscrupulous auto mechanics, it had come to perceive the entire Sears chain (not just the automotive centers) as a rock of reliability, America's store. This perception kept the chain going in spite of drab stores, less than contemporary products, and mediocre sales people. Sears wasn't pretty, but it offered a fair deal. The automotive repair crisis shattered the perception, once and for all, that you could trust Sears. In addition, it hammered home to headquarters that in order for Sears to survive, the company would have to compete on the basis of price and quality in every product, not just automotive repairs. This forced Sears into a radical modification of its vision. It shot down marginal stores, dropped old lines of merchandise, and retained sales personnel. Future customers would come for quality and price, not just out of loyalty and habit. The decision to modify its vision radically saved Sears from slow but inevitable financial starvation as its market share dwindled each year. After just 36 months of intense change, the company remarkably turned the corner toward restored profitability.

In the next section that deals with practical application, we talk about using vision to develop an approach to crisis that automatically results in the accurate typing of crises. Once management accomplishes accurate typing it can then match the most appropriate form of crisis management to that type. After all, you don't weather a hurricane with an umbrella, nor do you board up your windows during a summer shower.

Determining Crisis Intensity

When you call your friends on the phone, you usually begin the conversation with, "How are you?" But if your friend happens to be your psychiatrist, you might well start off the conversation with, "How am I?"

Vision provides the means of determining the intensity of the crisis, answering, in a way, the question "How am I?" It facilitates a sort of "organizational psychoanalysis," which enables you to gauge how well you have adjusted to a violation of your vision. While intensity separates a common from an unthinkable crisis, it also involves issues beyond the type of crisis you're facing. Common crises themselves vary in intensity. In the area of nutrition, McDonald's encountered a common crisis that turned out to be quite intense. Almost every senior McDonald's manager, from CEO Michael Quinlan on down, has spent time flipping burgers in a McDonald's outlet.

175

Even the chief operating officer of a premier international public relations firm put in his hours over the grill after winning a contract to represent the firm. Understanding customer expectations at the point of purchase preoccupies McDonald's management. From appealing to the newfound purchasing power of senior citizens to attracting budget-conscious parents of children eager to dig into a Happy Meal, the company has kept innovating its menu at every turn. Yet, despite its dedication, McDonald's found itself in the midst of a common crisis involving the nutritional content of its food.

When nutrition-conscious consumers began to distance themselves from red meat and fat, McDonald's noticed the trend but kept its menu centered around the hamburger. As other chains added chicken and salads to their menus, the giant chain stayed staunchly with red meat. As a result, once loyal customers and those not pressured by their children for Happy Meals, began deserting McDonald's for the competition. Now, the slight drop in market share did not pose a destructive threat to the long-term vision of the company, but any drop in market share attracts the attention of the legion of analysts who scrutinize McDonald's every move and report even the smallest anomaly to the business media. Thus, although the crisis falls into the common category, it took on rather intense proportions. With its usual focus and style, McDonald's made innovative corrections to its menu, adding chicken and salads. Not to be outdone, however, they went a giant step further by introducing a seaweed burger, The McLean.

In contrast to an intense common crisis, consider the unthinkable crisis that lacks intensity. A lack of intensity can make an unthinkable crisis extremely dangerous if the organization does not marshall appropriate counter-measures to solve the problem. During the last days of John Akers' administration of IBM, even the immensely talented Akers misread the intensity of the crisis that faced his company. Initially, Akers suggested that he might step down sometime in the "immediate future," but industry analysts pointed out that in the fast track computer industry, entire companies can come and go in the wink of an eye. Gerald Meyers, former chairman of American Motors and IBM director, commented that if IBM had waited another 90 days to make executive changes (by replacing Akers) "this place [would] be very close to being in ruins." Somehow IBM misread the intensity of its crisis, assuming Big Blue could afford more time to modify its vision than it really had.

Where the type of crisis determines the depth of vision modification needed to meet the challenge, intensity sets the timetable. Even an accurate reading of the type of crisis and your subsequent response can fail if you misread a crisis' intensity. This error cost Roger Stempel his job as CEO of General Motors. After only two years in office, Stempel was asked to resign, not because he did not reset the organization in the proper direction, but because he changed the vision too slowly. In a crisis, timing can make all the difference in the world.

The Five–Minute Audit

For every manager in every organization, time marches on in precise increments unfettered by any other considerations. An hour at General Mills flashes past at exactly the same speed as it does at Geneva Steel Mills. The clock ticks at the same 10 minutes in Tokyo as in Bonn. But five minutes of crisis can seem like five minutes in hell, and hell keeps its own time. Crisis tends to speed up or slow down the clock simultaneously, making every day feel like a second, every minute like an eternity.

This paradox arises because during a crisis your future stands in jeopardy, but you enjoy so little time to bring analysis to bear on your situation. Edward Van Den Ameele, Union Carbide's press manager and duty officer, on the morning of December 3, 1984, was awakened at 4:30 A.M. by a reporter from CBS radio. The reporter wanted a reaction to a news report from India that deaths had resulted from a leak at a Union Carbide pesticide plant in Bhophal. From that very moment, the media would scrutinize every action (and non-action) the company took to address the crisis. With the media constantly clamoring for information, Union Carbide found itself forced to make judgments without the luxury of formal analytical tools. Even the tiniest delay could make the company look lumbering and unconcerned, while, on the other hand, precipitous action during the early stages of crisis might result in the wrong moves. Under these conditions, management can and should assess its situation quickly and informally with what we call "the five–minute audit."

The five–minute audit doesn't necessarily take five minutes. You can complete it in less than 60 seconds or you can conduct it for several hours. Regardless of the time frame, it provides a *relatively* rapid assessment tool that does not require formal study but relies on the information at hand, however sketchy it may be. The audit serves three purposes. First, it provides immediate structure to the chaos surrounding the crisis. The structure may be shaky, but at least establishes a starting point for translating crisis thinking into action. As more and more accurate information becomes available, you can strengthen the structure constantly. Second, the five–minute audit puts the organization on yellow alert. You may lack enough valid information to launch a full-scale red alert response, but you can prime the organization for action and keep the rank and file from panicking. Third, the five-minute audit provides the basis for initial contact with the media. Since you get few second chances to correct first impressions, the audit enables you to deal with the media appropriately, but without committing yourself to a set crisis response. With these objectives in mind, let's test drive the five-minute audit.

The five-minute audit identifies the type of crisis and specifies its intensity even when little formal data has come to light. Since the integrity of the data will change as the crisis progresses, you will, of course, conduct a series of audits throughout the crisis. The need for such periodic updates argues for keeping the audit quick and simple. A word of caution, however: The audit does not replace the need for more formal analysis *as time allows.* Nevertheless, experience teaches that a crisis allows you so painfully little time at the front end that the audit buys you some valuable time as you take immediate action until conditions stabilize.

Type Determination

When determining the type of crisis you've encountered, in the absence of formal data, you concentrate on one single issue: How much does this crisis violate our vision box? To view the question graphically, imagine a straight horizontal box representing your organization's vision:

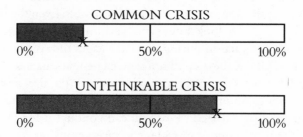

The dark bar represents the percentage of your vision that the crisis will violate. The 100 percent mark at the far right represents a crisis that threatens an entire vision. The X represents how much of the vision appears threatened at the point of the five-minute audit. If the X sits to the left of the midpoint of the box, you're facing a common crisis. If the X falls to the right of the box's midpoint, then you're under attack from an unthinkable crisis. The actual position of the crisis within the common or unthinkable quadrant suggests its intensity. For example, a common crisis that threatens 10 percent of a vision is less intense than one crisis that compromises 45 percent. However, given the importance of gauging the intensity of a crisis, you want to make a far more accurate assessment than this bar graph permits.

Intensity Determination

To precisely pinpoint the intensity of a crisis, you do not so much consider the level of danger it poses as you do the *rate* at which the crisis is playing out. Again, a crisis can be common, yet very intense, or unthinkable, yet not so intense.

The precise determination of intensity matches the level of urgency against internal and external factors. An internal crisis plays out within the confines of the organization and involves fewer consequences to the outside world. For example, an industrial accident on the shop floor presents an internal crisis. In contrast, a poison gas leak that requires the evacuation of houses near the plant poses an external crisis. Each entails its own level of urgency. The following grid combines the level of urgency with the internal or external nature of the crisis to produce a measure of intensity.

	INTERNAL	EXTERNAL
URGENT	•Borden Mgt. struggles with poor earnings	•American Airlines strike (Thanksgiving)
	LEVEL THREE	**LEVEL FOUR**
	•United Airlines employee buyout	
	•Exxon Louisiana explosion—two workers killed	•*Exxon Valdez*
	•American Express spins off Lehman Brothers	•GM Recalls S-10 pickups × 120,000
	LEVEL ONE	**LEVEL TWO**
NOT URGENT	•Cummins must meet new environmental requirements	•CBS loses NFL rights

An internal crisis that does not entail great urgency occupies Level One. An external crisis that entails little urgency occupies Level Two. A Level Three crisis is both urgent and internal, while the most intense crisis, Level Four, is both urgent and external.

The five-minute audit thus isolates eight subcategories of crisis: Common Level One, Two, Three, or Four, or Unthinkable Level One, Two, Three, or Four.

The Five Years Behind the Five-Minute Audit

Any organization, regardless of size and sophistication, can apply the five-minute audit. Its effectiveness depends, however, on linking it to the organization's vision.

If a company maintains a visible, viable, and clearly articulated vision, then the five-minute audit accomplishes far more than simply determining the type and intensity of a crisis. Rather, it enables the organization to zero in on the specific aspects of a crisis that require the utmost attention. While you want to gauge the extent to which a crisis violates a vision, you want to pinpoint the *specific* parts of a vision that have come under attack, because your specific crisis solution depends on that knowledge. Looking again at the five-minute audit, let's apply it to a well-documented crisis, the *Exxon Valdez* oil spill. In retrospect, Exxon's response to the oil spill suggests that the company responded to the crisis as a Common Level Four problem (i.e., an urgent, external crisis, but not one that posed a serious threat to the company's overall vision). After all, it wasn't even serious enough for Lawrence Rawl, Exxon Corp.'s CEO, to visit Alaska during the initial stages of the crisis. From a production and financial perspective, this typing of the crisis may have made sense at the time. The sheer size of the company rendered the potential loss of dollars and oil relatively insignificant, a logic that reflected Rawl's background in oil production. He holds a petroleum engineering degree from the University of Oklahoma, and he spent much of his career with Exxon's domestic operating unit. However, in hindsight, we would suggest that the company really should have typed the crisis as an Unthinkable crisis, Level Four problem. Our assessment flows from Exxon's responsibility toward the environment and the public perception of that responsibility, and this interpretation places Exxon's vision in extreme jeopardy. Unlike its reserves of cash and oil, the company had built up very little goodwill in terms of the public's concern for the environment. In fact, following the disaster, *Business Week* suggested that Rawl "made plenty of enemies" with his handling of the spill. First, he "was slow to appear on the scene," and then "he was criticized for ending the clean-up too quickly." Then the federal office of Technology Assessment, after Exxon had claimed victory in the cleanup, announced that less than 8 percent of the oil had been recovered. Upon hearing the estimate, Alaska Governor Steve Cowper allegedly responded, "I don't think it's cause for celebration."

What makes the *Valdez* oil spill unthinkable, according to *our* five-minute audit, is our belief that the company will not be able to weather another major spill without incurring public outrage, huge legal consequences, and government intervention. These forces could financially cripple the giant organization.

When assessing a crisis against specific parts of the company's vision rather than the vision as a whole, the five-minute audit should take into account three particular variables.

First, do you pursue a specific vision? As we stated earlier, every organization pursues a vision, but not every vision displays the same degree of detail. For example, one company may formulate a vision of attaining a number-two or -three position in a particular market, but it may not include the specific role that the accounting function will play in turning the vision to reality. In contrast, another company may create a similar vision but has thought out what each function within the company must accomplish in order for the vision to succeed. When a crisis strikes, the second company can far more easily assess its specific impact, not only on the vision as a whole, but on all individual functions. For example, not until *after* the spill of the *Valdez* did Exxon create a vice presidency for environment and safety. How could the dominant player in the American oil industry not *specifically* account for environmental issues until forced to do so?

Second, do your key players interpret the vision the same way? An organization can concoct a dynamite vision that key players interpret differently. While this type of conflict may seem surprising, it happens all the time, particularly between CEOs and boards of directors. For instance, when Baxter International president James Tobin resigned, it turned out that he and other top managers had disagreed over the future direction of the hospital supply company. Now, as a Fortune 100 company, Baxter is hardly the type of organization where the CEO shows up one day declaring that he does not agree with the company's vision. In all likelihood, the rift between interpretations occurred gradually but never got resolved in the form of a modified vision. It took a crisis in the form of a $1 billion restructuring to force the differences to the surface. Interestingly, as chairman Vernon Loucks fills in temporarily for Tobin, how will *he* interpret the company's vision?

Without a shared interpretation of vision, a company cannot possibly arrive at a consensus as to the type and intensity of a crisis it faces. A single individual can easily type a crisis as common or unthinkable, intense or not, but convincing another executive (or an entire board) of that conclusion can be difficult or even impossible.

Third, do all your activities relate to your vision? Corporate vision has become something of a management buzz phrase, with many organizations feeling that they must own one the same way they own dark business suits or laptop computers. Such superficial approaches to vision inevitably result in a yawning gap between the stated vision and day-to-day activities. Thomas Brown, writing for *Industry Week,* estimates that 90 percent of managers know their organizations have a specific and detailed vision, but only 50 percent or fewer have received a written copy of the vision, and, amazingly, only 5 percent connect their day-to-day work directly with the details of the vision. Brown's work suggests a performance relationship between how well a company articulates its vision and how much the vision affects daily operations. Take local government as an example. Almost without exception, government employees can recite their obligations as "servants of the people." In fact, you can find that exact phrase displayed on banners and posters in offices throughout the country. However, a mere 10 minutes standing in line at your local driver's license bureau or even less time with an IRS clerk during tax season will quickly convince even the most skeptical that a significant gap exists between the stated vision and day-to-day tasks.

Does a wide gap between the details of a vision and the details of day-to-day tasks suggest an insincere vision? Not necessarily. In our experience, most organizations do not lack sincerity but, instead, simply do not bind everyday activities with their vision. In many cases, the subject of vision comes up only once a year at the annual corporate retreat, sandwiched between golf and cocktails. If an organization hammers out its vision this way, then it will lack the ability to determine what activities during the pressure of crisis it should protect and which it should not.

Our three guidelines do not lend themselves to short-term consideration but should, in fact, take years of effort to establish within an organization. The five-minute audit may occur within these ticks of the clock, but it won't reveal much if the organization has not invested years of effort *prior to crisis conditions* in creating a powerful shared vision bound up inextricably with what that organization's people do day in and day out to implement that vision.

The True Value of the Five-Minute Audit

The five-minute audit *is not* brain surgery. Nor is it a buzz word for the next century. It is not a plan of action, an explanation, or a deep philosophical insight into the karma of crisis. It *is* a superquick and extremely effective tool for crisis management. To put the audit in perspective, imagine yourself sitting in the cockpit of a 747, and all the instruments lose power. Imagine, too, that all of the backup systems have failed. The failure leaves you with just two nonelectrical instruments: a compass that indicates direction, and the artificial horizon that tells you whether your aircraft is going up or down, right or left. Under these crisis conditions you do not put off making decisions or taking action until all the main, high-tech, computer-driven mechanisms come back on-line. Instead, you immediately glance at the manual instruments and make two determinations: the aircraft is flying in the right direction and it is flying straight and level. It takes less than a few seconds to determine these two important points, and once you have determined them, you can then proceed to assess the situation in greater detail and begin to work out an action plan. Every few minutes or so, you will again glance at the two manual indicators, then return to working out your crisis plan.

The dynamics of crisis often cut off an executive team from the management wizardry they use in day-to-day operations: the committees, the meetings, the information, the laptop computers, the dog-and-pony presentations, the power lunches, power suits, and supporting layers of middle management. Under crisis, the executive becomes like the 747 pilot with all the high-tech instruments down, flying by the seat of his or her pants. Under these circumstances, managers must rely on only their experience, their training, their wits, and the five-minute audit. Like the manual compass and artificial horizon, the five-minute audit provides an instant frame

183

of reference, a starting point from which more important decisions will flow, from damage assessment to action plans, from internal communication to media interaction. To try to make anything more of the five-minute audit damages crisis management's effectiveness by confusing the audit with a magic potion, but, by the same token, not taking the audit seriously hinders organizational effectiveness during the crucial initial moments of any crisis. Specifically, the audit makes two invaluable contributions. First, it articulates the language of crisis. Second, it provides multilevel organizational focus.

The Language of Crisis

During the blazing speed of a developing crisis, the five-minute audit offers a form of management shorthand, compressing pages of memoranda and hours of meetings into a five-second verbal burst: "We've got an Unthinkable Crisis, Level Four!" The simple statement, even spoken in front of a hundred microphones, conveys to everyone inside and outside the organization that the crisis threatens the company's future and people or property outside of the company, and that it demands immediate attention. The simple message also works wonders when the drama does not run nearly so high. Take, for example, a shift change in a manufacturing company where a piece of important machinery has gone down and a shipment of locking washers has not arrived. Management quickly calls one crisis a Common Level One, the other a Common Level Three. The designations reduce the risk that miscommunication occurs while passing on the crisis from one shift to the next. Regardless of the type or intensity of the crisis, a common vocabulary provides the basis for both effective communication and unified action.

Organizational Focus

In a company where all the employees work in the same building or even the same room, you can fairly easily coordinate a crisis response, say to a malfunctioning piece of equipment. However, the larger the organization becomes, the harder it becomes to focus the organization in a specific direction. This small detail ruffled the feathers of IBM during the transition from 1993 to the 1994 new year. The concluding months of 1993 brought an avalanche of negative publicity to the computer company as it continued to lay off thousands of "lifetime" employees. In the midst of the bloodletting,

184

another department of IBM, operating 3,000 miles away in Los Angeles, plunked down over $200,000 on a Tournament of Roses Parade float. The gaudy float, highlighted on national television, seemed at odds with the layoffs. IBM appeared to be sending vastly mixed signals in terms of its ongoing crisis.

As we mentioned earlier, the five-minute audit does not give you a plan of action, but it does enable you to warn the world that action plans will be forthcoming. The signal puts the entire organization on alert. If different divisions see the crisis differently, then the state of readiness will differ across the entire company, and the organization will squander valuable time getting everyone up to speed.

The five-minute audit's ability to provide a crisis vocabulary and an organizational focus sets the stage for eventual crisis management techniques. The terms "common" and "unthinkable" and the designations of Level One through Level Four reflect quick personal choices, but they do get a crisis response off on the right foot.

One-Half of a 10-Minute Perspective

The five-minute audit occurs *before* formal crisis management activity commences. The few minutes it takes to determine the type and intensity of a crisis make a significant difference to the ultimate outcome of crisis management efforts. In our experience, few organizations fail at crisis management because they are stupid, lazy, or inept. Rather, they expend too much energy without really getting a firm handle on the unique crisis conditions they face.

However, the five-minute audit solves only half of the equation. The other half involves values. Just as you use vision to determine the type and intensity of crisis, you use values to determine the solutions you'll use to resolve the crisis. This leads us to the second rule of effective crisis management: *values*—say it all, say it fast. Together these two activities provide the 10-minute perspective needed to prompt appropriate crisis action.

CHAPTER 12

Values—Say It All, Say It Fast: The Five-Minute Valuation

The Vulnerability of Values

The best solutions to a crisis evolve from an organization's values.

Consider the plight of a college senior anticipating a failing grade that will block graduation and violate her vision of enrolling this fall at the prestigious Ivy League law school that has already accepted her. Can you imagine a short list of possible solutions to her crisis?

She can hope that she can take the same class during the summer and boost her grade. Or she might approach her professor and arrange to complete a special project in return for a passing grade. Perhaps, too, the university might award her a degree with the condition that she pass a different class over the summer. Finally, she might contact the law school explaining the situation and work out an agreement whereby she would complete the class sometime during her first year of law school. Any one of these solutions might work. However, the list could also contain some "creative" solutions. The professor might accept cash in return for a passing grade. The student might agree to exchange sexual favors with a clerk in the academics office for an altered grade. Ultimately, she might opt to hire a thug to rough up the professor, threatening even greater harm if he doesn't issue a passing grade.

Every one of the potential solutions might solve the crisis, but most people would dismiss the last three possibilities as unethical and illegal. Their violation of values makes them unacceptable. In any given crisis, *the number of potential solutions always exceeds the number of solutions acceptable to the prevailing value systems.* Therefore, an organization's value system ultimately dictates the range of viable crisis management alternatives. Let's apply this role to some real-life situations.

We talked about the Harding-Kerrigan incident in the previous chapter. Tonya Harding and Nancy Kerrigan were competing for two spots on the U.S. figure skating team that would represent the United States at the 1994 Winter Olympics. Possible alternatives that might provide a competitive edge for either skater include training harder, developing more innovative routines or engaging in performance-enhancing physical and mental exercises. However, key members of Harding's staff suggested additional alternatives that fell within the acceptable limits of *their* values. They admitted to plotting and eventually implementing a plan to maim Kerrigan in order to keep her from competing in the Olympic trials. Their value system allowed them to act in a way the public and other athletes would condemn.

We could cite many instances in which organizations have adopted solutions to crises that clearly violate the law, but such behavior occurs infrequently in relationship to the huge volume of business activity. Instead, organizations quite frequently act against their values in ways that violate their values without actually breaking the law. Consider the case of British Airways.

The giant airline found itself embroiled in a competitive crisis with upstart Virgin Atlantic, offering attractive fares in an effort to woo a small pool of transatlantic travelers. While British Airways developed crisis measures that reflected its stature and reputation and drew from an established history of strong values, a small group within the airline felt compelled to act beyond those parameters, placing calls to passengers scheduled to fly on Virgin Atlantic and trying to persuade them to switch to British Airways. When this tactic failed, they met passengers at the airport, deliberately misleading them into thinking that Virgin Atlantic had canceled its flight, then booking them on a British Airways alternative. Outraged by these activities, Virgin Atlantic sued, and British Airways ultimately paid a stiff settlement, all because a small contingent within the organization violated their company's values.

Most managers we interview express initial surprise when we tie crisis solutions to corporate values. That connection somehow gets lost during the duress of crisis conditions, but a little analysis makes the linkage quite clear. Consider four issues: First, a network empowers every organization; second, each member of the network relates to the organization in terms of established values; third, crisis actions manifest organization values; and fourth, members of the network reaffirm or realign their relationships during and following every crisis. Let's look at these elements more closely.

A Network Empowers Every Organization

Think for a moment about a well-run company like Coca-Cola, the largest soft drink producer in the world, selling products in over 160 countries. The day-to-day existence of Coca-Cola depends on a network that includes consumers, employees, suppliers, investors, bankers, governments, and so on. Each member of the network in some way contributes toward the successful operation and profitability of the company. Now consider for a moment the theoretical (and remote) possibility that the relationships between Coke and all of the governments in its network suddenly and totally sour to the extent that all 160 countries make it illegal for their citizens to possess or drink any of Coke's products. Unless black-market sales replace once legal avenues of distribution, the company's international presence would wither and die. This unlikely scenario demonstrates the company's dependency on the government agencies that license its products for sale in their respective countries. In a literal sense, the agencies *empower* Coca-Cola to operate in their jurisdictions. In fact, the entire network surrounding an organization empowers that organization to exist. Try to imagine a company that, for whatever reasons, cannot secure relationships with workers, suppliers, investors, bankers, distributors, and even lawyers. From a practical perspective, that company could hardly survive such disruptions of its network.

While our Coca-Cola scenario may strike you as pretty farfetched, in the real world various members of a network quite often attempt to *unempower* an organization. Employees withdraw their empowerment by calling strikes, consumers cease to empower a company by initiating or supporting boycotts, the FDA withdraws its approval of a company's products, and entire populations stop empowering governments by acts of mass resistance or disobedience. All organizations derive their power from the networks that surround them. Separated from their networks, organizations become isolated and stranded.

During the 1993 Thanksgiving season, a group of American Airlines employees staged a strike, withdrawing their empowerment of the organi-

188

zation. For a brief period, American Airlines ceased to function. When banks and shareholders refused to lend or invest more money in Pan American Airlines, it went out of business. When the U.S. government temporarily banned silicon breast implants for cosmetic purposes, production of the implants declined measurably. By the same token, as Colombian drug cartels have learned, you can replace disrupted networks. The U.S. government, some 90 years earlier, withdrew its empowerment of cocaine as an additive in soft drinks, but the Colombian drug cartels remained empowered by installing a network of illegal producers, distributors, and consumers.

Each Member of the Network Relates to the Organization in Terms of Values

In the business world, money obviously links each member of the network to the organization. The link takes the form of wages (workers), debt (banks), taxes (governments), prices (consumers), fees (accounting firms), and other financial transactions. However, behind these transactions lies a bond forged by values. For example, when an organization must add a formal auditor to its network, the Big Six accounting firms (formerly the Big Eight) all look pretty much alike. Although fees might vary considerably during the bidding process, seasoned executives know that it all comes out roughly the same in the end. Further, all of the Big Six must operate within generally accepted accounting principles. So how do the Big Six differentiate themselves? Through values. Some exude values of quality and thoroughness. Others pride themselves on emphasizing the big picture and relating accounting procedures to larger business issues. This same type of differentiation occurs throughout any network. IBM looks for a certain type of employee. Consumers prefer a certain name-brand product, although scores of identical alternatives exist in the market. One organization values East Coast over West Coast law firms. Some executive road warriors believe that American Airlines differs from United Airlines in more ways than just routes and hubs. The list could go for pages, but this handful of examples shows that differentiation always boils down to values.

Of course it matters to an environmentally sensitive consumer that Toys-R-Us is not owned by a chemical company involved in the manufacture of a hotly debated pesticide, and it makes a difference to a racially sensitive bank customer that its bank does not redline black neighborhoods. In each case, the relationship between an organization and members of its network goes beyond the black-and-white realm of money into the gray area of values. Perhaps nowhere does the issue of values become more evident than in the world of minimum-wage employment.

As we write this book, the United States has developed an acute shortage of labor for minimum-wage jobs. Since all the jobs in this category pay the same basic wage, a worker's choice involves considerations such as location, work environment, and even dress codes. McDonald's, for one, knows that values play a big role in a job applicant's decision.

Extremely dependent on a minimum-wage workforce, McDonald's entices potential employees with a chance to become part of the "McDonald's team." What makes working for McDonald's team any different than the local mall janitorial team? The established values that dictate how McDonald's treats its employees. Once hired, an employee can count on those values.

Crisis Actions Manifest Organizational Values

As we discussed in Chapter 10, crisis conditions always expose the values of an organization. Under the pressure of crisis, organizations most likely respond in ways that afford insight into their value system. For example, in the immediate aftermath of the 1994 earthquake that caused over $30 billion damage in Los Angeles, consumers caught a glimpse of the values of local retailers. Basically, the actions of the retailers fell into three categories. One group opened their doors and distributed free or heavily discounted goods to needy consumers. Another group simply opened their doors and sold goods at the exact same prices as before the quake. A third group took advantage of the crisis and systematically increased prices on desperately needed goods. In the absence of the crisis brought on by the quake, all three groups of retailers, offering similar products at similar prices, appeared almost identical to consumers. No more. The crisis put retailers' value systems on the permanent record. As a result, 7-Eleven announced that it was pulling six franchises from owners for price gouging.

The beacon of values displayed during crisis attracts the attention of all members of the network. In addition to 7-Eleven's management, the press, government agencies, and, most importantly, local consumers also took note of the unfair pricing practices. While the level of attention accorded values varies with the intensity of the crisis itself, every crisis draws an alert audience.

Members of the Network Reaffirm or Realign Their Relationships During and Following Every Crisis

When singer Michael Jackson contained the crisis of alleged sexual abuse of a minor with a multimillion-dollar settlement, the intensity of the crisis began to decline. In the aftermath, both Pepsi and Disney decided not to renew their respective relationships with the popular singer, claiming that they had initiated their decisions before allegations of sexual misconduct surfaced. The public bought neither of these explanations. Most observers assumed that the crisis forced Pepsi and Disney to reaffirm or realign their relationships with Jackson, and both chose to realign.

At IBM, thousands of employees with pink slips in their hands gained an appreciation for the values of the computer company toward its workers. Faced with both a financial crisis and a crisis of confidence among investors, Big Blue took actions that dispelled forever the notion of lifetime employment and undying employee loyalty. Certainly surviving employees have gone through the process of reaffirming or realigning their loyalty to the organization, with more people changing rather than maintaining their former views.

During the 1990s, network members from consumers to governments have caught a naked glimpse into the values of some leading American organizations, and the revelations have been downright ugly. Exxon's true commitment to the environment was revealed as it addressed the *Valdez* oil spill. Union Carbide's actual values concerning victims of chemical accidents came to light as the company dealt with the Bhopal disaster. The reaction of plastic surgeons to the silicon breast plant crisis showed just how much they value the long-term safety of their patients over their own short-term income. On the other hand, and in refreshing contrast, the makers of Tylenol left little doubt about how much they valued their network members, voluntarily disposing of millions of dollars' worth of product to protect the long-term relationship they had formed between the company and its consumers.

Not every decision to reaffirm or realign contains the drama of the Michael Jackson case, nor are such decisions so easy to spot. Regardless of the scope of the crisis, however, any organization that thinks a crisis, even the most common and least intense, will not prompt network members to reaffirm or realign makes a monumental blunder. When a production glitch forces a late shipment of parts to a customer, even this garden-variety common crisis causes the customer to rethink his or her relationship with the manufacturer. The process to reaffirm or realign might take less than 30 seconds, but for 30 seconds the fate of the relationship hangs in the balance.

Since values play a crucial role in governing the relationship between network members and an organization in crisis, management must carefully consider the exposé of values during its crisis. No decision making should occur without thinking through the consequences an action might produce in terms of values and network relationships.

Organizational Values versus Religious Values

Don't confuse organizational values with religious values. While some organizational values do derive from religious or philosophical beliefs (such as *honesty, human rights, integrity,* and other aspects of ethics and social responsibility), when we speak of organizational values we refer to beliefs, issues, or concepts that the organization deems important within the context of its business conduct. They do not so much address right or wrong, good or bad, but issues that pertain to organizational success. In this sense, most Japanese car manufacturers value quality, Paramount and other American movie makers value creativity, and the armed forces value order. Other organizational values might include punctuality, thoroughness, team building, horizontal structures, participative management, long-term return on investment, and an endless variety of preferences that an organization might view as important. Differentiating organizational from religious or philosophical values allows us to clarify the nature of organizational values! First, values come in degrees; second, values are not inherently good or bad; and third, values are intangible until actions reveal them.

Differing Degrees of Values

While most people strongly associate Japanese car companies with quality, most also agree that American car manufacturers respect some degree of that value. In fact, Detroit does value quality—just not to the extent that Tokyo worships it. It's all a matter of degree.

While we have documented some public outrage over Exxon's handling of the *Valdez,* we cannot claim that the giant oil company does not value the environment at all. Doing so would ignore Exxon's history of environmentally supportive activities. Still, we would agree that Exxon does not value the environment to the same degree as the Sierra Club or the Audubon Society.

All this argues that most organizations should worry at least as much about the degree to which they honor a value as much as the nature of the value itself. Most Fortune 500 firms value their employees to some extent, but not all value their employees enough to land on the list of *The 100 Best Companies To Work For In America* with the likes of Motorola.

Values Are Not Inherently Good or Bad

Surely every organization values creativity. Yet, if you think about it, you don't want your accounting department or your auditors to place too much emphasis on creativity. Excessively creative accounting often irritates the SEC and IRS to the point of criminal prosecution. The Dallas Cowboys, winners of back-to-back Super Bowls, may not desire much creativity in their established and proven system and may not make any immediate creative changes. Similarly, an established market leader in a mature industry such as canned soup production may not put as much of a premium on the value of risk taking as would a small startup electronics company in Silicon Valley. Again, the values of creativity and risk taking are not intrinsically good or bad. It all depends on the specifics of your business and what it takes to establish and maintain a competitive edge. One vision might demand emphasis on one set of values, while another may suggest an entirely different emphasis. So, unlike religious values, which tend to mirror absolute beliefs, organizational values gain their value from the role they play in getting results.

Values Are Intangible Until Revealed by Actions

In the remake of the classic movie, *The Invisible Man,* Chevy Chase became invisible after an industrial accident and could only be seen by his pursuers when outlined by rain or, in one case, powdered concrete. Values are much the same. We really can't tell what an organization deems important, until some action or series of actions outlines a value.

193

Take, for example, Chrysler under Lee Iacocca. An examination of Iacocca's '80s rhetoric in conjunction with the company's advertising suggests that Chrysler put a premium on the value of U.S.-produced products. In a television commercial, with jet planes streaking overhead and leaving red, white, and blue contrails, Iacocca blared "Here's to you, America!" Yet on closer examination, Chrysler's actions reveal a far different value. In response to the crisis brought on by U.S. consumers buying more and more Japanese cars, Chrysler shifted production to Mexico, incorporated a higher percentage of foreign parts in its cars than either Ford or GM, and invested heavily in Mazda. Even the jet planes used in the commercial were not made in America, but in France. Chrysler's actions made it perfectly clear how much it valued goods made in the United States, regardless of what it said over the airwaves.

These four characteristics of organizational values set the stage for a closer look at exactly *how* values bind members of a network together.

Shared and Established Values

There are two types of values that bind networks together: those that are widely shared, and those that are firmly established.

Shared Values

Values held in common esteem by network members provide the best foundation for any productive relationship. This holds true for individuals as well. In fact, to fully understand the importance of this thought, think about it in terms of your individual relationships.

No two individuals look or behave exactly alike. Each person operates as a package of unique talents, experiences, beliefs, and perspectives. For all practical purposes, people differ as much as individual snowflakes. Yet, for all of their individuality and differences, we humans function quite well in groups. Part of that success derives from an ability to identify and honor shared values. Take the U.S. Congress as an example. Clearly, individual representatives and senators bring radically differing, and often opposing, visions, views, and agendas to Congress. However, all share certain common beliefs. Rarely does a senator refuse to vacate his office after losing an election, a simple reality that points to the shared belief that politicians do not own their offices. As simple as this belief may be in the United States, however, officials in some countries do not respect it at all. The gun, not the vote, creates their power.

The more an organization and its network share values, the more likely the relationship will prosper. When Sharon Lambly was interviewing with Hershey Foods for the job of vice president of human resources, her hosts first took the 25-year IBM veteran to the Milton Hershey School, an orphanage caring for over 1,000 youngsters. More than a beneficiary of the company's charity, the Milton Hershey School holds a lot of Hershey Company stock and votes a whopping 77 percent of the shares outstanding. At a company with such a shareholder, not to mention two movie theaters, a museum of American life, a sports arena, five golf courses, and a theme park hosting almost 2 million visitors each year, a prospective manager had better feel a sense of strong community and family values or apply elsewhere. In contrast, McKinsey, the highly successful consulting firm, does not exude nearly that same sort of family and community values. In fact, Ron Daniel, a former managing partner of the firm, admits that they look to hire people who feel "insecure and thus driven by their insecurity." Beyond any question, both Hershey and McKinsey field productive workforces, but ones built on radically different shared values.

During crisis, many managers overlook the fact that shared values bind *all* members of a network together, because many relationships are not nearly as obvious as the relationship between a company and its workforce. As an example, many viewers will not watch the "CBS Evening News" with Dan Rather due to the perceived liberal bent of the news organization. Similarly, hordes of listeners religiously tune in Rush Limbaugh for the opposite reason: to hear a more conservative viewpoint. Contributors to Greenpeace support the organization almost exclusively on the basis of shared values; whereas, the same contributors might not support "pro-life" causes, because of a lack of shared values. Wise executives never suspend the analysis of shared values with obvious groups such as workers or consumers, but extend it to all other key network members, especially to the government and the media.

The relationship between government agencies and other members of a network has become particularly touchy because shared values can change from one administration to the next. During the Bush years, shared values supporting *less* government were the vogue. With the election of Clinton, *more* government involvement become the watchword—a considerable shift in shared values. The media may seem at first much more consistent than the government in terms of shared values, but on closer inspection, the media's response to a given situation looks highly fragmented. The values relating to the vices and virtues of big business at *The Wall Street Journal* differ noticeably for those at *The New York Times*. Furthermore, contrasting the content of both news organizations leaves little doubt that values influence their respective perceptions of the same events.

Established Values

Not all the values that bind networks together come in the form of shared values. In reality, many values *not* held in common provide a strong binding effect. In the case of the IRS, most Americans share the value that they must pay their taxes, but few Americans share the values exhibited by the IRS's actual collection process. Here, *established,* not shared, values provide the glue.

Without sharing an established value, people nevertheless willingly support it within clear-cut and pre-agreed guidelines. Look again at the IRS. Most citizens willingly tolerate the values of the IRS, even when they manifest themselves in the form of rudeness, zeal, and an apparent love of their disagreeable task. But if IRS methods turned toward greater levels of intimidation and fear, that would violate the established values and ignite a fervent public backlash. As an aside, the IRS has, to its credit, taken great strides toward making the tax collection process a less unpleasant experience—a smart move from established to shared values with its network.

Established values derive their power from the fact that you can count on them. While they may not invoke the same warm emotions as shared values, they do respect definite boundaries. Dennis Rodman of the San Antonio Spurs is a talented and driven basketball player that (non-Spurs) fans love to hate. Sporting a different hair color (blond, purple, red, black, or blue) almost every other game, and adorned with a navel ring and nine tattoos, Rodman does not exactly look like the All-American boy. But he plays so well, with fierce defensive skills and determination, that crowds tolerate his deviance from the norm because his activities fall within established limits despite some rough play, banter with fans, and media statements that do not enhance the image of pro basketball as family entertainment: "My image is me and I don't care if I fit in or not." Now, consider what would happen if Rodman exceeded the established boundaries. What if he spit on fans, made obscene gestures to kids during games, and cavorted with known figures involved in organized crime. His relationship with his team, the fans, and the NBA would come to a screeching halt, all because he did not respect the boundaries of

196

established values. In the case of Michael Jackson, Pepsi and Disney could live with the established limits of crotch grabbing, but they drew the line at the mere allegation that Jackson imposed that same behavior on someone else.

You can appreciate the subtle importance of established values by considering the cookie crisis that stole up on the Girl Scouts of America. Every year, thousands of Girl Scouts descend on U.S. neighborhoods, selling boxes of cookies. Customers tolerate the hard sell by soft scouts because it falls within established limits, due largely to shared values that scouting serves the needs of growing girls. But when the public heard allegations that the Girl Scouts of America were allocating more and more of the proceeds to administrative overhead, customers felt the organization had stepped beyond the parameters of established values, resulting in a crisis of public confidence.

The binding of networks through shared and established values make values a prime consideration when you begin developing crisis solutions. An organization's crisis response must not inadvertently run contrary to the shared and established values of its network.

The Violation of Values

Just as a crisis violates vision, the response to it can violate shared or established values, causing network members to reevaluate their relationships with the organization. When violation occurs, members either reaffirm their relationship, perhaps with new definitions of shared and established values, or they realign with another network. The issue of violated values lies at the heart of the national health-care debate. Consider the logic.

For years, consumers willingly let physicians and insurance companies decide health-care issues because there existed between consumers and these two groups common values regarding the delivery and payment of health care. However, over time, consumers grew less and less trusting of their doctors and their insurance carriers, perceiving that the entire health-care profession was making too much money and lacked sufficient interest in the public well-being. Consequently, the relationship shifted from one based predominately on shared values to one held together by established values. Consumers would tolerate certain limits of greed and price gouging in return for what they still considered one of the best health-care systems in the world. But then, the providers exceeded even the established values. Insurance companies jacked up rates and then tried to evade payment for health-care services. The doctors and hospitals pushed every expense increase onto consumers, compensating for administrative mismanagement and the increase in non-paying patients. Pharmaceutical companies sold miracle drugs with huge mark-ups, citing the cost of research and government interference. In the end, consumers turned their backs on both shared values and established values and *realigned* their relationship, shifting their allegiance from the health-care establishment to the government.

The reality that every crisis causes reaffirmation or realignment for network members suggests that an organization must rapidly determine how a crisis and the resulting crisis solutions will affect shared and established values. Like using vision to determine the type and intensity of a crisis, you can use values to measure how much a crisis might affect your relationships with your network. As with vision, you can conduct a quick and dirty assessment, but one you can enhance considerably by following a set of pre-crisis guidelines involving values.

The Five-Minute Valuation

After conducting the five-minute vision audit, you should spend another five minutes auditing values. Combined, both five-minute audits create a *10-minute perspective,* which can serve as a gathering point for all your crisis management activities.

Like the five-minute vision audit, you should apply the five-minute valuation quickly, bearing in mind that the valuation provides only an assessment tool, not a means of either affirming or shifting organizational values. The five-minute valuation addresses two issues. First, what specific values has the crisis called into question? Second, how might prospective solutions affect the shared or established values held by each major constituent?

Value Determination

When Marge Schott, owner of the Cincinnati Reds baseball team, allegedly made demeaning remarks about African-Americans, she put the value of racial equality into question. Period. It doesn't matter what she actually said, or even what she really meant. When an O-ring failure resulted in the explosion of the *Challenger* space shuttle, the crisis questioned the commitment to safety of NASA and its subcontractors.

The FDA recall of Albuterol, an asthma drug, brought to light a number of flaws in the testing and manufacturing of the drug, and the crisis directly affected the public perception of how much Copley Pharmaceutical, Inc., really valued the stringent development guidelines that protect consumers from dangerous drugs. Crises can and do violate every imaginable value, and even the smallest can do damage. Consider a machine failure at a national insta-print chain. The customer comes in to pick up the order only to learn that it will be an hour late. At that very moment, the disgruntled customer mentally questions whether the organization values efficiency and honoring its commitments. It is a small crisis that causes a small violation of values, but such incidents can add up quickly. McDonnell Douglas Corp. landed the contract to build the C-17, a $300-million-per-plane cargo transport. As the contract played out, McDonnell Douglas allegedly failed to meet the guidelines set by the government. First, costs escalated, then quality problems cropped up, and, ultimately, the company couldn't deliver the plane on schedule. In each instance, one more "little" crisis chipped away at the government's perception of McDonnell Douglas as a reliable contractor. Finally, the government put the company on heavy probation and threatened to terminate the contract.

To identify potentially violated values, you should quickly list those values that seem most vulnerable during an evolving crisis. These make up a *watch list* of values on which you should concentrate until you bring the crisis to a conclusion. For example, you might graphically portray a chemical spill by a pesticide plant like this:

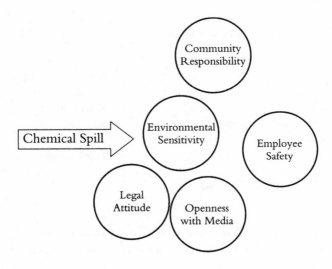

Remember, you should draw up the list quickly and record it simply. Then the management team can compare lists and isolate those values that the entire team feels are in the greatest jeopardy.

Relationship Grid

The next task in the five-minute valuation involves identifying those members of the network who are (or will be) most affected by the crisis. For the sake of illustration, consider a massive open ocean oil spill off the coast of California and make a quick list of those constituents it might affect.

NETWORK	
Local residents	
EPA	
Fishing industry	
Coastal commission	
Direct consumers	
Media	
Employees	

With the list complete, then identify the shared and established values that bind each constituent to the organization.

NETWORK	SHARED VALUES	ESTABLISHED VALUES
Local residents	Jobs, economic stimulus	
EPA	Doesn't want to appear anti-business	Smooth cleanup, look cooperative
Fishing industry		$ Settlement
Coastal commission	Economic stimulus	Keep spill offshore at all costs
Direct consumers	Need products	
Media		Fair treatment in exchange for information flow
Employees	Need jobs	

You have now completed the five-minute valuation, pinpointing the relationships most vulnerable to the crisis and your crisis management efforts. In addition, the valuation also points out those values and constituent relationships your crisis management actions might strengthen. For example, John Hall, the chairman of Ashland Oil, Inc., used the crisis of an oil spill to establish his organization's values relating to the environment. His efforts (which are detailed in Chapter 10) convinced a skeptical set of constituents that his company sincerely cared about environmental protection. In addition, Hall used crisis to promote other values, such as community responsibility. In the midst of the crisis, Hall publicly acknowledged that "you have to treat people the way you'd treat your next-door neighbor." That said it all.

Say It All, Say It Fast

Crisis communications enable network members to assess their relationship with an organization in trouble. This applies especially to the media. Since you rarely get a second chance to make a first impression, you must take special pains to communicate effectively at the onset of a crisis. However, your communication must address *all* of your constituents. During the *Valdez* imbroglio, Exxon responded to a number of constituents but appeared to overlook the impact of the crisis on its own employees. One Exxon manager admitted that "whenever I travel now, I feel like I have a target painted on my chest." *Fortune* reported that Exxon's crisis management efforts left workers "confused, embarrassed and betrayed." The company's people would not have suffered that fate had Exxon followed one simple rule: *Say it all, say it fast.*

In this age of virtually instantaneous worldwide communication, it's hard to keep a lid on crisis. You simply must assume that sensitive information can and will be broadcast, no matter how hard you might try to keep it under wraps. From interested whistle-blowers who must heed their consciences to lawyers armed with the court's permission to ransack your files to gain full disclosure, the world now conspires to make even an organization's most private moments public property. Under these conditions, saying it all and saying it fast no longer represents one viable option for an organization in crisis, it represents the *only* option.

Complete and clean disclosure governs the new crisis-speak. However, don't make the mistake of thinking that getting it all out quickly automatically elevates your organization to a higher ethical or moral plane. Rather, full disclosure serves simply as a positive crisis management tool, which, if used properly, can actually create competitive advantage out of even the most severe catastrophe. Don't be fooled. We're not saying, "When life hands you lemons, make lemonade." That's a Pollyanna attitude best reserved for Amway conventions. Instead, we suggest that crisis communications can serve other purposes than the media's thirst for scandal. Three in particular deserve note. First, you can use crisis communications to reinforce key organizational values. Second, you can use them to edify, unify, and motivate the rank and file. Third, you can use them to create *industrywide* change. Of course, using crisis communication in these three ways will vary from crisis to crisis.

Reinforcing Values

In a speech given in Brussels, Philip Morris executive vice president Craig Fuller used crisis communications as a platform to communicate some little-known information about the giant conglomerate. Since, these days, the controversy over cigarettes makes every public event a potential crisis activity for Philip Morris, its executives always speak guardedly. However, in Brussels, Fuller boldly seized the opportunity to discuss certain values dear to his heart that no one seems to notice: his firm's commitment to its employees, the almost fanatical emphasis it places on quality in its food products line, and its contribution to the community. Fuller illustrated each value with careful, yet disclosing, documentation. The speech caught the audience and the media by surprise because everyone had expected the usual defensive posture of an organization in crisis.

A crisis offers prime-time opportunity to display positive values. This holds particularly true with respect to a high-profile crisis, in which the organization can tap millions of dollars' worth of free media coverage, worldwide. Certainly, no sane person would intentionally engineer a crisis for the sole purpose of displaying values, but once a legitimate crisis erupts, why not swallow hard and act to convert a difficult situation into a positive result? This approach seems directly counter to legal advice, which invariably advises an organization to admit nothing and make all decisions with an eye on limiting liability. However, the legalistic approach breeds ill will with a suspicious press and a public all too accustomed to corporate arrogance. Using crisis communications to underscore values, on the other hand, maximizes advantage by squeezing goodwill out of a difficult situation. The traditional legal approach limits your options; the new one expands them. One seeks only to preserve the status quo; the other tries to create a better future out of the present problems.

Subordinating legal caution to effective display of values during crisis would not make sense, of course, unless doing so leads to hard financial results. By that measure, believe it or not, value display still wins, hands down, for two reasons. First, goodwill is not cheap. When you consider that a major crisis can negate millions of dollars' worth of corporate advertising and contributions, it stands to reason that preserving goodwill during crisis literally saves dollars. Second, goodwill can be a form of legal caution. With so many trials hinging on the emotions of a jury, the right record of crisis communications stressing values can make all the difference in the world. Without this display of values, it may appear to a jury that the company exists only to cause environmental damage, sell improperly tested drugs, or fly passengers in unsafe aircraft.

Edifying, Unifying, and Motivating Employees

Let's face facts. Workers represent the most important network member during any crisis. Yet, companies rarely make them the object of crisis communications, even *internal* crisis communications. These reasons argue that you should.

First, employees, not management, actually solve problems. Like all organizational activity, management may plan and coordinate all crisis responses, but workers must carry out those plans. When workers were steam-scrubbing rocks in Alaska to break down the residue of an oil spill, you didn't see a single senior vice president on the beach. When J&J decided to pull a painkiller off the shelves in response to a few tainted capsules, the press footage showed workers, not senior managers, doing the job.

Employee productivity makes as much of a difference during crisis management efforts as at any other time. Consequently, you must follow the same rules of increasing productivity under crisis conditions as you do the rest of the year. Using crisis communications to edify, unify, and motivate employees can contribute greatly toward a happy ending for any crisis.

Second, employees often know the real story. Executives hate to step up to the podium and admit that they screwed up, even when they know their employees know that the organization did, in fact, screw up. An organization's press version of the crisis should match the employees' understanding of the situation. If it doesn't, you inadvertently display a new value to your workers; accuracy and forthrightness don't matter. Always treat your workers with the same respect you show the press.

Third, employees make convincing witnesses. During the period immediately following the Los Angeles earthquake, an innocent, yet revealing, set of interviews took place. During one television interview, a senior official representing a state government transportation agency described the damage to the freeway system as relatively minor, claiming that the entire system had held up extremely well, and that commuters should not worry about driving to work the next morning. Just after that, on another network, a lowly employee for the *same* agency faced cameras and insisted that the overpasses were poorly constructed and that *he* wouldn't risk driving on them. The employee's assessment seemed much more credible because he spoke with honest conviction, unlike the manager, who struggled to uphold his own reputation.

In a worst-case scenario, an employee can become a whistle-blower, feeling the obligation to disclose publicly what the organization itself has failed to communicate. Federal laws protect this right, and it can prove a tremendous embarrassment to an organization trying hard to bury certain elements of a crisis.

Create Industrywide Change

Johnson & Johnson's management of the Tylenol crisis has become a model for many crisis management experts. The company really did do a terrific example job in that case. However, the most instructive lesson comes from the fact that the company used the crisis to force an industrywide change.

When J & J put Tylenol back on the shelves, the product sported a new look: caplets. The fused packaging of the pill's contents not only protected it from tampering but also made the medication easier to swallow. With it, Johnson & Johnson set an industry standard, forcing all other competitors to follow suit. In a sense, when crisis served J & J a lemon, the company made its competitors choke on it.

Exxon could have seized the same opportunity during the *Valdez* crisis if it had admitted to the press that it had learned important lessons about the need for increased safety and environmental protection measures. Exxon could have announced a 10-year program to convert its fleet to double-hulled tankers, which would greatly reduce the risk of a major spill. While doing so, the company could have made it clear that it assumed all oil tankers operating out of U.S. ports should do the same or stop shipping oil. The move would have cost billions, but the largest oil company in the United States could have more easily swallowed that lemon than many of its competitors. In reality, however, Exxon missed a golden opportunity to get the public, the media, the EPA, and even the Sierra Club behind its values.

The Five Years behind the Five-Minute Valuation

The five-minute valuation, like the five-minute audit, provides a quick and informal analysis. If the initial valuation turns into a formal analysis or demands a series of committee meetings, then it loses its usefulness. During the breakneck pace of a breaking crisis, you must move quickly, delaying the formal stuff until later.

Even though the valuation should take no longer than one to five minutes, an organization can take three steps prior to a crisis that can make the quick valuation even more worthwhile. First, you should write down and thoroughly articulate values for all levels of your organization. Second, you should identify the values of all key members of your organization's network and make sure management understands them. Third, you should affirm shared values and document established values.

Articulating Values

Values, like vision, inhabit every organization. Everyone might not always agree with the values of an organization, but that does not diminish their role in determining how that organization functions. Even the least-organized street gang exhibits certain values in terms of how members view nonmembers and their property. Those values govern gang activities. Look into any organization and you can *work backwards* to identify the predominant values, tracing any action or set of actions back to the values that spawned them. In this regard, note how actor Woody Allen has consistently presented a shy and introverted personality to the public. Amazingly, he displays these traits at prearranged press gatherings. These actions seem contrary to the claims themselves. Why would a supposedly shy and introverted individual willingly engage in a profession that requires the antithesis of introversion? The value behind his actions? The careful orchestration of a public persona. Woody Allen values publicity. For another example, consider the teaching profession.

As a group, public school teachers staunchly oppose the testing of teachers to determine competency, claiming that tests do not accurately indicate a teacher's true ability. Teachers reject the value of testing. Yet, ironically, the entire profession relies almost solely on testing to determine the competency and potential of students. Why do they think tests given by teachers are more accurate and less subjective than tests taken by teachers? The actions of the profession with respect to testing argues that testing is, in fact, a strongly held value. This leads to the conclusion that teachers, taking a position contrary to the claim that tests do not reveal competency, simply find the notion threatening to their own well-being.

While every organization possesses values, not every organization can describe them specifically. Furthermore, not all parts of the same organization would necessarily agree on the priority among even identified and articulated values. During crisis, not knowing or agreeing on an organization's values severely limits the coordination of an effective crisis response, with one understanding of a particular value leading to a certain crisis management activity that violates the perceived values of another part of the organization. In 1993, an operating subsidiary of General Electric came under fire for some possible wrongdoing. Ensuing media reports revealed a visibly agitated Jack Welch, who was upset not because his company was implicated, but because a manager operating under GE's value system could even consider an activity that the value system deemed improper. In Welch's mind, strong commonly held organizational values mean as much to the company as its vision.

Obviously, a crisis does not afford the most opportune time to *begin* articulating the values of an organization. During crisis, an organization should be reinforcing, not defining, its values. Thus, organizations should make value definition a constant exercise long before any sort of crisis strikes. You can define values three ways.

First, write them down. Formalizing values into a written statement by no means ensures that everyone will follow them, but it does provide a starting point from which acceptance can grow. Furthermore, written values tend to hold an organization's "feet to the fire" during crisis because they have created some degree of expectation in terms of how to handle a crisis. For instance, during the confrontation between North Korea and the United States over the production of nuclear weapons, the United States considered a number of options for resolving the crisis. However, it never contemplated one option: a first strike. The established values guiding the military, formally written and taught at military colleges, upholds the American aversion to starting wars, a value not accepted by many other countries.

Second, discuss values. Since values only exist in peoples' minds, their development should entail a lot of mental exercise. Discussion provides that exercise. To operate as a team, members of an organization need to know what goes on in the minds of fellow managers and workers. During crisis, you can't afford to guess what people think. Therefore, you should constantly assess through discussion how people perceive organizational values. Ongoing dialog both refines and builds commitment to values. The more specific and honest the dialog, the more fully people will embrace values and use them to drive their crisis management activities.

Third, constantly monitor the relationship between values and actions. Values relate to actions like the chicken to the egg. On one hand, values create actions, but by the same token, actions create values. Which comes first? Imagine an individual who sincerely values honesty but then consistently engages in dishonest activities. From the viewpoint of actions, you would assume that the individual does not really value honesty at all. Yet, looking at the situation from another angle, if the person holds on to the value of honesty, he or she might eventually act in accord with the value.

Although we cannot answer the chicken-and-egg riddle, we do know that actions out of harmony with stated values cause problems. The disharmony either indicates false values or dysfunctional actions. Regardless of the root cause, a lack of harmony between values and actions demands that you modify one or the other. By constantly relating actions back to values, an organization can see whether the gap between the two narrows or widens. A narrow gap suggesting harmony deserves praise; a widening gap indicating disharmony requires prompt attention.

A former client of ours strove almost obsessively to force his organization onto the cutting edge of crisis management. He appeared to deeply value creativity and wanted all crisis management solutions to reflect this value. Yet, not a single action taken by people in his organization during non-crisis moments indicated that they sincerely embraced that value. The lack of harmony between the stated value and actions suggested to us that our client needed to alter one or the other. When we told the CEO what type of actions we felt he needed to instill in order for his people to demonstrate the value of creativity, he expressed dismay. His organization, part of a government agency, could never operate "so informally." It turned out that the CEO really did not value creativity, but simply liked to talk about it because doing so made him appear progressive to his peers.

Writing values down, discussing them constantly, and measuring them against action comprise a routine that results in shared values throughout the organization. When a crisis strikes, the routine improves the odds that all crisis solutions will reflect the shared values of the organization.

Identify the Values of Network Members

Every network member possesses its own set of values. Since values spawn action and vice versa, then knowing these values provides some clue as to what response you might expect from a particular member during a crisis. In the midst of the Los Angeles earthquake, one national news organization appeared obsessed with fixing the blame for the collapse of a number of freeway overpasses, and every reporter's question seemed geared to surfacing a clue or piece of information that would prove negligence on the part of the agencies responsible for the freeway system. If *properly* constructed overpasses *should* withstand any earthquake, then it naturally followed that someone had built them improperly. The actions of the network underscored a media trend toward zeroing in on deliberate wrongdoing. News organizations that do so appear not to value a story unless they can turn it into a scandal. Expect this same approach when crisis strikes your organization.

Since networks consist of extensive sets of relationships, you should prioritize them and focus on the most important ones. You cannot fully assess the values of every member of every organization that interacts with ACME Enterprises. Consequently, we suggest a basic set of five network members that every organization should worry about most: consumers, the government, the press, employees, and shareholders. We cannot think of a major crisis that has not involved these five players in one way or another.

The value assessment of these five members should not take the form of a complicated psychological profile because you simply want to know what each group values most. For example, the environment now represents a value held by most consumers. Where sensitivity toward the environment once exclusively preoccupied activists and extremists, environmental concern has mainstreamed into schools and religious organizations. If a crisis involves the environment, then an organization should pay attention to this value. Similarly, any crisis that catches the attention of a powerful special interest group will almost certainly result in some form of government intervention in the form of sanctions or increased regulation. Developing a sense for where key values may affect crisis management contributes powerfully to effective crisis solutions.

Reinforce Shared and Established Values

As part of the five-minute valuation we suggested that you construct a grid indicating the shared and established values that exist between your organization and key network members. While the grid gives you a quick handle on the situation during a crisis, you can also apply it during non-crisis conditions.

The grid used during the five-minute valuation helps you keep crisis solutions from unnecessarily or inadvertently violating the shared and established values that bind a member to your organization. During non-crisis periods, a more extensive and detailed grid can help you engage in two relationship-building activities that we call making deposits and mending fences.

Making Deposits.   The relationship between two members of a network works very much like a bank account. All the activities that generate goodwill and build shared values post credits to your account. A crisis posts debits. The smart investor creates big deposits so no crisis can drain the account to zero or create a deficit.

Public education across the nation has come under fire for years. Since the government first published its report, *A Nation at Risk,* in 1983, network members have attempted reform after reform in an effort to turn the education establishment toward a particular objective, be it lower-cost education, more comprehensive education, more socially aware education, or just plain better education. Since most of the reform efforts arise *outside* the education establishment, members inside the establishment view them as crisis. Ultimately, each major reform makes its way to voters, who have ended up supporting the establishment and, for the large part, maintaining the status quo. Since the education system forms a core of U.S. culture, it has built up a considerable bank account of goodwill, trust, and shared values, but each crisis has reduced the account, with deposits never fully replacing the depletion. Now, most of the talk about education involves crime, incompetent teachers, and overpaid administrators. Consequently, each new reform movement that goes before the voters gains more receptiveness. If the bank account turns negative, the next major reform initiative might finally break the bank. In 1993, California voted on a bill that would allow students to attend the school of their choice by presenting vouchers that would in turn determine how much tax dollars each school, public and private, would receive. The bill failed, but not by much, suggesting that a variation will almost certainly appear on the next ballot.

Making deposits amounts to engaging in activities that add to the goodwill and shared values between members of the network. During a period of intense competition between domestic airlines, Delta employees made a big deposit to Delta Air Lines by donating a new aircraft to the fleet. Employees across the company pitched in to purchase the plane. When the competition crisis achieved critical mass and airlines shed employees by the thousands, Delta hung on to its people, partly because the relationship between the organization and the employees had enough value in the bank to weather the difficult times.

The specific types of activities that accrue assets in the bank will vary from one member to the next, and the activities themselves matter less than that depositors reinforce shared values during times of relative calm and stability. The chaos of crisis simply does not afford you the time to *begin* the process of building relationships.

Mending Fences. Relationships held together by established values function quite differently from those based on shared values. The former work much like the boundaries established in cattle country, where barbed wire fences clearly mark the limits of cooperation. But like bank deposits, even fences require mending from time to time.

A fence surrounds an established value, clearly marking a line that network members, in order to preserve the relationship, agree not to cross. However, as time passes, the line can blur to the point where members no longer know for sure where established values begin and end. A running battle has broken out in the NCAA over alleged discrimination against African-Americans. Although African-Americans represent over 80 percent of Division One basketball players, fewer than 10 percent hold head coaching jobs. This ratio of players to coaches has created a touchy issue for the NCAA. The relationship between the NCAA and African-American athletes and coaches has, until recently, been held together by an agreement over established values. However, when the NCAA ruled that schools must eliminate one scholarship per school, African-American coaches perceived the act as discriminatory because in 80 percent of the cases, the lost scholarship would have gone to an African-American player. The new ruling blurred the boundaries surrounding established values and African-American coaches (as well as other coaches) threatened to boycott the season. Fortunately for college basketball fans, the NCAA short-circuited the boycott by agreeing to reexamine the issue, in a sense, reestablishing the boundaries of established values.

While mending a fence compares in concept to building a bank account, it differs greatly in application because you reinforce established values not by activities but by negotiation. To strengthen an established value, you must constantly clarify the boundaries that surround it. Consider the relationship that exists between the police department and the African-American community in post-riot-torn Los Angeles, which does not depend on shared values at all. Rather, the fragile alliance hinges on established values renegotiated after the riots. In short, the established value that the police operate with a soft touch binds the community together. Any step across the line by either party will most likely result in a crisis.

An organization that articulates its own values, identifies the values of other network members, and sincerely tries to reinforce the shared and established values that bind it to the network can make the five-minute valuation an instinctive task performed with little effort. Like riding a bike, it takes time to master, but once mastered it becomes second nature, whether you're riding the bike on a smooth road or one riddled with potholes.

The 10-Minute Perspective

The five-minute audit and the five-minute valuation combine to create a 10-minute perspective. In relationship to the hours, days, and months that a crisis might run, 10 minutes amounts to very little time. Yet, those 10 minutes can make all the difference in the world. You develop effective crisis management the same way you create a winning batting average: success in both endeavors demands attention to small details. For every 10 trips to the place, three hits produces a .300 average, which management considers very good, but just one more hit for every 10 times at bat earns close to a .400 average, a star performance worth millions of dollars and induction into the Baseball Hall of Fame. Good hitters take the time to prepare mentally before each trip to the plate. The solitary and informal preparation takes little time compared to the two to three hours it takes to play a nine-inning game. During crisis, the 10-minute perspective provides just such mental preparation. However, in business, as in baseball, you sooner or later find yourself standing at the plate three runs down in the bottom of the ninth inning with a 3-and-2 count, two outs, and bases loaded. Will you hit a home run or strike out? In that sort of crisis, preparation can make or break the game. Still, no matter how perfect your preparation, effective crisis management ultimately comes down to *management* and our third rule of crisis: *change it all, change it fast.*

CHAPTER 13

Versatility—Change It All, Change It Fast

The Forced Journey

Every crisis forces a journey. Michael Silva took one on a crisp spring morning in Preston, Idaho, as he hunched under cow number 17, moving on autopilot. Each cow in the herd of 120 went through the same routine: you press the feed button, close the stall gate, chlorine scrub the udder, attach the milkers, move to the next cow, disconnect the milkers, open the stall, usher in a new cow, press the feed button, close the stall gate, chlorine scrub. The routine was numbing, particularly at 4:30 A.M., when your breath turned to ice in the morning cold. Of course, that's just when a crisis chose to strike. Suddenly, cow number 18 stubbornly refused to enter the stall. Smacking it between the horns with a two-by-four, Michael watched helplessly as the cow bolted in the other direction and out of the milking barn. At this point, consider three points. First, the year was 1970, and with people killing people in Vietnam, animal rights activists had not yet equated animals with people. Second, cows surpass only the lowly amoeba in terms of innate intelligence, with solid bone where a brain should be, making a blow by a two-by-four a purely symbolic gesture. Third, you must milk dairy cows *twice* a day or they get uncomfortable, ornery, and, of course, susceptible to milk blockage and infection. This meant that after milking the remaining 102 cows, Michael had to round up cow number 18 and bring it back for its milking.

Now, runaway cows just don't hang around the milking barn awaiting your pleasure, especially after having been whacked with a board, and, while not socially adept, they do like to mingle in herds. This makes it really hard to spot number 18, a small three-inch band on its ear, nestled among 240 identical ears. When you finally locate number 18 the creature lacks the gray matter to remember the two-by-four experience, but, regardless, it resists being led to the milk barn. Catching the cow and completing the milking process takes almost two hours for a city-bred college student, relatively new on the job.

Although one missed milking hardly poses a calamity, it did violate Michael's vision of a hot breakfast and a little hard-earned rest before sunrise, and it did cause a crisis because it violated what Preston ranchers call the *way of the day* or how things were supposed to happen. The violation forced a journey.

Just such a journey occurs whenever a crisis forces an organization out of the comfort zone of its vision in order to deal with the problem. In the case of cow number 18, the journey was short, relatively safe, and not very taxing. But not all journeys take so little toll. Some are long, dangerous, and *never* allow you to return to your comfort zone.

Service Merchandise Co., based in Nashville, Tennessee, is a $3.8 billion merchandising company. With almost 400 catalog stores and a glossy 600-page catalog mailed to over 15 million households, the company has grown at a healthy clip. However, it has not always enjoyed a smooth journey. In the mid-1980s, the company expanded into a retail war zone somewhere between cheap discounters and more expensive department stores. Its operations included computer stores, home improvement outlets, lingerie shops, and toy stores. Unfortunately, however, Service Merchandise failed to bring a unique skill, approach, or product to those already oversaturated markets. As a consequence, profits plummeted and the stock sank to $1 a share in 1987, down from $10 per share in the early 1980s. Confronted by the losses, the company found the path to its vision completely blocked, forcing a journey that amounted to a massive operational migration. It discontinued all of the retail operations, with the exception of the catalog stores, then it borrowed heavily and refocused on catalog operations. Fortunately, the journey concluded successfully, with Service Merchandise returning to profitability. That success came only after the company became an accidental tourist in a financial travelog that might not have ended so happily.

From the simplest element of a rural dairy operation to the most complex financial aspect of a classy catalog company, crisis always forces an organization to travel, and, since crisis sooner or later attacks all organizations, you must master the rules of the road.

Road Warriors and the Rules of the Road

In this era of global competition, virtually every corporate activity requires some amount of business travel, if only to an occasional conference. Some business people, however, have elevated business travel to an art form. These road warriors log upwards of 100,000 miles per year in an endless cycle of airports, planes, hotels, and meetings. Because of the sheer volume of travel, road warriors pick up subtle tricks that elude most travelers. For instance, when an airline cancels a flight, most passengers stand in the appointed line for booking on another flight. But the road warrior bypasses the line, heads for a check-in counter of a flight that has just departed where no line exists, and asks the agent to book the needed flight. Same airline, same computer system, same flight schedule, but not the 45-minute wait in the line assigned by the gate agent. It's the easiest of travel tricks, but still it takes a few thousand miles of experience to figure it out.

Crisis, like business travel, has created a class of road warriors, executives who have spent more than the normal amount of effort on crisis-ridden journeys and have learned a few tricks that make crisis travel less painful. Three executives, in particular, exemplify this new class: William Weiss, Michael Walsh, and Jack Welch. Their combined experience suggests that organizations in crisis travel light, travel straight, and travel fast.

Travel Light

On forced journeys you must, first and foremost, travel light. While an organization may want to take everything along for the ride, sooner or later, the baggage becomes a burden. At AT&T, the inclination to, as William Weiss put it, "hang on to the things that kept us so secure in the past" represented a particularly heavy piece of baggage, a fact that did not escape the attention of Weiss, former CEO of Ameritech and a seasoned crisis road warrior.

215

Ameritech is an $11-billion-a-year Bell operating company, serving 12 million customers, mainly in the Midwest. When the government terminated AT&T's communications monopoly, Ameritech joined a myriad of offspring forced on the road toward their own corporate identity. However, much of the offsprings' management wanted to undertake the migration to a new identity with the same luggage that had served them well as a monopoly. According to Weiss, "we were the ones that made the rules, and we had rules for everything."

Realizing that the game had changed, Weiss "decided to drop a bomb," taking a close look at the baggage left over from AT&T's days as a monopoly and tossing it to the curb. First, when he found that the organization's culture "had no instinct for competition," he jettisoned that entitlement philosophy. In a year of record earnings, Weiss trimmed management ranks by 7 percent. Second, when he identified the tendency to avoid "hard decisions" and "bold transformational change," Weiss forced management to "take each other on," replacing committee meetings that had become gentlemanly affairs, dealing more with affirmation than transformation, with confrontational meetings. Finally, when Weiss noticed that senior managers had become tradition bound, he turned over the leadership group several times until he found people who could implement the kind of change he felt the company needed. Seeing crisis on the horizon, the road warrior forced the organization on a journey before the journey forced itself on the organization.

Since every organization carries its own unique collection of baggage, the baggage it needs to leave behind varies. The baggage may be valuable, but you can't carry it all when crisis forces a journey. Furthermore, a one-time organizational housecleaning of old baggage does not suffice. You must engage in the process constantly in a ruthless reexamination of every item that can weigh down your forward momentum. In an interview with *Fortune*, Weiss advised that the journey progresses "like a race where you run the first four laps as fast as you can—and then you gradually increase the speed."

Travel Straight

Forced journeys present such challenges, you can't afford to wander around in circles. Tenneco CEO Michael Walsh, another veteran road warrior, admits that "large organizations try to wear you down, or wait you out."

Both tendencies represent an effort to forestall the inevitable journey, with management trying to make their efforts look like a trip, without really moving at all. The result, if plotted on a map, amounts to two steps sideways and four steps back for every step forward.

In crisis, many large organizations try to circumnavigate their problems in the hope that all roads eventually lead back home. If their managers believe that after all the crazy competition, insane economic pressure, off-the-wall consultants, and nutty new management have come and gone, the organization can then move back to its old neighborhood, why not travel a circular path that never takes them far from the comfort of home? As a staunch opponent of circular routes, Walsh warns against "two kinds of businesses in the United States: those that are heading for the cliff and know it, and those that are heading the same way but don't know it." In Walsh's mind, there is only one viable option, traveling in the straightest possible line toward a new vision.

Walsh gets particularly annoyed when "people who call themselves leaders just slow things down." He genuinely worries that senior executives "aren't willing to deal with the arteriosclerosis that's weakening the organization." With those words, Walsh was not referring to Tenneco, the $13 billion conglomerate he transformed as CEO, but to organizations in general.

At Tenneco, Walsh focused on not "talking better than they play." He cut the company's sacrosanct dividend in half, sold $700 million worth of assets, cut 10,000 jobs, lowered expenses by a whopping quarter of a billion dollars and increased operation profit by over 30 percent, all in the same year. Clearly, he didn't let the company wander around in circles. In fact, Walsh suggests that all people in key management positions see themselves as mini-CEOs. He advises them to, specifically, look for executives with a "burning desire for change."

Traveling straight flows from the realization that the wrecking ball will soon level the old neighborhood. Given that eventuality, why hang close by and eat dust as the demolition proceeds? According to Walsh, an organization should face reality and "get on with it."

Travel Fast

In an interview with *Fortune,* a reporter asked General Electric CEO Jack Welch what he most regretted, in hindsight, about his management accomplishments. Welch responded simply, "I should have done it faster." Akin to a Formula One racer craving more horsepower or Emmet Smith hankering for more speed, Welch's desire to move more quickly sounds like Einstein longing for particles faster than the speed of light. Nicknamed Neutron Jack, road warrior Jack Welch handles corporate change at the same rate photons travel. Why the regret? Because the only thing moving faster than Jack Welch is the rate of global change that challenges General Electric. Says Welch, "If you're not fast and adaptable, you're vulnerable."

Most managers understandably wish to approach change at an incremental pace, a tendency that Welch says ignores the fact that the journey will be "ten times worse than they've admitted to themselves." Not moving fast enough can negate the accomplishments of traveling light and in a straight line. The entire airline industry knows that it must escape the burden of high labor costs, unprofitable routes, and resulting high fares, but it has tackled those problems incrementally. Incremental means slow. As a result, upstart competitors have sprung up in region after region, gobbling up prime slices of market share and leaving the giants to dominate routes that might never turn profitable. In the airline industry, incremental spells doom.

Unfortunately, as Einstein knew, speed is relative. Most often an organization measures the rate of change against its own pace of change. Consequently, an established 60-year-old corporation can think it has broken the sound barrier when it has in actuality moved forward at a snail's pace. They mistakenly believe they still lead the pack when in reality smaller competitors have moved so far in front of them that they cannot even see them. As a cure for this condition, Welch suggests that management learn that "change is a continuing process, not an event." He warns that "changes are always bigger than you initially sense." If he's right, then the race belongs to the swift.

The organization moving in slow motion kids itself about its real progress on its journey. Oh, it does keep changing, tackling the hard issues one by one, making sacrifices every day, and generally restructuring itself for the next level of competition, but only it thinks it's speeding ahead. Imagine then, the disappointment when the new destination comes into view, and the competition has already folded its tent and left for yet another new neighborhood.

Traveling light, traveling straight, and traveling fast demand that organizations incorporate two traits into their culture: the willingness to travel and the skills to do so.

Change It All, Change It Fast

Since all crises violate vision, then during crisis you must alter either the violation or the vision as quickly as possible. As long as both remain unchanged, the crisis will remain unmanaged and uncontrolled. Any delay can kill you. Since every crisis thrusts you off the path established by your vision, why hang around? Managers of an organization with a Hyatt vision who find themselves suddenly forced to stay at the Lotel motel don't like the thought of wading into a 3 by 7 unheated pool, bringing their own towels and sleeping on a cot. Confronted with these circumstances, they long to escape back to the road that leads to the Hyatt. By the same token, the journey back to the Hyatt should not end up at a Holiday Inn. Since half-measures during crisis get an organization only halfway back on an acceptable path, so during a crisis you should not cut corners in either the depth of solution or the rate that you apply the solution. In other words, you must *change it all, change it fast*. To do so you must travel willingly and develop the skills to travel well.

The willingness to travel requires a mental commitment, but that commitment itself won't lead you anywhere unless you possess the skills to travel well. The NBA's annual Senior All-Stars competition provides a good case in point. Every year, the best *retired* professional basketball players gather for a big game. While they bring sharp minds, a wealth of experience, and tremendous knowledge to the contest, they take to the contest weary legs and lungs. They play with a lot of heart, but not with the old skill. In contrast, some organizations still display superb skills, but have lost the will to play. The computer industry boasts the best organizational talent the business world has ever seen. These companies brought the world computer literacy by taking the nation from cash registers to central processing units in the 1950s and 1960s. Sadly, however, they have lost heart. Unisys, DEC, IBM, and Nixdorf have, in terms of innovation, become mere spectators at a game that, ironically, they invented. Certainly, these giants with their assets and cash reserves possess the horsepower to accomplish transformation; they just don't seem willing to travel.

The willingness to travel and the skill to travel will require two organizational skills: profiling and versatility.

Profiling

This skill involves the *constant* assessment of the market and the competition. Like the answer to the vaudeville question, "How's your wife?," the

219

response is "Compared to what?" many organizations define their journeys by relating them to the journeys of others. For example, California has seriously considered mandating that a certain percentage of new cars sold in the state use electrical power, with quotas for the number of electric cars possibly going into effect by 1998. California has embarked on this journey in response to its air-quality crisis, and where California travels, so must Detroit, Tokyo, and Bonn. In order to sell gas-powered cars in California, a car manufacturer must also offer electric alternatives. The 1998 deadline would come far sooner than Detroit would have liked, but in reality, the company will either accept the itinerary or risk missing the trip altogether.

Since profiling can make or break a company, we find it amazing that so many established organizations know so little about their competitors and their markets. Take, for example, the luggage industry.

The roller-board represents the hottest piece of luggage to come out of the industry since the two-suit garment bag. Once the sure sign of a flight attendant, the roller-board or what amounts to a basic carry-on with small wheels and a retractable handle, has become popular with frequent flyers. Oddly, just about every luggage manufacturer jumped into roller-board production, except Hartman. As the Porsche of the luggage industry, Hartman could certainly afford to delay offering one of the few innovations in a very mature industry. However, the company actually appeared stunned by the success of the new line and then struggled to get their meager two models to the market a full four years behind everyone else. The Hartman roller-boards did not boast any special features that caused the delay, so we can only assume the company profiled the situation poorly.

Those companies that actively profile do so for a number of reasons, but the most successful do so because they relentlessly long for any excuse to shed the status quo and start traveling. To these companies, the profile merely quantifies what their instincts have already suggested: It's time to change. On the other hand, companies that do not profile usually do so because they hope that change will shrivel up and die. These companies often sit at the peak of their markets, and any change means more competition, more product variation, and a challenge to their market share. A profile might turn up something they take seriously, and they just don't want to do that. In fact, however, every organization exists within a larger network, which constantly bombards the organization with factors that influence how it must operate in order to prosper within the network.

To view an organization, no matter how large or how powerful, as beyond the influencing factors of its network represents an extremely myopic approach, akin to a goldfish actually believing that it leads a life independent of those who change the water in its bowl. The goldfish feels independent swimming in seemingly isolated surroundings, but objective observers outside the bowl appreciate the interdependency that exists among the fish, the bowl, and the surrounding environment. That same interdependency links the world's car manufacturers with the state of California, the oil and chemical industry with the Sierra Club, the American health-care establishment with the Clinton administration, the National Education Association with parents, and corner lemonade stands with passersby. Since no organization is an island unto itself, it stands to reason that every organization ought to figure out what's happening in the surrounding sea. You figure that out with accurate profiling.

Versatility

While you should analyze influences beyond your organization's boundaries, that knowledge will do little good unless you can put it to work, adapting to it in a creative and timely fashion. Adapting demands versatility.

A versatile organization embraces and participates in an ever-fluctuating world. This sounds obvious, and, in fact, a great many organizations simply take their versatility for granted, but not all organizations really perform that way.

Paradoxically, a lack of versatility often results from exposure to too much change. In the last three decades, organizations have so wholeheartedly incorporated the term "change" into their managerial vocabulary that most every executive in any size organization can eloquently recite the role that change plays in organizational life. Change has become the universal common-denominator in the mathematics of management. Unfortunately, familiarity breeds contempt; these same executives mouth the words without acting as if they really believe in them. Essentially, they just rattle off the times-tables without really contemplating their implications. Even those proficient in advanced math stutter if asked to multiply big numbers. Quick, what is 1263 × 847? Crisis doesn't involve 2 × 2 but more complicated numbers that require more thought and less rote recitation.

We have found an alarming condition in almost every organization with which we have come in contact. Organizations have become very skilled at handling 2 × 2-type change, those the organization encounters most often, but 1263 × 847 throws them into a dither.

A graph of specific types of change results in three different curves, as suggested below.

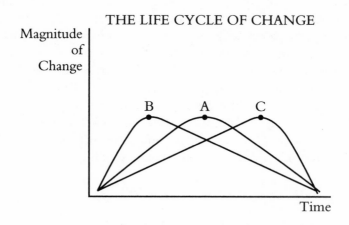

THE LIFE CYCLE OF CHANGE

The A curve graphically represents symmetrical change, that is change that takes as long to decline as it does to build up. The two sides of the curve mirror each other. The development of the fast-food industry resembles an A curve. Change began slowly in the 1960s as outlets, usually single-location outlets or small regional chains, cropped up across the country. Change accelerated and peaked during the early 1980s with the dominance of such companies as McDonald's, Wendy's, and Burger King. The last 10 years have witnessed a gradual deceleration in the growth of the industry as it matures.

Curve B plots revolutionary change, that is, a sudden shift in direction followed by years of trying to figure out what the shift means and how it will affect all concerned. The deregulation of the airline industry has followed a B curve change. It occurred relatively suddenly, peaking early on. Now the airline industry, responding to the sudden decompression of rules and government control, has found the rate of change gradually stabilizing.

The C curve reflects evolutionary change. This is a change with a long, slow, and almost imperceptible buildup, and then—wham—a sudden and deadly strike. This particular curve can be somewhat misleading. The quick drop in the magnitude of change after the peak suggests that the rate of change has slowed. Yes and no. Yes, it has in the sense that the change portrayed by the curve has suddenly dropped off, but no, it hasn't in the sense that another curve will spring up to take its place, most often a B curve. Take health care and education as examples. Both institutions have played important roles in the development of our nation. For over 100 years, these systems have undergone incremental changes which have fine-tuned, adjusted, and aligned them to fit changing times and circumstances. However, for a variety of reasons, incremental change during the last 10 years has failed to bring either system more in line with current demand. Thus, after peaking, both systems have significantly slowed their rate of effective change, sending the curve slanting downward. Now both systems have reached a critical mass of stagnation (in terms of effectiveness) and will find themselves propelled onto a B curve, with quick and radical change (massive reform) followed by years, perhaps decades, of sorting it all out.

Differentiating among the three types of change curves relates directly to the skill of versatility. We have found that an organization that meets the demands of curve C change with versatility does not necessarily do so as well with equal curve B change. In reality, not many organizations can deal as well with all three, or even two, of the curves. Consequently, even the most talented organization can find itself blindsided by even an obvious and easy-to-identify change. This explains why General Motors, long accustomed to curve C change, can't tolerate the presence of Ross Perot, who preached a B curve approach to GM's lethargy.

Real versatility during crisis means that an organization can combat a crisis even when it feels extremely uncomfortable with it. During crisis, you seldom enjoy the luxury of dealing with the sort of change your organization has come to know and love. Dealing with this type of change has become second nature and rarely poses a real threat. Ironically, while even curve B type change does not take an organization that is used to it by surprise, that same organization can fail miserably with demands of a more gradual curve C change. The DeLorean car company gave the world a radical organization with a radical new definition of a performance automobile (curve B), but it could not meet the demands of establishing an effective production, parts, financing, and dealer organization (curve C). In the end, the boring stuff, not its radical vision, killed DeLorean.

The skills of profiling and versatility allow an organization to structure a crisis management approach that allows it to change it all, change it fast, but the approach must incorporate the three components of crisis.

Three Crisis Components

Every crisis, whether common or unthinkable, consists of three components: those you can directly control, those you can only indirectly control, and those that defy control. Isolating these components provides the means by which anyone can more effectively manage crisis.

Direct Control

You can exercise a great deal of direct control over a crisis when the solutions to it fall well within the scope of your organization's capabilities. For example, if a crisis arises from an assembly line, a manufacturing company can easily resolve the situation because that sort of crisis crops up all the time. Based on experience, management can easily profile the probability of such an event and address it with a certain amount of versatility.

Indirect Control

Those elements of a crisis over which you can only exert indirect control occur outside the organization and *affect* other members of the network. When a chemical spill forces the evacuation of a neighborhood, a company can only indirectly control those elements of the crisis involving the community. Since the company lacks the jurisdiction and power to demand that a neighborhood comply with its crisis management program, it can only *influence* the decision of the neighborhood to cooperate. During the Union Carbide poison gas leak at Bhopal, India, the company wielded no official power or authority to direct the community response to the leak and thus could only try to shape the directions of the community's decisions. Similarly, during the cleanup operations after the *Valdez* oil spill, Exxon could not directly control the methods other organizations employed to fight the spill. Each cleanup action, particularly those involving the use of chemicals, detergents, or bio-organisms, required approval of federal and state government agencies. Exxon could rely only on persuasion.

No Control

You cannot control at all these elements of a crisis that fall completely beyond the realm of practical solutions. During the Los Angeles earthquake, the various California state agencies could only sit by helplessly awaiting the inevitable aftershocks. No one could anticipate them or prepare for them.

Not all uncontrollable events involve acts of nature. For example, during the 1970s the OPEC oil cartel conspired to raise prices, and American auto manufacturers could only helplessly sit back and watch events unfold. Delta Air Lines experienced a more recent example of this when Mexican revolutionaries calling themselves *Zapatistas* attacked Acapulco and several other towns in Mexico. Media coverage of the incidents caused tourists to scuttle travel plans to Mexico, which in turn affected the airline. Delta could do little but hope the Mexican government solved the crisis.

Any given crisis may consist of one or all of these categories of control. For instance, when Chrysler launched its new Neon line of automobiles, it discovered a major engine flaw before the cars left the factory. The crisis demanded a series of solutions, all of which fell within the direct control of the company. American defense companies have gotten swept up into a crisis that forces them to trim back operations (direct control), improve relationships with the Pentagon (indirect control), and learn to live with the competitive economic warfare brought on by peace between the United States and the former Soviet Union (no control).

In order to develop effective crisis management, you must identify the direct-control, indirect-control, and no-control components of a given crisis. A management approach that works well in direct-control circumstances may fail miserably in a no-control situation. For example, animal rights groups have been putting considerable pressure on consumers wearing fur coats. The pressure poses a serious crisis for ranchers and retailers whose financial well-being depends on the fur industry, and that crisis lends itself to indirect control. Representatives from the fur industry cannot convene and pass a resolution restraining animal rights groups from speaking out. That approach would fail. However, ranchers and retailers could exert direct control over the situation by converting to other products. The ranchers could raise non-fur-bearing animals, and retailers could offer synthetic alternatives. Once you identify the control elements of a crisis, then you can weigh your options in terms of control, indirect control, and no control.

In our consulting, we use a simple chart that demonstrates the options that arise when an organization encounters either a common or the unthinkable crisis. Each box in the chart represents that specific area management must address while contemplating solutions:

	COMMON	UNTHINKABLE
DIRECT CONTROL	POLICIES AND PROCEDURES	COMPETENCIES
INDIRECT CONTROL	METHODS OF INFLUENCE	VALUE SYSTEM
NO CONTROL	STRATEGY	VISION

For example, you can see that the direct-control component of a common crisis requires that management review and change some aspect of the organization's policies and operating procedures. Likewise, the indirect-control component of an unthinkable crisis demands that the organization change some aspect of its value system. Note that dealing with a direct-control component of a common crisis differs radically from dealing with the same component of an unthinkable crisis. The fact makes the five-minute audit so valuable because it helps management quickly determine what type of solutions they should consider. Let's take a closer look at the different management approaches demanded by both common and unthinkable crises.

Managing Common Crises

The effective management of a common crisis requires attention to these distinct elements, each of which corresponds to the direct-, indirect-, and no-control components of a crisis: policies and procedures, methods of influence, and strategy.

Policies and Procedures

The direct-control component of a common crisis requires that management review and subsequently change some aspect of the organization's policies and procedures. To put it more simply, they must reconsider the way they operate. All direct-control problems flow from some malfunction in the process of making and delivering products and services. Once you have pinpointed the malfunction, then you can correct the problem and end the crisis.

Common crises that lend themselves to direct control and subsequent policy and procedure solutions are by far the most frequent crises faced by organizations. These day-in, day-out problems attack the agendas, quotas, and short-term goals of every organization, and although they rarely make the news, they do make up the bulk of any organization's crisis management activity.

Changes to internal policies and operating procedures fall totally within the control of management. A perfect illustration of this fact comes from America Online, an information service competing with CompuServe and Prodigy, which had increased its base 165 percent in a single year to over 600,000 subscribers. Having originally designed its system to handle up to 8,000 users at a time, the growth of the subscriber base swamped the system's capacity, greatly slowing down response and access times. As a solution, America Online reviewed and modified their guidelines controlling subscriber access to the system and quickly put common crisis to rest.

Methods of Influence

When a crisis includes an indirect-control element, an organization must wrestle with a more complex level of crisis management. Unlike a direct-control problem you can solve by addressing issues totally within your control, you can only manage an indirect-control common crisis by changing the methods you use to influence others.

Consider a fairly indirect control portion of a common crisis that occurred in 1994 when the Teamsters called a nationwide strike against United Parcel Service. The union struck in protest against a new UPS rule requiring drivers to handle packages up to 150 pounds, more than twice the old limit of 70 pounds. With the union involved, the crisis took on an indirect-control component. UPS could not directly control the Teamsters but could only influence them. To do that, UPS initiated a $5 million damage

227

claim against the Teamsters. For our purposes, it doesn't matter so much whether or not the damage claim was a smart move, but whether or not it worked. Within 48 hours, two parties settled the strike, with UPS agreeing to label packages weighing more than 70 pounds and accepting that two employees handle packages exceeding the 70-pound limit. While UPS ended up changing its policy and procedure, the company clearly used influence to get the Teamsters to go along with the changes. UPS dropped its $5 million damage suit and agreed not to punish union members who had honored the strike—less than 20 percent of the workforce. Simply put, UPS successfully changed its method of influence in order to achieve its objective.

Indirect-control crisis components always involve relationships between the organization and at least one other person or group outside of the organization's control. This limits crisis management efforts to those activities that push or pull the relationship toward a desired objective. Interestingly, crisis management efforts often break down when indirect-control components come into play, largely because of an organization's discomfort and lack of skill when it must deal with issues that it cannot merely change by executive order. The skills demanded by the need to influence a relationship clearly differ from those required to review policies and procedures analytically and make the necessary adjustments. Sadly, Carl Karcher learned this lesson the hard way.

As the founder of a 649-outlet fast-food chain, Carl's Jr., Karcher managed his organization with ironclad efficiency. Building the organization from a single barbecue stand in 1956, he offered a healthier menu of chicken and salads before any competitor, but then crisis struck in the form of declining sales and a $5.5 million loss in 1993. Ordinarily, Karcher would single-handedly have weathered the storm with a stream of executive orders. However, the board of directors, many of whom he had handpicked, thought of other ways to manage the crisis, and their input posed an indirect-control challenge for Karcher, who could not silence the board by executive order. Still he tried, forcing various programs on the board in the same way he liked to force them on the operating organization. In short, Karcher used a style more fitted to direct-control than to indirect-control issues. In the end, his inability to alter his methods of influence pushed fellow directors to throw him off the board and ban him from the very company he had created.

Strategy

A no-control element of a crisis calls for changing the organization's strategy. No other alternative exists. To appreciate that fact, consider the following anecdote so often repeated in military management training circles. In the days before radar, a navy battleship was proceeding cautiously through dense fog when a lookout spotted the lights of another ship directly in the cruiser's path. The fleet commander ordered the signal man to flash a warning for the other ship to veer and make way for the cruiser. The offending ship flashed in response, "please change your course 20 degrees port." Incensed, the commander told the signal man to respond, "I am a fleet commander, and you change your course 20 degrees." The response: "I am a seaman second class, and I suggest you change your course 20 degrees port." By this time, the fleet commander was livid. Embarrassed by the flash communication that everyone on the bridge could see, the commander then ordered the following signal: "I command a battleship; it is in your interest to change course." The response came immediately: "I am the maintenance seaman of this *lighthouse,* and I strongly suggest you change course."

All too frequently, an organization actually believes that its strategy should prevail even when pitted against a no-control crisis component. During the OPEC oil squeeze of the early 1970s, American automotive executives tried to convince the federal government to intervene militarily in the Middle East so that Detroit could continue its production of gas-guzzling cars. In effect, they wanted the lighthouse to move so their battleship could proceed as planned. Everyone knows the result of that stubborn adherence to traditional strategy.

By definition, you cannot take charge of a no-control crisis component. Faced with such a circumstance, you can only change those portions of your strategy that the no-control problem affects. Bernard Schwartz, chairman of Loral Corp., understands full well the implications of a no-control element in a crisis.

One of the nation's largest defense contractors, Loral faces the financially dismal prospect of peace between the United States and the host of former communist-dominated countries. Understanding the Cold War thaw and the resulting peace dividend as a no-control issue, Schwartz has radically altered Loral's strategy to match reality. In a bold move, he acquired IBM's Federal Systems Co. for $1.57 billion, a surprising and swift move that posi-

229

tions Loral to go after lucrative electronic systems contracts that will fill the void that the decline in armaments contracts will certainly create.

Understanding the three control components of a common crisis and matching them with the appropriate type of solution provides the structure needed to keep focused under trying circumstances. In your search for solutions, you must consider changing policies and procedures, methods of influence, and strategy or risk losing the battle. However, modifying policies and procedures, methods of influence, and strategy, while effective in confronting a common crisis, do little good when you run smack up against an unthinkable crisis.

Managing Unthinkable Crises

The control components of a crisis apply to an unthinkable crisis as well, but they lead to very different types of solutions. When facing the unthinkable, an organization must consider changing its competencies, its system of values, and its vision.

Competencies

The direct-control component of an unthinkable crisis, like that of a common crisis, falls directly within the control of the organization. However, in the case of an unthinkable crisis, the fate of the organization hangs in the balance.

During the aftermath of the poison gas leak at Bhopal, India, the tragedy so mesmerized the media and the public that they failed to notice three other Union Carbide accidents that occurred the very next year. Ironically, the leaks occurred at plants that Union Carbide officials, testifying before congress, assured the American people were immune from a Bhopal-like disaster. Then on August 11, 1985, the Union Carbide plant at Institute, West Virginia, suffered a toxic gas leak that sent 135 area residents to the hospital. Just two days later, on August 13, the Union Carbide plant in South Charleston, West Virginia, leaked over 1,000 gallons of toxic chemicals. And on August 26, the same South Charleston plant suffered yet another leak, this time of hydrochloric acid. Since the safety systems were virtually the same for all the plants, including the Bhopal operation, Union Carbide faced an unthinkable crisis, a portion of which invited direct control.

Improving the safety of its plants lay strictly within the power of Union Carbide's management team, but it would take more than merely tinkering with policies and procedures to set things right. Four toxic leaks in less than a year suggested that the company needed to go further and review and improve its competencies from top to bottom, specifically its skills relating to plant safety.

When we contrast policies and procedures with competencies, you might think we are playing a game of semantics. But consider again the Bhopal disaster. Union Carbide's own report found 31 plant employees negligent in their duties, thus creating the conditions leading to the leaks. Thirty-one negligent workers indicate a need for more than just fine-tuning safety procedures, and, in light of three additional leaks, it logically follows that considerably more employees lacked sufficient plant safety skills. This situation argued not for small adjustments, but for whole new competencies. The result? On August 28, 1985, Union Carbide announced a $100 million safety program and the termination of 4,000 employees.

System of Values

The indirect-control component of an unthinkable crisis hinges the fate of the organization on how outsiders perceive and interpret its values. You cannot merely adjust your methods of influence; you must, instead, rethink your values from top to bottom, changing your system of values or risking rejection from your network (consumers, government agencies, the media, etc.). The indirect-control component of an unthinkable crisis struck hard at Friendship Air.

Friendship Air was a fledgling airline applying to the Department of Transportation for permission to operate four planes between Boston and Atlanta. Strongly capitalized and sporting a precise business plan, the application seemed a shoo-in. So, why did the government deny the request? The vision of Friendship Air stalled on the runway. It seems that the Department of Transportation did not like the airline's dominant stockholder, the notorious Frank Lorenzo. The government's ruling claimed that Lorenzo lacked the skills to manage an airline and wouldn't likely play by the rules. The Department of Transportation just didn't like Frank Lorenzo. His legacy as the union-busting chief of Texas Air Corp., parent of Continental and Eastern Airlines, had made him the least-loved of all of the unions' most-wanted list of hated executives. Ultimately, Friendship Air saw no choice but to avert the crisis by changing its values, bringing them more in line with those of the Department of Transportation. More specifically, they changed Mr. Lorenzo to a position of minority ownership, and reapplied.

Similar to the case of Friendship Air, Shawmut National Corp., parent to Shawmut Bank, found its values significantly out of synch with members of its network. The successful banking organization caught the ire of the Justice Department and the Federal Reserve Board for actions that appeared to suggest racial discrimination in the bank's lending practices. As a result, the Justice Department sued the company and the Federal Reserve Board doomed its application to acquire New Dartmouth Bank of Manchester, New Hampshire. In order to placate the two powerful government bodies, Shawmut paid a $1 million settlement and agreed to make the changes necessary to avoid the appearance of discrimination. In essence, Shawmut changed more than its policies, but altered its values with respect to minority and "red-line" lending practices in order to solve its crisis.

Regardless of its power or size, an organization depends on the various members of its network, from consumers to regulators, in order to thrive. When the network does not accept a particular system of values, then only two alternatives exist: change the values or change the network. The latter option rarely represents a practical choice. The increased environmental concern of the U.S. public forces on oil companies like Exxon only two choices: change their values to reflect increased environmental awareness or change their network by moving the company to Afghanistan, which doesn't care so much about the environment. Which option seems most impractical?

Vision

Perhaps an organization's worst nightmare involves the no-control elements of an unthinkable crisis. Here, the entire future of the organization comes into harm's way because management can neither control nor influence events. Under these conditions, the organization can do nothing but change its vision.

The education establishment offers a prime example of a group facing crisis that consists of not just one, but a whole slew, of no-control elements. More children come from homes of working or single parents. At the same time, the population of students has steadily become more diverse in terms of social status, economic backgrounds, language, parental support, and even basic nutritional needs. Violence plagues schoolyards, and tax dollars are getting harder and harder to appropriate for education. Organizations like the National Association of Teachers can do little to control any of these trends. Yet, each trend exerts huge pressure on the education establishment, leaving educational institutions across America with only two choices: change their vision of education to incorporate the trends or get out of the business altogether. Speaking of business, one trend that will surely force education to change its vision is the requirement that school systems operate more efficiently, a sacrilege to traditionalists who feel that the high ideals of education should not be governed by something as morally bankrupt as money. Since the nation's taxpayers think otherwise, the vision of education will assuredly have to change.

Similarly, the American workforce, if viewed as an organization, faces the no-control element of corporate downsizing. Pick up the business news on any given day. KODAK TO CUT 4,500 JOBS. SMITHKLINE SETS 1,600 JOB CUTS. BORDEN SHEDS 65 PLANTS AND 7,000 JOBS. MATTEL TO PARE PAYROLL BY 14%. 700 NBC EMPLOYEES DISMISSED. WESTERN UNION TO ELIMINATE 25% OF STAFF. BANKAMERICA TRIMS 5,000 STAFFERS. J.P. MORGAN PLANS 10% CUT IN WORK FORCE. UNISYS SLICES 6,000 JOBS. AT&T TO LAY OFF 14,000. The vision of starting at the bottom, working hard, and retiring comfortably with the same company has evaporated, and company loyalty has become an icon of a previous era that exists only in rhetoric. Under these no-control crisis conditions, workers and managers can only change their vision to include flexible or multiple careers, perhaps in differing fields and geographical locations, prior to retirement.

The consequences of succeeding or failing to meet the demands of direct-control, indirect-control, and no-control components of an unthinkable crisis force managers to approach an unthinkable crisis differently than they would a common one. With the future of the organization on the line in an unthinkable crisis, the same management techniques that work during a common crisis simply won't work. You must know the difference between the two types of crisis, but making that determination foils many an established and powerful organization that underestimates the severity of a crisis until the crisis devalues the entire organization. The list of blue-chip enterprises that have skated close to collapse while we were completing this book reads like a who's who of corporate America. If you look closely at the crisis remedies they have attempted, you quickly see that they misread the scope of their problems.

Obviously changing competencies, value systems, and visions entails a lot more risk and effort than modifying procedures, methods of influence, and strategies, but desperate times call for desperate measures, and desperate measures require artful preparation.

Crisis Preparation

Like much in life, an ounce of preparation prior to crisis can provide a pound of cure once crisis strikes. In most of the major companies with which we have come in contact, we have seen encouraging signs of crisis preparation. Certainly, contingency and emergency plans can help you deal with the media, but these tactical activities, while useful, do not represent the radically different level of mental preparation we encourage. That preparation must accomplish two goals: differentiating between primary and preferred activities and monitoring fat, slack, and flexibility.

Primary versus Preferred Activities

All organizations consist of activities, assets, and values, some primary, some only preferred. We emphasize the distinction. A well-fed person might *prefer* to eat salmon rather than steak or soup rather than salad, but to someone lost in the desert without provisions these culinary preferences dissolve during the search for any food that will sustain life. Most people consider their health a primary asset. Yet, when a logger got pinned beneath a tree miles from help, he cut off his own leg with a Swiss Army knife in order to save his life (true story). In his moment of unthinkable crisis, his leg suddenly became a preferred rather than a primary asset.

All unthinkable crises, and some common crises, require that organizations make the same choice as the logger. In order to survive, an organization might need to cut away preferred assets, activities, or traditions in order to protect and keep alive those things on which its life really depends. The business community shook its head in astonishment when Sears closed down its catalog operation, but Sears saw no alternative to jettisoning an American institution in order to protect more valuable parts of the organization. Similarly, IBM, once involved in every computer market, has found itself forced to decide which niches it really wants to dominate and withdraw from all others.

234

Your sense of what you deem primary and what you merely prefer should come prior to the heat of crisis. Obviously, the absence of crisis pressure allows for calmer, less emotional analysis. Don't misconstrue the word "analysis." We're not suggesting formal analysis and statistical documentation so much as a thoughtful reexamination of organizational culture. Is it a primary requirement that IBM keep its headquarters in New York? What about moving to Dallas or Silicon Valley? Is it absolutely essential that the airlines maintain their hub systems? Or does management merely prefer that approach? Must public schools be managed by educators or can they be administered by a for-profit company under contract? Why not contract out to the private sector every state-run organization? Of course, anyone could drum up countless arguments pro and con for each suggestion, but in the end, you want to weigh what really counts. Knowing what really counts prior to crisis allows you to make the very best crisis decisions.

Fat, Slack, and Flexibility

Imagine a talented executive stranded by a plane crash in a remote region of the Rocky Mountains. With limited food, no radio, and approaching bad weather, the executive must figure out how to survive on her own for weeks. Confronted by the problem, she realizes that she possesses three assets she had not previously afforded much attention. First, her body enjoys a comfortable layer of fat. While she had thought the fat didn't match her Italian business suits, she now realizes that it will keep her alive until she can trap or dig up some food. Second, she discovers that the crisis itself has elevated her self-awareness, noticeably increasing her level of energy, probably due to a big dose of adrenaline. Finally, she finds that she can do things she never before imagined, such as fashion the airplane's seat covers into a reasonably warm outer jacket. Within 10 days, a search party finds the stranded executive. Expecting to find a starving, helpless city slicker, instead the rescuers encounter a trim, alert, adequately nourished survivor, who has successfully transformed her predicament into a survival strategy that could have kept her alive for weeks, perhaps months. Crisis can do the same for organizations.

Only a fool welcomes unthinkable crisis, but when it strikes—and it will—management can trust *that the crisis is worse than it appears, and that the organization is far more capable of confronting the crisis than it thinks.* Even before crisis strikes, however, you can arm yourself with an understanding of three organizational facts of life: fat, slack, and flexibility.

Fat. Every organization, without exception, carries some fat, by which we mean the margin between the resources an organization possesses and the resources it needs. If organizations operated at peak efficiency, then every thinkable crisis would wipe them out because they could apply no reserves to resolving the crisis. In people, as well as organizations, fat has gotten a bum rap, with the debt-conscious always trying to get rid of it. Actually, however, fat serves a vital function by providing active people with fuel even when they skip a meal or two. Frankly, if you found yourself stranded on a desert island, you would rather own a body like that of Roseanne than of the cover model in *Sports Illustrated*'s swimsuit edition. A larger person could go days without food, precious days that could spell the difference between life and death.

Now, in no way do we suggest that organizations intentionally maintain a layer of fat. They don't need to because they instinctively maintain a fat layer whether they want to or not. Remember when the *endaka* crisis struck Japan? *Endaka* arises when the yen is valued strongly against the dollar, a condition that makes Japanese cars more expensive for American consumers. In response, Toyota announced that it would cut organizational expenses by six percent. Wait a minute. Didn't Japanese firms operate at peak efficiency? Where did they find the six percent cuts? They cut fat instinctively accumulated over the years despite all efforts by management to trim it. During a crisis, an organization always enjoys more resources than it realizes. Since the fat exists somewhere, you merely need to locate it.

Slack. Slack means the difference between the actual output of an organization and its full capacity. This amounts to excess energy you can apply to crisis solutions.

The intensity of crisis conditions drains organizational energy faster than a frigid winter night saps a car battery. Therefore, you always welcome extra energy during a crisis. Like fat, organizations store energy by maintaining an instinctive gap between what an organization can perform under normal conditions and what it can perform if really pushed. At a distance, a rope may look taut, but on closer examination you can see just a bit of sag. Under special conditions, you can pull that rope just a little bit tighter.

When Lee Iacocca took over Chrysler, he noticed a considerable amount of slack. From the outside, the car company looked stretched to the limit, but Iacocca saw the slack internally and exploited it during his transformation of Chrysler.

Flexibility.   Organizations adapt remarkably, even when management strives to keep them rigid and rule-bound. When U.S. companies began to utilize team-building concepts with employees, they noted significant improvements in performance. Sensing success, managers then tried to quantify and qualify the team-building techniques that contributed the most to increased performance. They did not like what they found: that increased performance came about when management did not interfere and let the workers, who really understood the process, make shop-floor decisions. Chrysler employees involved in assembling the Neon car line noted that the 300 or so fasteners required at least nine different fastening tools, which significantly slowed down the assembly process. When they recommended universal fasteners requiring the same tool to management, management balked. Fortunately, however, the engineers listened and the changes significantly improved performance.

In every organization's workforce there exists a latent power that can be tapped to improve organizational performance. But you must tap that power with great sensitivity, because an employee will feel little need to increase performance when management will end up taking the credit, often in the form of fat bonuses. In addition, it doesn't take a brain surgeon to figure out that if a productivity enhancement results in increased quotas, it won't take long before workers remain silent about potential improvements.

Taking the time to differentiate primary from simply preferred activities and understanding the elements of fat, slack, and flexibility will multiply the range and scope of solutions available to you when crisis forces you to change your organization's competencies, value system, and vision.

The End of the Beginning

We decided to conclude this last chapter with a few observations on the difference between principles and practices.

Principles guide practices the same way moral guidelines guide behavior. A few principles, such as "Do unto others as you would have them do unto you" govern innumerable behaviors. This book has tried to suggest a few simple principles that should guide the practice of crisis management. Basically, these amount to the five myths, three errors, two dangers, and three rules related to crisis as an organizational phenomenon. This relatively small set of principles gives rise to a much larger set of potential practices.

In other words, *how* an organization translates the suggested principles into specific actions or practices will vary as much as organizations themselves vary. No single management approach will work for everybody, even though the principles of crisis apply to each and every crisis that afflicts each and every organization.

Franklin Planners, a successful time-management company, provides a great example of principles combined with practices. Franklin preaches a set of principles directly related to the task of time management, just as this book has tried to do with crisis. Then Franklin takes a further step. They also provide the specific practices related to their beliefs in the form of day calendars that they feel most effectively implement the principles they preach. Scores of competing management agenda calendars saturate the market, all of which appear to put Franklin's principles into practice, but Franklin has won a dominant position because it has so well harmonized its practices with its principles. The sources of your crisis management will depend on the same sort of harmony.

We conclude on this note because we have watched the impact of other management books on organizations in the 1980s. Every week a talented company picked up the latest theory, applied its precepts step by step, then reaped disaster, all because management confused practices with principles and applied a cookie-cutter approach to every unique situation. Think of us as consultants, not managers, and accept the burden that only you can implement an effective crisis management approach suited to your unique organizations. We hope we've helped you make a beginning. Only you can write the ending.

INDEX